T0350636

CHOOSING BETWEEN UNINCORPORATED ENTITIES IN ARKANSAS

Carol R. Goforth
University Professor
Clayton N. Little Professor
School of Law
University of Arkansas

Choosing Between Unincorporated Entities in Arkansas

Copyright © 2012

All rights reserved

Printed in the United States of America

ISBN 978-1-55728-637-6

Printed on recycled paper

PREFACE

In the past several years, there has been unprecedented change in Arkansas's business statutes. We not only have new general partnership and limited partnership acts, but we now recognize three options for unincorporated business entities that were not in existence when I began my legal career. The rapid changes and developments have left many practitioners in a state of confusion about the new rules and new options. Frankly, for those busy with a general practice and not blessed with the time to focus on these developments, that is not at all surprising.

This book seeks to provide general guidance about the current rules governing the following unincorporated business entities in Arkansas: general partnerships, limited liability partnerships, limited partnerships, limited liability limited partnerships, and limited liability companies. While the focus is on the Arkansas business statutes, various chapters also offer a general comparison between the business choices, a very basic overview of tax considerations, conversion between various entities, and the issue of piercing the veil of limited liability. To assist the practitioner in further research, the text and footnotes provide citations to the Arkansas Code and various other relevant authorities.

I would like to give special thanks to the University of Arkansas School of Law, for supporting my research and scholarship. Thanks also to my children, who sometimes managed to make it a joy for me to get in to the office. And at other times, made it a real pleasure to return home.

CHOOSING BETWEEN UNINCORPORATED ENTITIES IN ARKANSAS

CHAPTER ONE.
INTRODUCTION. 1

I.1.   **Scope and Purpose.** 1

I.2.   **Format and Structure.** 2

I.3.   **Overview of Business Enterprises.** 4
      I.3.1.   **The Sole Proprietorship.** 4
           Assumed Name. 5
           State and Local Business Licenses. 5
           Labor Laws.. 6
           Verification of Employment Eligibility. 6
           Employer Federal Taxpayer ID Number.. 7
           Employer's Payroll Withholding Taxes.. 7
           Estimated Tax Installments. 7
           Arkansas Workers' Compensation. 8
      I.3.2.   **The General Partnership..** 10
      I.3.3.   **The LLP.** 17
      I.3.4.   **The Limited Partnership..** 18
      I.3.5.   **The LLLP.** 25
      I.3.6.   **The LLC.** 26
      I.3.7.   **The Corporation..** 33

CHAPTER TWO.   CONSIDERATIONS IN CHOOSING
BETWEEN ORGANIZATIONAL OPTIONS. 43

II.1.   **Developing an Enterprise Profile.** 43
      II.1.1. **What is the Nature of the Enterprise?** 43
      II.1.2. **Is a New or Existing Enterprise Involved?** 46

i

II.1.3. What is the Likely Duration of the Enterprise?... 48

II.1.4. What are the Likely Capital Needs of the
         Enterprise?................................. 48

II.1.5. What are the Needs for Management Expertise?... 49

II.2. Who are the Investors?........................... 49

II.2.1. Number of Investors. 50

II.2.2. Types of Investors. 52

II.3. Identifying Investor Expectations/Objectives........... 53

II.3.1. Participation in Management................... 53

II.3.2. Personal Risk Comfort Level. 55

II.3.3. Distributions--When are Profits Paid Out, in What
         Amounts and to Whom?..................... 59

II.3.4. Profit Allocation............................ 62

II.3.5. Allocating Losses. 63

II.3.6   Liquidation of Investment...................... 65

CHAPTER THREE. TAX IMPLICATIONS OF CHOICE OF
ENTITY. 69

III.1 INTRODUCTION TO TAXATION OF BUSINESS
       ENTITIES... 69

III.1.1. Tax Status Versus State Law Business Label. ... 69

III.1.2. Very Broadly, Why it Matters. 71

III.1.3. Default Rules About how a Business is Classified
          for Tax Purposes. 71

III.2 SUPERFICIAL OVERVIEW OF PARTNERSHIP
       TAXATION. 75

III.2.1. The Problem of Terminology. 75

III.2.2. Overview of Partnership Tax–Essential
          Concepts. 78

Entity Versus Aggregate Treatment for Tax 78
Partnerships. 78
Time Frame in Which Taxes Are Imposed. 79
General Operation of the Code–Calculation of
Income. 80
How Allocations are Made for Tax Purposes. 81
Allocation of and Limitation of Deductibility of
Losses. 83
III.2.3. "Capital Accounts". 87
III.2.4. Special Allocations and "Substantial Economic
Effect". 94
III.2.5. Recap of Partnership Taxation. 99

III.3.   EQUALLY SUPERFICIAL OVERVIEW OF
CORPORATE TAXATION. 101
III.3.1. The Traditional C Corporation. 101
III.3.2. The Subchapter S Election. 104

III.4.   CONCLUSIONS. 107

CHAPTER FOUR.   THE GENERAL PARTNERSHIP AND
THE LLP. 109

IV.1.   Statutes–A Bit of History for Context. 109
IV.2   Formation and the Partnership Agreement. 112
IV.2.1. Proof of Formation. 112
IV.2.2. The Value of a Partnership Agreement (Preferably
Written). 113
IV.2.3. Mandatory Rules. 122
IV.2.4. Optional Documentation. 125
IV.3.   Management, Authority, and Fiduciary Duties. 129
IV.4.   Liability of Participants in a General Partnership. 134
IV.5.   Sharing of Profits and Losses; Distributions. 138

IV.5.1. Profits and Losses Generally............. 138
IV.5.2. The Services-Only Partner. 138
IV.5.3. Distributions. 140
IV.6.   Partnership Interests.......................... 146
IV.6.1. Nature of Partnership Interests.............. 146
IV.6.2. Issuance of New Interests (Becoming a Partner).148
IV.6.3. Sales and Voluntary Transfers of Interests by
         Existing Partners......................... 148
IV.6.4. Creditors and Charging Orders. 150
IV.7.   Leaving the Partnership (Dissociation). 151
IV.7.1. Effect on the Partnership.................... 151
IV.7.2. Events that Cause Dissociation. 152
IV.7.3. Events that Cause Winding Up of the
         Partnership................................. 154
IV.8.   Continuation of the Partnership Business when a Partner
         Dissociates...................................... 156
IV.8.1. The Process................................. 156
IV.8.2. Buying out a Withdrawing Partner. 157
IV.8.3. Wrongful Withdrawing Partners............. 160
IV.9.   Winding up a General Partnership. 161
IV.9.1. The Process................................. 161
IV.9.2. Wrongful Withdrawal. 163
IV.10.   Electing to Become an LLP......................... 165
IV.10.1. What is an LLP.............................. 165
IV.10.2. How to Elect. 167
IV.10.3. Annual Reports............................. 169
IV.10.4. Unauthorized Election. 171

CHAPTER FIVE.   THE LIMITED PARTNERSHIP AND THE
LLLP.. 173

V.1.   Formation and the Partnership Agreement. 173
V.1.1   A Word about the Arkansas Statutes............ 173

	V.1.2	Forming a Limited Partnership. 174
	V.1.3	Continued Existence. 177
	V.1.4	The Partnership Agreement. 179
V.2	The General Partners. 189	
	V.2.1.	Becoming a General Partner.. 189
	V.2.2	Management and Authority. 190
	V.2.3	Fiduciary and Similar Obligations.. 195
	V.2.4	Personal Liability.. 199
V.3.	The Limited Partners.. 201	
	V.3.1	Default Power and Authority. 202
	V.3.2	The Historical Problem of Control.. 203
	V.3.3	Fiduciary and Similar Obligations.. 206
	V.3.4	Rights of Limited Partners. 207
	V.3.5	Limited Liability. 210
V.4.	Erroneous Belief in Status as a Limited Partner. 210	
V.5	Sharing of Profits and Losses; Distributions.. 211	
	V.5.1.	General Rules.. 211
	V.5.2.	Timing of and Limits on Distributions. 214
	V.5.3.	Right to Distributions. 219
V.6	Partnership Interests.. 220	
	V.6.1	Nature of Partnership Interests. 220
	V.6.2	Issuance of new Interests (becoming a partner). . 221
	V.6.3	Transfers of Interests by Existing Partners.. . . . 223
	V.6.4	Creditors and Charging Orders.. 225
V.7.	Leaving the Partnership (Dissociation). 227	
	V.7.1	Limited Partners. 227
	V.7.2	General Partners. 231
V.8.	Continuation of the Limited Partnership following Dissociation of a Partner.. 236	
V.9	Winding up a Limited Partnership. 239	
	V.9.1	The Normal Process.. 239
	V.9.2.	Judicial Dissolution. 242
	V.9.3.	Administrative Dissolution. 243

V.9.4. Winding up Process........................246
V.9.5. Creditors, Claims, Liabilities and Contribution.. 248
V.10 Electing to become an LLLP........................254
V.10.1 What is an LLLP..........................254
V.10.2 How to Elect..............................256
V.10.3 Termination of Election....................257

CHAPTER SIX.   THE LIMITED LIABILITY COMPANY.. 259

VI.1. Background and Overview.........................259
VI.2. Formation and the Operating Agreement............260
VI.2.1. Formation and the Articles of Organization. ... 260
VI.2.2. The Operating Agreement...................265
VI.2.3. Mandatory Rules. 277
VI.3. Management, Authority, and Fiduciary Duties. 279
VI.3.1. The Member-Managed LLC.................280
VI.3.2. The Manager-Managed LLC. 286
VI.3.3. Hybrid Management. 288
VI.3.4. Duties Owed by Those with Management
          Authority..............................290
VI.4. Liability of and Contributions by Participants
       in an LLC.....................................292
VI.5. Sharing of Profits and Losses; Distributions.........295
VI.5.1. Profits and Losses Generally.................295
VI.5.2. Distributions..............................298
VI.6. Membership Interests. 308
VI.6.1. Nature of Membership Interests..............308
VI.6.2. Issuance of New Interests
          (Becoming a Member)......................308
VI.6.3. Sales and Voluntary Transfers of Interests by
          Existing Members. 309
VI.6.4. Creditors and Charging Orders. 311
VI.7. Leaving the LLC (Dissociation). 316

VI.7.1. Effect on the LLC
VI.7.2. Events that Cause Dissociation. 317
VI.8. Winding up an LLC. 320
VI.8.1. Events that Cause Winding Up of the LLC. 320
VI.8.2. The Winding Up Process. 322

CHAPTER SEVEN–
CONVERTING FROM ONE BUSINESS FORM
TO ANOTHER. 329

VII.1. History and Overview. 329
VII.2. Structure of the Statutes. 332
VII.3. Conversions. 335
VII.3.1. General Partnerships and LLPs. 335
VII.3.2. Limited Partnerships and LLLPs. 340
VII.3.3. LLCs. 345
VII.3.4. Corporations. 348
VII.4. Mergers. 351
VII.4.1. General Partnerships and LLPs. 352
VII.4.2. Limited Partnerships and LLLPs. 356
VII.4.3. LLCs. 361
VII.4.4. Corporations. 365
VII.5. Effects of Converting or Merging. 370

CHAPTER EIGHT
PIERCING THE VEIL OF LIMITED LIABILITY IN
ARKANSAS. 373

VIII.1. What does it Mean to "Pierce the Veil". 373
VIII.2. Traditional Piercing of the Corporate Veil. 376
VIII.3. Piercing the Veil of Limited Liability for other
Entities. 387
VIII.4. "Reverse Piercing". 389

CHAPTER I.   INTRODUCTION

I.1.   Scope and Purpose of Materials.

These materials have been selected, edited and prepared with the hope of offering attorneys some guidance in helping clients choose the optimal form of organization for their business enterprise. Corporations were the prevalent form of business venture for decades (primarily because of the fact that investors did not automatically face the risk of personal liability), and the corporate statutes in this state have not undergone wholesale revision in recent years.[1] This book therefore focuses on unincorporated business options, with the presumption that the corporate option is basically familiar to most legal practitioners.

It is worth emphasizing that this book has been written for attorneys who already possess a basic understanding of the most common forms of for-profit business ventures, the role of statutes in our legal system and rules of statutory construction, as well as basic principles of legal drafting. This is not written for the lay person seeking to form his or her own business, and anyone considering how best to structure a planned enterprise is urged to seek the advice of legal counsel, as business structure can have a profound impact on the way in which a business operates. Some attorneys will feel comfortable providing tax advice as well, but if this is not the case, individuals seeking to choose the best form of business should also consult a tax advisor. In fact, even where the attorney can provide general tax advice, it is generally an excellent idea to consult an

---

[1]   The most recent substantial revision to our corporate statutes occurred in 1987 with the enactment of the Business Corporation Act of 1987, which is now codified at Ark. Code Ann. §§ 4-27-101 to -1706. Certainly there have been numerous amendments to that statute in the years since it was originally promulgated, but the basic structure and functioning of corporations in this state have not undergone the same sort of changes that the other unincorporated forms have in recent years.

individual tax professional, such as a C.P.A., who is familiar with the client's particular tax situation.

The options considered in these materials are limited to unincorporated enterprises authorized under Arkansas law and do not cover certain specialized forms of organization such as cooperatives, real estate investment trusts, or non-profit organizations. This book emphasizes common issues that are likely to be relevant in helping your client decide between unincorporated business forms for new ventures being organized in this state. The hope is that these materials will help bring attorneys who do not specialize in entity formation up to date with the myriad of recent statutory developments in this area in a way that is beneficial to clients generally.

These materials focus on the Arkansas business statutes, and not upon federal law or other federal or state regulation. However, it is virtually impossible to exclude consideration of basic tax issues even if you make no claim of being a tax specialist, so some information is included here in order to help frame any discussion of choice of organization with your clients. Please remember that these materials are not designed to and will not be sufficient to train you to act as a tax attorney in most business settings. Ideally, however, the materials should be sufficient that you will be able to communicate with a tax advisor who might also be assisting in the formation of your client's business.

I.2.   Format and Structure.

The book is organized by first providing an overview of the various choices available to persons wishing to organize a for profit business in Arkansas (the last portion of this chapter), followed by an introduction to the types of considerations that are most likely to be significant in helping clients choose between the different options (chapter two). The third chapter provides an overview of the major

2

tax implications associated with choice of entity, primarily to place the detailed analysis of each kind of business form in context. The next several chapters provide a more detailed look at the various options addressed here: (the general partnership and the limited liability partnership (LLP) (chapter four); the limited partnership and the limited liability limited partnership (LLLP) (chapter five); and the limited liability company (LLC) (chapter six). Although the overview materials appearing at the end of this chapter do include some information about the corporate form, there is no separate chapter dealing with corporations in this book. In addition, even though chapter three collects the simple tax rules applicable to these various business options in one place, there are references to tax issues scattered throughout the chapters focusing on each of the options. Chapter seven deals with the issue of conversion to a different form of organization if a particular choice of organization is made and, for any reason, a client wants to switch to a different entity. Chapter eight governs the special rules applicable to piercing the veil of limited liability, or in other words the question of when a business creditor can successfully go after the assets of one or more business owners even though the statutes normally provide that they are not personally liable for business debts.

Because this book gives an overview of so many different organizational options, there will necessarily be a number of issues that can arise which are not covered here. Complicated business arrangements might involve choices that are not discussed here. Particular clients may have tax issues that are beyond the scope of these materials. Certain transactions may require the consideration of issues and regulations that are not even mentioned here. However, given the rapid pace of developments in the law applicable to business organizations in Arkansas, it made sense to include in one place an overview of current rules for basic organizational options.

I.3.   Overview of Business Enterprises

The starting point for this book is to provide a very general overview of the various organizational choices available for persons wishing to form a business in the state of Arkansas. These materials describe the options that will be considered in more detail in later chapters, as well as two that will not be examined in any detail–the sole proprietorship and the corporation.

I.3.1.   The Sole Proprietorship

A sole proprietorship is a business owned and operated by a single individual. While that individual may hire employees or other agents to assist him or her in conducting business operations, the proprietor is the sole owner of the business. Moreover, the business has no legal existence independent of the proprietor. There is no entity which can sue or be sued, or which can shield the proprietor from personal liability for debts arising out of the business.

Because there is no separate legal entity, there is no general statute governing the formation and operation of a sole proprietorship. It will be subject to state laws and regulations governing the operation of a business under a fictitious name, rules requiring licenses and permits for the operation of certain types of business, and general principles of agency and employment law when the sole proprietor hires agents or employees to assist with business operations.

In general, the proprietor has sole control over the business and all decisions relating to its operation (although these can be delegated to others under general agency law). All debts of the business are also debts of the proprietor, and in fact, business assets can also be seized to pay for personal debts of the proprietor.

4

Because the business has no legal existence apart from the proprietor, the proprietor will be able to use business assets for personal purposes and personal assets to meet business obligations. There need be no segregation of assets or income. All earnings or losses are attributed and taxed directly to the proprietor. There is no need for formal distributions from the business.

The foregoing discussion should not, however, be taken as evidence that a sole proprietorship can legally operate without regard to any legal formalities. Such is simply not the case. In fact there are a number of important formalities required of sole proprietorships (and every other form of business enterprise). To introduce you to some of these considerations, consider the following list of items:

Assumed Name

If the sole proprietor plans to transact business under a name other than his or her own, he or she must complete an assumed name filing with the county clerk for the county in which he or she plans to operate. Ark. Code Ann. § 4-70-203. The filing of an assumed name does not, in and of itself, protect the name for the proprietorship, and just because the name was used by a sole proprietor, that does not mean the name can be used by the proprietorship in other businesses. For these reasons, the sole proprietor may need to consider trade name protection or similar protective measures.

State and Local Business Licenses

Many trades, professions, businesses, and occupations are regulated by the State of Arkansas. The state requires that owners meet various qualifications before granting certain certificates of registration or business licenses. The Arkansas Department of Finance and Administration can provide information about various required state level licenses. Many cities also require that enterprises doing business within the city limits obtain a local business license. The city governments in question should be consulted for more particular information about this issue.

Labor Laws

Employers are required to comply with numerous state and federal laws that regulate employment conditions. These include, without being limited to, the following: National Labor Relations Act (with regard to the organization of unions); Fair Labor Standards Act (minimum wage, overtime pay, etc.); Americans with Disabilities Act (discrimination against the disabled); Civil Rights Act (discrimination in employment based on factors such as race or religion); Age Discrimination in Employment Act (age discrimination); Arkansas Labor Code (minimum wage, overtime pay, manner of payment); Occupational Safety and Health Administration (OSHA) requirements (safety); and common law rules (such as case law that provides a remedy in the event of wrongful discharge). This is intended neither to be an exclusive listing of such laws nor sufficient explanation of what these laws entail; the list merely puts you on notice that such requirements exist and are potentially applicable to sole proprietorships as well as other forms of business enterprise.

Verification of Employment Eligibility

Employers are required by the Immigration Reform and Control Act of 1986 ("IRCA") to verify the work authorization of each person hired within three business days of the date of hire. An employer must complete and maintain INS Form I-9 for all employees, whether they are temporary, part-time, or full-time workers.

Employer Federal Taxpayer ID Number

A new business is required to obtain an Employer Identification Number from the IRS The number must be used on various federal tax returns and documents. Application is made on Form SS-4 and should be filed with the IRS as soon as possible after the business begins or in time to include the number on any return or document to be filed with the appropriate IRS office. On line filing is permitted. Until a number is received, the business may file forms by stating that the business has filed for the number and giving the date on which the application was filed.

Employer's Payroll Withholding Taxes

Under federal tax laws, an employer generally must withhold both income and social security tax from an employee's taxable wages. The procedures to be followed for these withholding taxes are explained in the IRS publication IRS Circular E, "Employer Tax Guide." Willful failure on the part of an employer to collect, account for, and pay withholding taxes can subject the employer to a significant monetary penalty. The sole proprietor or others responsible for remitting the withholding tax may be held personally liable for failure to act.

Although Arkansas withholding procedures are similar to those of the federal government, there are some significant differences between the two systems. The Arkansas Department of Finance and Administration maintains information about Arkansas withholding rules.

Estimated Tax Installments

Both federal tax laws and Arkansas income tax laws require individuals to pay estimated taxes. This includes income from a sole proprietorship owned by an individual, since the proprietorship is not a legally separate entity apart from the proprietor. Information about estimated tax installments can be obtained from the IRS web page.

Arkansas Workers' Compensation

Most Arkansas employers are subject to the Arkansas Workers' Compensation laws. The laws subject an employer to liability for accidents that occur during the scope of employment, regardless of the employer's negligence. On the other hand, the laws also preclude employee lawsuits which could potentially result in large damage awards. However, in certain narrow situations, the employer may also be liable for damages in a civil suit. The laws provide a schedule of benefits to be paid to the disabled employee for injuries or, if the employee is killed, to the employee's dependents or heirs. Most businesses can and should obtain sufficient workers' compensation liability insurance from an authorized private carrier of workers' compensation insurance or from the local office of the state agency.

This listing is not intended to suggest that the sole proprietorship is more complicated than other forms of business. Quite the contrary. However, the fact that the sole proprietorship is easy to form does not mean that there are no formalities, and the preceding list should give you some idea of the potential complications that can be raised by plans to go into business as a sole proprietorship or in any of the other business forms discussed in these materials. By way of concluding this relatively brief overview of the sole proprietorship, here are some of the relative advantages and disadvantages of this form of enterprise.

Advantages:
The sole proprietorship is very easy and inexpensive to form. No particular forms need to be prepared or filed, although this

changes if the business is to have employees or is to do business under a fictitious name. However, the formalities here are clearly less than for most other forms of business. The taxation of a sole proprietorship may also be a significant advantage. A sole proprietorship has no separate tax status. It is not an entity recognized under the Internal Revenue Code. Rather, it is treated as an extension of the owner (proprietor). The proprietor is required to report all items of income and expense on his or her personal tax return. There is a separate schedule on which to calculate profit and loss from a business, but there is no separate tax on income earned from such an enterprise. Rather, the income is added to any other taxable income attributable to the proprietor. Similarly, if there is a loss from the business, such loss can generally be deducted from other taxable income earned by the proprietor. Because everything is reported on the proprietor's returns, the cost of record keeping and tax preparation are generally less with this form of business than with any of the others that will be discussed in this book.

Disadvantages:

In addition to the unlimited personal liability, which is the most obvious disadvantage to the sole proprietorship, there are other potential drawbacks to the sole proprietorship. First, there can be only one owner, which limits equity contributions to those by a single individual. This in turn is likely to significantly hamper any fund raising. The sole proprietorship also presents significant problems in the area of estate and liquidity planning. By definition, the sole proprietor has no other equity owners. Since it is other owners who may be the most likely to be in a position to buy out a business interest upon the death of a co-owner, this lack may be a significant hurdle to heirs who may be more interested in the value of the business than the business itself. Quite aside from this problem, the after-death valuation of a "going concern" organized as a sole proprietorship may be exceptionally difficult to anticipate, leaving substantial uncertainty as to the cash needs of the estate to meet its estate tax liabilities. The uncertainty may also increase the risk of litigation in the event the executor of the estate and the IRS cannot agree upon a fair estimate of the value of the business. Finally, the sole proprietorship is an unwieldy vehicle for fragmenting ownership or making lifetime transfers of interests in the business if such transfers would aid in either estate or business planning.

I.3.2. The General Partnership

A general partnership is an association of two or more persons acting as co-owners in a business for a profit. No particular formalities are required to form a general partnership. This form of business is governed by a relatively detailed set of default rules. In Arkansas, the applicable statutes are currently codified at Ark. Code. Ann. §§ 4-46-01 et seq.[2] These provisions are modeled after the Uniform Partnership Act (1996), which commentators still tend to refer to as "RUPA" (i.e. the Revised Uniform Partnership Act). Most of the regulatory requirements applicable to sole proprietorships also apply to partnerships (and all other forms of business enterprise). For example, all businesses are required to register fictitious names if they operate under anything other than their legal name;[3] state and local business licenses must be obtained and maintained; labor laws must be complied with; employment eligibility of all employees must be verified; an employer federal taxpayer identification number must be obtained; employer's payroll withholding taxes must be paid and reported; and Arkansas workers' compensation laws must be obeyed.

---

[2]   Rather than using a footnote to provide a direct citation to statutory authority, these materials will simply provide a shorthand code cite to the Arkansas Code in the textual materials, unless some additional explanation is required, in which case the materials will be footnoted.

[3]   While the Business Practices provision referenced in the sole proprietorship materials (Ark. Code Ann. § 4-70-203) does not by its terms apply to corporations, limited partnerships, or LLCs (Ark. Code Ann. § 4-70-201), the applicable statutes include their own requirement that fictitious names be registered.

The partnership is not a taxable entity, and therefore does NOT need to make estimated payments; however it IS required to report taxable earnings, and to allocate all items of income, loss, etc. to partners, who must make appropriate arrangements to pay their taxes. This discussion will not review in depth these kinds of requirements, and instead will briefly review the most important provisions of partnership law itself.

Speaking very generally, no written documents need be prepared and nothing need be filed in order to form a general partnership. The association of two or more persons as co-owners to carry on a business will form a partnership, even if this is not the intended legal consequence of such action. § 4-46-202(a). In fact, the sharing of profits by two or more persons creates a presumption of partnership status. § 4-46-202(c)(3).

All partners are agents of the partnership with apparent authority to bind the business. § 4-46-301. The partnership is liable for all acts taken by partners with either actual or apparent authority (§ 4-46-305), and the partners are personally liable for debts of the partnership as well. § 4-46-306(a). The partnership can sue or be sued (§ 4-46-307), but in order to recover against the partners personally, they would also need to be named in the law suit. § 4-46-307(c).

Absent agreement to the contrary by the partners, general partners have equal management rights and may only change the way they do business if a majority (in number) of the partners agree. § 4-46-401(f). If the act is outside the ordinary course of business or involves a change in the partnership agreement, unanimous consent is required. § 4-46-401(j).

Partners are presumed to share profits equally, and to share losses in proportion to their share of profits. § 4-46-401(b). Absent agreement to the contrary, partners are not entitled to remuneration for services, except for reasonable compensation for services in connection with winding up the partnership business. § 4-46-401(h). Partners have no right to receive distributions in kind. § 4-46-402.

Contrary to the very broad standards of fiduciary obligations imposed under common law (a "punctilio of an honor the most sensitive," per Meinhard v. Salmon, 164 N.E. 545 (NY App. 1928)), the modern general partnership statues impose limited fiduciary duties on partners. In essence, the duty of care owed by partners in the conduct and winding up of the partnership is limited to refraining from grossly negligent or reckless conduct, or intentional misconduct, or a knowing violation of law. § 4-46-404(c). A partner's duty of loyalty is limited to the obligation to account to the partnership for profits derived from the use of partnership property, acting as or for a party with an adverse interests, or competing with the partnership in the conduct of the partnership business prior to dissolution. § 4-46-404(b). A partner must also act consistently with the obligations of good faith and fair dealing (§ 4-46-404(d)) although this is not technically a fiduciary duty. Unlike most of the provisions of the general partnership statute, these provisions may not be freely modified. § 4-46-103. The partners can define what does not constitute a violation of the duty of loyalty (§ 4-46-103(b)(3)), and may restrict the duty of care, but not "unreasonably." § 4-46-103(b)(4). They may also adopt standards for what will constitute good faith and fair dealing, but may not eliminate this obligation. § 4-46-103(b)(5).

Absent consent of all other partners, the only part of a partnership interest that is transferable is the partner's interest in profits and losses. § 4-46-502. Such a transfer does not constitute dissociation of the transferee or dissolution of the partnership. § 4-46-503. If the partnership agreement restricts this kind of transfer, a purported transfer of even the economic interest is ineffective if the purchaser has notice of the restriction. § 4-46-503(f). A transferee can get a charging order that would constitute a lien on the partner's interest, and this is subject to foreclosure to protect the transferee's rights. § 4-46-504.

A partner is dissociated from a partnership if: (1) the partner announces withdrawal for any reason, even in violation of an agreement; (2) an event specified in the partnership agreement as causing dissociation has occurred; (3) the partner is expelled pursuant to the partnership agreement; (4) the partner is expelled by unanimous vote because it is unlawful to continue the business with that partner; all of that partner's economic interest has been transferred, or the partner is an entity that is dissolving; (5) a court expels a partner for engaging in wrongful conduct, or for persistently breaching the partnership agreement or because the partner has made it impracticable to carry on the partnership; (6) the partner becomes bankrupt; (7) the partner dies or becomes incapacitated. § 4-46-601.

Dissociation of a partner always triggers a technical dissolution of the partnership (because those partners are no longer associated together as co-owners), but the business is not necessarily wound up just because a partner dissociates. If the business is NOT wound up, the dissociating partner is to be bought out, unless the partnership agreement provides a different process or result. § 4-46-701. The purchase price is to be the amount that would have been distributable to the partner if the assets were sold on the date of dissolution for the greater of liquidation or going concern value without the dissociated partner. § 4-46-701(b). Damages owed from the dissociating partner are offset against the purchase price. § 4-46-701(c). If the partnership was to last for a particular term or undertaking, payment is due when that time or even occurs (with interest from the date of dissociation) unless with dissociating partner can prove undue hardship as a result of such delay. § 4-46-701(h). Otherwise, the buyout is apparently expected to occur at the time of dissociation.

The rules change somewhat if the partnership business IS wound up. Such winding up occurs only in the following circumstances: (1) if there is dissociation of a partner in a partnership at will (§ 4-46-801(1)); (2) in a partnership for a definite term or particular undertaking, a partner dies or otherwise terminates, all partners agree, or the term expires or the undertaking is completed (§ 4-46-801(2)); (3) an event agreed to in the partnership agreement occurs (§ 4-46-801(3)); (4) something makes it illegal for the business of the partnership to continue and the illegality cannot be cured within 90 days (§ 4-46-801(4)); (5) a court has determined that the economic purpose has become impossible, or a partner has engaged in wrongful conduct making it impracticable to carry on business; or for any reason it is not practical to carry on business (§ 4-46-801(5)); or (6) if a transferee of all of a partner's transferable interest convinces a court that it is equitable to wind up the partnership (§ 4-46-501(6)). If you do have winding up, the partnership continues for the purpose of liquidating assets, paying off debts, and distributing the remainder to partners. § 4-46-802. Partners other than those who dissolved wrongfully may participate in the winding up. § 4-46-803. In the winding up process, obligations to creditors must be satisfied first (including paying partners who are creditors). § 4-46-807(a). Then, payments to partners are made in accordance with their capital account (§ 4-46-807(b)), which start out with the value of their contributions (§ 4-46-401(a)) and are then increased by the partners' share of profits and charged with the partners' share of losses as well as any distributions actually made to the partners over time. § 4-46-401(b). Partners must pay in to the partnership any amounts by which their share of losses exceeds the amounts credited to their account (§ 4-46-807(b)), excluding any amounts for which they are not personally liable. The other partners must step up and contribute any amounts that another partner fails to pay in. § 4-46-807(c).

14

There are other provisions in the partnership statute, and some of the details about partnership operations have been omitted here. Nonetheless, this is a brief review of the basic rules applicable to general partnerships in Arkansas. Frankly, the fact that general partners have unlimited personal liability for debts of the business makes this an unpopular business choice now that LLPs (limited liability partnerships) are available, but it is also worth considering briefly the primary advantages and disadvantages of this form of business.

Advantages:

The general partnership is very easy and inexpensive to form. No particular forms need to be prepared or filed, although this changes if the business is to have employees or is to do business under a fictitious name. In addition, although a partnership can operate under an oral partnership agreement, it is always preferable to have a written document in the event a dispute or disagreement arises. It is however true that the formalities here are clearly less than for most other forms of business (albeit not the sole proprietorship). The taxation of a general partnership may also be a significant advantage, at least when compared with a corporation. A general partnership does not pay taxes at the entity level. It calculates and reports items of income, gain and loss, but those are all allocated to the partners in the year that they occur, and the partners are to report those amounts on their individual returns. Thus, there is only a single layer of tax (imposed at the owner's level), and business losses may also be deducted against the partners' individual incomes (subject to loss limitations such as the passive activity loss rules, basis limitation rules, and other considerations that are beyond the scope of this book). Because partnership tax is well understood, and meshes so well with traditional rules applicable to general partnerships, the cost of record keeping and tax preparation are generally less with this form of business than with LLCs or S corporations.

Disadvantages:

In addition to the unlimited personal liability, which is the most obvious disadvantage to the general partnership, there are other potential drawbacks to this form of business. It is not well suited to a business where one expects to have passive investors, as all owners have at least apparent authority to bind the business by acts that appear to be carrying on the usual business of the enterprise. You cannot take away a partner's ability to quit at any time, which triggers at least a technical dissolution of the business, and you will have to do extensive drafting in a partnership agreement to cover all possible contingencies about when a partner's withdrawal, death, incapacity, termination (for non-individual partners), or bankruptcy triggers winding up or the right to continue, and what pay outs are required upon a partner's departure for any of those reasons. Finally, although the lack of entity-level taxation and pass through of losses to the partners are generally advantageous, remember that partners must pay tax on partnership income in the year that the income is earned by the partnership—and this is true even if the income is not passed through to the partners. Thus, income earned but placed in a retirement account (even if it does not vest immediately) is taxed immediately. Income earned but retained by the business for future expansion is taxed immediately. And because all partners have management rights under the default rules and at least apparent authority to bind the business, all income is treated as employment income and is subject to employment taxes, including Medicare and Medicaid taxes. This inability to have portions of income treated as a return on investment may be disadvantageous in some circumstances.

Note that the first of the disadvantages I listed was the unlimited personal liability of all partners. You may recall from basic business organizations that a relatively recent statutory innovation has addressed this particular limitation. This is the option to register a general partnership as a Limited Liability Partnership, or LLP. Because some rules are different for an LLP, let's treat that as a separate form of business.

I.3.3. The LLP

Arkansas law authorizes LLPs in subchapter 10 of the Uniform Partnership Act (1996), codified at Ark. Code Ann. §§ 4-46-1001 to -1003. These provisions allow a general partnership to qualify as a limited liability partnership upon the filing of a statement of qualification. § 4-46-1001 (c). The statement has to include the name of the partnership; its principal executive office or a street address of an office in the state or if none, the name and address of the registered agent for service of process; a statement that the partnership elects to be an LLP; and a deferred effective date, if any. *Id.* The name of an LLP must end with "Registered Limited Liability Partnership, "Limited Liability Partnership," "R.L.L.P.," "L.L.P.," "RLLP," or "LLP." § 4-46-1002. (LLP is by far the most common in Arkansas.) An Arkansas LLP is required to file an annual report containing the name of the partnership, its state of organization, and the current address as required in the initial statement. § 4-46-1003. If the LLP fails to make this annual filing, the Secretary of State may administratively revoke the statement of qualification after 60 days' written notice. § 4-46-1003(c). Such a revocation ends the partnership's status as an LLP, not its existence as a partnership. § 4-46-1003(d). Even after such a revocation, however, the partnership can retroactively reinstate its status as an LLP by making the required filing within two years. § 4-46-1003(e).

The sole substantive effect of registering a general partnership as an LLP is that the partners are NOT personally liable for debts of the enterprise incurred while the partnership is an LLP solely by virtue of being a partner. § 4-46-306(c). Note that partners are still liable for their promised contributions, for any injury caused by their personal misconduct, for any debt that they personally guarantee, or (presumably) if the veil of limited liability is pierced. This is exactly like limited liability enjoyed by limited partners in a limited partnership, members in an LLC, and shareholders in a corporation.

ALL other default rules applicable to general partnerships apply to an LLP. Thus, partners continue to have equal management power (unless otherwise agreed); apparent authority to bind the business (no matter what they actually agree); ability to transfer only their economic rights in the partnership (absent unanimous consent of all other partners); and the absolute power to quit at any time (even if that violates the agreement of the partners). The partnership agreement is not required to be in writing (although a written document certainly makes things easier to prove in the event of a later disagreement).

All the advantages and disadvantages of the general partnership continue to apply, EXCEPT the partners in an LLP do not have personal liability for all partnership debts.

I.3.4. The Limited Partnership

The next form of business to remember is the limited partnership. This form of business is governed in Arkansas by the Uniform Limited Partnership Act (2001), codified at Ark. Code Ann. §§ 4-47-01 et seq. This statute is modeled on the model Uniform Limited Partnership Act promulgated by the National Conference of Commissioners on Uniform State Law (NCCUSL).

A limited partnership is an entity with at least one general partner and one limited partner formed under the Uniform Limited Partnership Act. § 4-47-102(11). It is an entity distinct from its partners and can be organized for any lawful purpose; its duration is presumed to be perpetual. § 4-47-104.

As with all forms of business offering limited liability to at least some owners, there are requirements for naming a limited partnership. It must contain the phrase "limited partnership," or abbreviation "L.P.," or "LP" and not the words "limited liability limited partnership" or "L.L.L.P.," or "LLLP" unless it has registered as a limited liability limited partnership. § 4-47-108.

A limited partnership is formed in Arkansas when a certificate of limited partnership is filed by the Secretary of State, unless a delayed effective date is specified. § 4-47-206(c).[4] In order to be filed, a certificate of limited partnership must be filed in duplicate, along with the required fees, and must include the name of the limited partnership; the address of an agent for service of process (required not by the limited partnership statue any longer, but by the Model Registered Agents Act which can be found at Ar. Code Ann. §§ 4-20-101 et seq.); the name and street mailing address of each general partner; whether the limited partnership is an LLLP; and any other elective information the partners choose to include. § 4-47-201(a). All general partners listed in the certificate must sign. § 4-47-204. If the certificate contains errors or the information changes, an amended or restated certificate may be filed. § 4-47-202. The statute also provides both civil and criminal penalties for false information in a certificate of limited partnership. § 4-47-208. As with an LLP, a limited partnership must file an annual report, but the statute does not include penalties for failure to comply. § 4-47-210.

The big difference between a limited partnership and general partnership is the presence of limited partners. Limited partners do not have any statutory right or power to manage or bind the

---

[4]   Section 4-47-201(c) adds a little confusion to what would be a straight-forward rule by stating that the limited partnership is formed upon filing IF the certificate is in substantial conformity with the statutory requirements. However, a cross reference to § 4-47-206 should mean that the certificate will be effective upon filing.

partnership. § 4-47-302. They can be given actual authority, but that takes agreement of the general partners. They do not have any apparent authority to bind the business by virtue of their status as limited partners, and they owe no fiduciary duties. § 4-47-305. They are also, by statute, insulated from personal liability for debts of the business solely by virtue of their role as limited partners. § 4-47-303. They have rights to certain information (§ 4-47-304), some of which must be maintained and available at the offices of the limited partnership (§ 4-47-111).

Obviously, the limited liability of limited partners is a big deal, and there are special rules for what happens if a person erroneously believes him- or herself to be a limited partner. § 4-47-306. If a person erroneously but in good faith believes that he or she is a limited partner, and he or she causes a corrected certificate to be filed or withdraws from future equity participation in the business that will end future liability. § 4-47-306(a). In addition, such person is liable to pre-existing creditors as a general partner only if the third person believed in good faith that the person was a general partner at the time the debt was incurred. § 4-47-306(b). A person acting diligently and in good faith may withdraw under this provision even if it would otherwise breach an agreement about withdrawing. § 4-47-306(c).

General partners in a limited partnership are much like general partners in a general partnership. They do have apparent authority to bind the business (§ 4-47-402); they are presumed to have equal rights to manage the business along with all other general partners (§ 4-47-406); they are personally liable for debts of the enterprise (§ 4-47-404); and they do owe the same fiduciary duties as general partners in a general partnership (§ 4-47-408). General partners can be sued either along with the limited partnership or in a separate action. § 4-47-405.

Unlike the case in a general partnership, however, distributions from a limited partnership are presumed to be shared on the basis of value (as stated in the required records of the partnership) of contributions received from each partner, unless the partners have agreed otherwise. § 4-47-503. Interim distributions are made only when the managers declare them, or the agreement calls for them to be made. § 4-47-504. The mere fact that a person dissociates does not mean that they are entitled to a distribution. § 4-47-505. The limited partnership statute also prohibits distributions that would leave the limited partnership unable to pay its debts as they come due, or if it would leave the partnership with debts exceeding its assets. § 4-47-508. Any general partner that declares an unlawful distribution is personally liable to creditors for up to two years. § 4-47-509.

The rules governing how a partner quits a limited partnership and what happens in the event of such dissociation differ depending on whether we are talking about a limited or general partner.

The language of our limited partnership statute is a little confusing with regard to limited partners. A limited partner does not have the right to dissociate as a limited partner prior to termination of the limited partnership. § 4-47-601(a). However, a limited partner is dissociated if the partner gives notice to the limited partnership of "express will to withdraw." § 4-47-601(b)(1). In essence, this gives a limited partner the "power" to dissociate, but not the legal right to do so, although one might have wished for slightly clearer language in the statute. A limited partner also dissociates: (1) as provided in the partnership agreement (§ 4-47-601(b)(2)); (2) if the partner is expelled pursuant to the partnership agreement (§ 4-47-601(b)(3)); (3) if there is a unanimous vote to expel the partner because it is unlawful to carry on the business with such person, or such person has transferred all of his or her economic interest in the partnership or the partner is a business that is being wound up (§ 4-47-601(b)(4)); (4) if

21

there is a judicial order of expulsion because of wrongful actions by the partner or because it is no longer practical to carry on the business of the partnership with such person (§ 4-47-601(b)(5)); death or termination of a partner (depending on whether the partner is an individual or entity) (§ 4-47-601(b)(6)-(9)); and sometimes upon the conversion or merger of the limited partnership (§ 4-47-601(b)(10)). Once a limited partner dissociates, the limited partner gains the status of a mere transferee. § 4-47-602.

A general partner is dissociated if: (1) the partnership is given notice of the partner's express will to withdraw (§ 4-47-603(1)); (2) an event specified in the partnership agreement occurs (§ 4-47-603(2)); (3) if the partner is expelled pursuant to the partnership agreement (§ 4-47-603(b)(2)); (4) if there is a unanimous vote to expel the partner because it is unlawful to carry on the business with such person, or such person has transferred all of his or her economic interest in the partnership or the partner is a business that is being wound up (§ 4-47-603(4)); (5) if there is a judicial order of expulsion because of wrongful actions by the partner or because it is no longer practical to carry on the business of the partnership with such person (§ 4-47-603(5)); (6) the partner becomes bankrupt (§ 4-47-603(6)); (7) death or termination of a partner (depending on whether the partner is an individual or entity) (§ 4-47-603(7)-(10)); and sometimes upon the conversion or merger of the limited partnership (§ 4-47-603(11)). A general partner's withdrawal is only "wrongful" if it violates the partnership agreement, or occurs by voluntary withdrawal, judicial expulsion, bankruptcy, or voluntary termination prior to termination of the limited partnership. § 4-47-604(b). A wrongfully withdrawing general partner is liable to the limited partnership and other partners for damages. § 4-47-604(c). Upon such dissociation, the general partner's rights to management and fiduciary duties terminate except as to matters that arose prior to dissociation. § 4-47-605.

With regard to transfer of partnership interests, partners (general or limited) may transfer their economic interest in the partnership without the consent of the other partners, unless the partnership agreement restricts this right. § 4-47-702(a)(1). The purchaser becomes a transferee, however, not a partner. § 4-47-702(b). The transferring partner is not dissociated, and retains the rights and status possessed prior to the transfer. § 4-47-702(a)(2). A transferor has very limited rights, which do not include any management powers unless they are admitted as a partner. § 4-47-703. The estate or a deceased partner is also treated as a transferee. § 4-47-704. A person (whether or not a transferee) becomes a general partner only as provided in the agreement, or if the person was previously a limited partner and all general partners have dissociated; or there is unanimous agreement of all partners. § 4-47-401. A person can become a limited partner in exactly the same way. § 4-47-301.

The limited partnership statute uses the word "dissolution" slightly differently than does the Uniform Partnership Act (1996). Under the Uniform Limited Partnership Act (2001), dissolution is the first step in the winding up process rather than it being a synonym for dissociation of a partner. Hence, subchapter 8 of the limited partnership statute talks about events that cause the limited partnership to be "dissolved and its activities . . . wound up. . . ." Such dissolution can happen without court order if: (1) something specified in the partnership agreement occurs: (2) all general partners and a majority in interest of the limited partners agree; (3) a general partner dissociates and a majority in interest of the partners vote to dissolve; (4) the last general partner dissociates and no replacement general partner is found and agreed to by at least a majority in interest of the limited partners within 90 days; (5) the last limited partner dissociates and no new limited partner is added within 90 days; or (6) there is an administrative dissolution by the Secretary of State for non payment of taxes, fees or other regulatory non-compliance. § 4-47-

801. A court may order dissolution if it is not reasonably practicable to carry on the partnership's business. § 4-47-802.

Winding up basically involves liquidating assets, paying off creditors and distributing the remainder to partners. § 4-47-803. Normally, the general partners would wind up, but if there is no remaining general partner, a majority in interest of the limited partners may select someone to wind up the partnership. § 4-47-803(c). The court may be asked to step in and appoint someone if the limited partners cannot agree, or if the applicant shows "good cause." § 4-47-803(d).

A dissolved limited partnership may send notice to known claimants, and if such notice is sent, the claimant has 120 days in which to perfect its claim against the partnership. § 4-47-806. For unknown claims, the limited partnership may publish notice of the dissolution, and this starts a five year statute of limitations. § 4-47-807. This parallels the dissolution procedures applicable to corporations.

As with general partnerships, creditors of a dissolved limited partnership are paid first (including partners who are creditors). § 4-47-812(a). After that, partners are paid in cash the amounts that they are entitled to receive, which under the default rules would be in proportion to the agreed value of their contributions to the partnership. § 4-47-812(b), 503. General partners may be required to make additional contributions if there are insufficient funds with which to pay creditors. § 4-47-812(c).

Advantages:
Under current tax rules, a limited partnership is presumed to be taxed as a partnership. This means that there is no entity-level tax, and that losses are passed through to the partners. Another tax benefit, not present with the general partnership, is the possibility of

structuring at least some of the return (particularly that paid to limited partners who do not provide substantial services to the business) in such a way that employment taxes are avoided. On the other hand, limited partners may have a harder time deducting losses due to at risk and basis limitations. Outside of tax considerations, this form of business also allows for the participation of passive investors, who have no personal liability for debts of the business, no responsibility for managing the enterprise, and no fiduciary duties owed to other owners. In addition, they will have no statutory authority to bind the business, so the managers of the business have less to worry with regard to unauthorized activities creating surprise liability. Finally, limited partners can quit without resulting in any obligation to immediately buy out their partnership interest, even under the default rules.

Disadvantages:

The primary disadvantage to the limited partnership form of business is that there must be at least one general partner with unlimited personal liability for debts of the enterprise. The only downside from a tax standpoint is that, as with any tax partnership, taxes must be paid on income when earned and not just when it is distributed. Limited partners might find themselves converted into general partners if all general partners withdraw. Withdrawal of general partners can trigger dissolution and winding up, unless a majority of the remaining partners can agree to continue the business.

Again, there is another option that does away with the first and primary disadvantage of the limited partnership: an LLLP eliminates personal liability of the general partners.

I.3.5. The LLLP

In Arkansas, a limited partnership can choose to be a limited liability limited partnership ("LLLP"), by the simple expedient of electing such status in the certificate of limited partnership. § 4-47-201(a)(4). The effect of such election is to change the required name so that it indicates the business's status as an LLLP (§ 4-47-108(c)), and to eliminate personal liability of the LLLP's general partners (§ 4-47-404(c)). In essence, this is the only substantive difference between LLLPs and limited partnerships.

There are two possible differences in disadvantages as compared to the limited partnership. First, the most important drawback to the limited partnership is eliminated because the LLLP does not subject its general partners to personal liability, except for loss of contributions, liability arising out of personal fault, personal guarantees, or if the veil of limited liability is pierced. The second is a new disadvantage, in that many states do not currently recognize the LLLP as a valid form of business. The issue of whether Arkansas law providing for limited liability of the general partners would be respected in the event of litigation arising out of injuries caused in a jurisdiction that simply does not recognize the LLLP has not been resolved. The risk that limited liability might not work creates a significant limitation on this option for partnerships that anticipate doing business across state lines.

I.3.6. The LLC

Many studies suggest that the most popular form of business for new start-up companies is the limited liability company ("LLC"). This is true not only in Arkansas, but all across the country. LLCs are designed to be very flexible and informal, to give all owners the same protection against personal liability that shareholders in a corporation enjoy, and to avoid entity-level taxation.

Arkansas' LLC Act has a very cumbersome official name called the "Small Business Entity Tax Pass Through Act," is codified at Ark. Code Ann. § 4-32-101. Our statute is not based on any uniform or model act, and not surprisingly has a number of idiosyncratic provisions that make it hard to work with. Hopefully, within the next few years, Arkansas legislators will adopt a model or uniform act to eliminate some of the nagging issues that currently plague LLCs in this state.

The name of an LLC must include the words "Limited Liability Company," or "Limited Company," or the abbreviations "L.L.C.," "L.C.," "LLC," or "LC," and the word "Limited" may be abbreviated "Ltd.," and "Company" may be abbreviated "Co." § 4-32-103(a). The name may not be confusingly similar to the registered name of any other business in Arkansas. § 4-32-103(b).

In line with the majority rule, the Arkansas statute permits formation of domestic LLCs by one or more persons by filing Articles of Organization with the Secretary of State. § 4-32-202. The Articles have to have a name for the LLC that is in compliance with the statutory requirements, and if the LLC is to be managed by its members, a provision to that effect must also be included in the articles of organization. § 4-32-202. Under the Model Registered Agents Act, the LLC is to have either in this document or in another filing, the information necessary for service of process on the LLC (i.e. a street address and name or title of an appropriate agent for service of process). (This Act is codified at Ark. Code Ann. §§ 4-20-101 et seq.)

In one of the irritating idiosyncracies caused by our non-uniform statute, unless a delayed effective date is specified, the LLC is formed when the articles are delivered to the Secretary of State, even if they cannot be filed at that time. § 4-32-206. So long as non-conforming Articles are fixed within 20 days after notice of the deficiencies are given by the Secretary of State, they are deemed filed as of the date of delivery. § 4-32-1308. It would be so much simpler (and in conformity with all of our other business entity statutes) if the

27

LLC simply came into existence when the Articles were filed, but this language does not currently appear in our statute.

Arkansas has two distinct provisions relating to management of LLCs. One deals with "agency power" or apparent authority to bind the business. In essence, in a member-managed LLC, members have default power to manage and unavoidable apparent authority to bind the business for acts apparently carrying on in the usual way the business of the LLC. § 4-32-301(a). In a manager-managed LLC (i.e. where the Articles specify that the LLC will be managed by managers), only the managers have such power and authority and the members do not. § 4-32-301(b). As to third parties with actual knowledge of any limitation on actual authority, the member or manager's apparent authority ends. § 4-32-301(d). On the other hand, when it comes to relations between the members of an LLC, it is the operating agreement and not the Articles that will control as to who has the ability to manage the LLC. § 4-32-401.

Perhaps this is the appropriate place to remind you about the Arkansas rules governing Operating Agreements. Buried amidst the harmless and generally helpful definitions section of the Arkansas LLC Act is the following language describing the LLC's "operating agreement": "'Operating agreement' means the written agreement which shall be entered into among all of the members as to the conduct of the business and affairs of a limited liability company." § 4-32-102(11). The problems with this provision are the inclusion of the word "written," and the apparent requirement that "all members" must enter into the agreement if it is one that governs "conduct of the business and affairs" of the LLC. While a careful review of the entire statute does not reveal anything that has to be in an operating agreement, the rules DO specify that an LLC has to have one, and it apparently has to be in writing. § 4-32-102(11). (The fear is that failure to comply with the minimal statutory formalities associated with an LLC might increase the risk that the veil of limited liability will be pierced.)

Turning back to the way in which LLCs operate, Arkansas adopts the universal default rule that members in an LLC are not personally liable for debts of the business. § 4-32-304. They can still be liable for their contributions, for debts guaranteed by them, for injuries that they personally caused, and in the event that the veil of limited liability is pierced. The statutes also make it permissible for LLCs to render professional service (§ 4-32-306), and to act as executors or fiduciaries (§ 4-32-307).

Unless the written operating agreement otherwise provides, the persons with management power (members in a member-managed LLC and managers in a manager-managed LLC) owe only the duty to avoid "gross negligence or wilful misconduct." § 4-32-402(1). Members and managers must account to the LLC for profits derived from transactions connected with the conduct or winding up of the LLC's business, unless one-half by number of the disinterested persons with management power consent. § 4-32-402(2). The operating agreement can, however, limit or eliminate the liability of members or managers for monetary damages arising out of breaches of such duties. § 4-32-404.

Absent a provision in the written operating agreement to the contrary, no formal voting is required in an LLC in order to make business decisions. § 4-32-403(a). Instead, the "affirmative vote, approval or consent" of more than one-half by number of the persons with management power is required. *Id.* Note that no record need be kept of such decisions. § 4-32-405 (requiring a list of members and managers and their addresses, copy of articles and amendments, copies of tax returns, copies of the operating agreement, a writing which can be the operating agreement setting out the agreed value of any contributions, the events upon which the LLC is to dissolve and anything else required by the operating agreement. Failure to keep these records, however, is not to be considered grounds for imposing liability on members or managers for the debts and obligations of the LLC. § 4-32-405(d)). On the other hand, the default rules do require a unanimous vote to amend the written operating agreement or to permit any member or manager to contravene any provision in an operating agreement. § 4-32-403.

There is no limit in the statutes on the type of property that can be contributed in exchange for membership interest (§ 4-32-502), but in order to be enforceable, an agreement to make a contribution in the future must be in a signed writing. § 4-32-502(a). If a required contribution is not made, the LLC may enforce the obligation or require that a cash contribution be made in lieu of promised services or property. § 4-32-502(b) - (c).

Unless otherwise provided in the written operating agreement, each member in an LLC is to be returned his or her contribution and then is entitled to share equally in profits. § 4-32-503. Interim distributions are made only as providing the operating agreement or when declared by whoever has management authority. § 4-32-601. The statute also says that, unless provided otherwise in the operating agreement, distributions are to be shared equally. *Id.* Although the language would appear to suggest this, I doubt that it really means that members would have to share distributions equally even if the operating agreement allocated profits in a different manner.

LLC membership interests are presumed to be transferable in the same way that partnership interests are transferable–an assignment is effective only as to economic rights (§ 4-32-704), absent agreement to the contrary or written consent of all other members. § 4-32-706. Persons become members only as provided in the operating agreement or by the written consent of all members. § 4-32-801. Transfer of all of a member's membership interest neither makes the transferee a member nor ends the transferor's status as a member, unless the other members remove the transferor or the operating agreement provides for such a change in status. §§ 4-32-704(4), - 706.

Absent agreement to the contrary, a member dissociates (i.e. ceases to be a member) only if: (1) the operating agreement allows a member to withdraw either at will or upon the happening of an event or expiration of period of time (§ 4-32-802(c), (a)(1)); (2) the member transfers all of his or her interest and the transferee is admitted as a member (§ 4-32-802(a)(2)); (3) the member is removed in accordance with the operating agreement, or removed after transferring all of his or her interest in the LLC (§ 4-32-802(a)(3)); (4) the member becomes bankrupt (§ 4-32-802(a)(4) - (5)); (5) death or incapacity of a member who is an individual (§ 4-32-802(a)(6)); or (6) termination of a member that is an entity (§§ 4-32-802(a)(7)-(10)). Absent agreement to the contrary, the LLC is to pay a dissociating member the fair value of the member's interest (based on the rights to share in distributions) within a reasonable time after dissociation. § 4-32-602.

In the context of the LLC Act, "dissolution" is the first step of winding up, and this happens only: (1) as provided in the operating agreement; (2) upon unanimous written consent of all members: (3) if there are ever no members for at least 90 days or such other period as the operating agreement provides; or (4) if there is judicial dissolution because it is no longer reasonably practical to carry on the LLC's business. §§ 4-32-901 to- 902. Anyone who had management power prior to dissolution will have authority to wind up, unless a circuit court takes over following wrongful conduct by such member or manager. § 4-32-903. Upon winding up, assets are to be paid first to creditors, then to return contributions, then in accordance with the members' right to receive distributions. § 4-32-905. An LLC can file articles of dissolution, and can give notice to creditors (by sending it to known creditors and publishing it for unknown claims), just as is the case with a limited partnership or corporation. § 4-32-906 to -908. These steps are optional but advantageous to the LLC because they contain relatively strict limitations on the time period in which claims may be made.

Advantages:

The LLC offers all members limited liability; while they can lose their contributions, anything they personally guarantee, anything which was their fault or a consequence of their misconduct, or if the veil of limited liability is pierced, they are not generally liable for any debts of the enterprise merely by virtue of being members. The LLC is also eligible to be taxed as a partnership, and is presumed to be a tax partnership unless a special election is made to obtain tax status or if the LLC ever becomes "publicly owned" under the tax requirements (i.e. ever has more than 500 members). This means there is no entity-level tax and losses pass through to the members. The LLC is both very informal (no meetings and few records are required) and very flexible, meaning that virtually all default rules discussed above are subject to the contrary agreement of the parties.

Disadvantages:

The LLC has the same potential disadvantages as other tax partnerships, in that members must pay taxes on all income from the business even if it is not all distributed to them. In addition, there is considerable uncertainty as to whether it is possible to structure an LLC so that passive members can avoid paying employment taxes on what they might prefer to see as amounts characterized as a return on investment rather than compensation. Some accountants tell clients that it is more expensive to do the accounting for an LLC than for a partnership or corporation, and this may also be a consideration for some businesses. Some of the default rules are unclear and potentially troublesome (particularly in Arkansas with its poorly worded statute and lack of case law offering any interpretive guidance), and this means that lawyers must take special care in drafting an operating agreement in order to protect the client's interests. While this is possible, the very flexibility that is potentially an advantage for clients can also be a disadvantage, when it takes more time and money to form the LLC to meet the client's needs. Because the LLC is relatively new, there is also some uncertainty about standards and rules, even where the statute seems to be clear or consistent with majority rules. There simply has not been enough time for a well developed body of case law on such topics as the practical extent of members' and managers' fiduciary duties, exactly what facts render an LLC vulnerable to piercing, what is a reasonable time for payout of a dissociating member's liquidating distribution, etc.

Even with these potential disadvantages, it does appear that the LLC is generally the vehicle of choice for new businesses.

I.3.7. The Corporation

The corporation retains such a dominant position in American society both because it is an operational choice of considerable longevity (having been around since the founding of this country, albeit not quite in its current form), and because it is the overwhelming choice for publicly held businesses, where wealth, power, and influence have been so concentrated. Even for new businesses, however, the corporation may be the vehicle of choice.

It seems appropriate to begin this section with a brief overview of tax considerations, because tax issues are different for corporations (which cannot currently simply elect to be taxed as partnerships). Corporations are generally taxed under subchapter C of the Internal Revenue Code. In fact, a reference to a "C Corporation" is only a reference to its tax status; the "C" does not stand for "Code," "Close," or "Closely Held." Under the general terms of subchapter C, a corporation is treated as a taxable entity distinct from its owners. It not only calculates income at the entity level (as do tax partnerships), but it pays taxes at the entity level (which tax partnerships do not). Losses are not passed through to the shareholders, but rather are used to offset corporate income. If there is insufficient income at the corporate level, the losses are "suspended" until there is sufficient income to offset the losses. In addition to this taxation at the corporate level, shareholders do pay tax on dividends when they are paid out. Traditionally, dividends were taxed as ordinary income. At the moment, dividends are taxed at the lower capital gains rate regardless of the taxpayer's income tax bracket, but this was one of the provisions enacted under President George W. Bush with a sunset provision. This means that after 2010, unless Congress acts to extend or otherwise change the law, dividends will once again be taxed as income, at whatever bracket the shareholder-taxpayer is in.

To avoid the negative consequence of double taxation and inability of shareholders to use corporate losses, Congress has authorized corporations meeting certain relatively rigid requirements to elect to be taxed as "S Corporations." "S" in this context does not mean "small," but rather that the corporation has filed an election to be taxed under subchapter S of the Internal Revenue Code. An S Corporation is taxed sort of like a tax partnership, although there are some technical differences that are far beyond the scope of this book. For your purposes, you should know that an S Corporation reports income but does not pay taxes on it; shareholders in an S Corporation pay tax on all corporate income in the year it is earned, not when it is distributed. Losses are also passed through to shareholders. The major drawbacks are the limits on which corporations are eligible to elect S status. First, the corporation may have no more than 100 shareholders (although this number has steadily been creeping higher and higher over the years). Second, all shareholders must be individuals, although in the event that a shareholder dies, there is a reasonable time for the shareholder's estate to hold the shares without triggering an automatic termination of S status. No shareholder may be a non-resident alien. And most importantly, the corporation may have only a single class of shares. Under treasury regulations, this means that every share must have the same economic rights as every other share. It does not matter if you have classes under state law (called whatever you want), or shares with different voting rights, but if you have different economic rights, that will automatically terminate a corporation's S election. Thus, a shareholder agreement that subjects some shares to differing transfer limitations, or buy-back requirements, would be a distinct class of shares, and would make Subchapter S unavailable.

Regardless of whether a corporation is taxed under subchapter C or S, the rules of the Business Corporation Act of 1987 will govern its formation and operation. Codified at Ark. Code Ann. §§ 4-27-101 et seq., this statute governs all for-profit corporations formed after 1987, and even those formed prior to that date if they elect to be subject to the more modern provisions.

A corporation is formed in Arkansas upon the filing of Articles of Incorporation, unless a delayed effective date is specified. § 4-27-203. The Articles must include an appropriate name (§ 4-27-202(a)(1), cross referencing the name requirements set out in § 4-27-401); the number of authorized shares with par value or a statement that the shares are without par, or if multiple classes of shares are allowed, the number of shares of each class with a statement of par for each such class (§ 4-27-202(a)(2)); a registered agent for service of process and appropriate address (§ 4-20-105(a)); the name and address of each incorporator (§ 4-27-202(a)(4)); and the primary purpose for which the business is established, for informational purposes only (§ 4-27-202(a)(5)). The Articles may, but need not name initial directors; limit the purposes or powers of the corporation; limit the power of directors consistent with law; or limit liability of directors or stockholders for monetary damages arising out of breaches of fiduciary duty. § 4-27-202(b). The name must include the word "corporation," "incorporated," "company," or "limited," or the abbreviation "corp.," "inc.," "co.," or "ltd.," or words or abbreviations of like import in another language, and must be distinguishable from the names of other entities in the records of the Secretary of State. § 4-27-401.

The Articles must contain all statutorily required information, may include optional information, must be typed or printed, must be in English with English letters or Arabic or Roman numerals, and must be executed by the appropriate person who must both sign and state the capacity in which the document is being executed. § 4-27-120. The form must also be accompanied by the required fee and an exact or conformed copy. § 4-27-201(i). The Secretary of State has the power to prescribe certain mandatory forms (including application for certificate of existent, certain applications by foreign corporations, and the annual franchise tax report. § 4-27-121. Copies of these and other sample forms may be located on the Secretary of State's web page,[5] as of the date this was written. It is a Class C misdemeanor to knowingly file a false document under the statute. § 4-27-129.

After incorporation the incorporators must select the initial directors if they are not already named in the Articles. § 4-27-205. The incorporators may also adopt initial bylaws. § 4-27-206(a). If the directors are named, they must hold an organizational meeting to appoint officers, adopt bylaws and carry on other business (presumably including the issuance of shares). § 4-27-205. Bylaws are the general rules that govern the day-to-day operations of a corporation. § 4-27-206(b).

Once organized a corporation has the power to engage in any lawful business. § 4-27-301. Extensive corporate powers (such as

---

[5]   As of the date this was written, these were located at <http://www.sos.arkansas.gov/business_entity_fees_forms_pro.html#dc>

power to appear in court, to own property, to enter into contracts) are presumed, and need not be recited in the corporation's Articles. § 4-27-302.

Ownership of an interest in a corporation is reflected in share or stock ownership (those terms are synonymous). Authorized shares may be divided into classes, and the Articles must specify how many shares are allowed in each class, and what the par value of those shares will be. § 4-27-601. Classes must have distinguishable names, and the articles must state (before the shares are issued) the preferences, limitations and relative rights of each class. § 4-27-601(a). At least one class must have unlimited voting rights, and at least one class must be entitled to have the net assets of the corporation upon dissolution. § 4-27-601(b). Optional classes can have special voting or economic rights. § 4-27-601(c).

Shares are to be issued when the board of directors authorizes their issuance. § 4-27-621. The corporation must receive at least par value for the shares (§ 4-27-621(c)), and must accept only money paid, labor done, or property actually paid over. § 4-27-621(b). Absent fraud, the determination of the directors about the adequacy and receipt of consideration is conclusive. § 4-27-621(d). Ownership of shares does NOT make a shareholder personally liable for debts of the corporation, except that a shareholder must pay the full consideration required as agreed. § 4-27-622. Of course, as with other forms of business, a shareholder is still liable for the consequences of his or her own misconduct, if he or she guarantees a corporate obligation, or if the veil of limited liability is pierced.

The presumption is that shares are readily transferable and may be sold at any time to anyone for whatever a selling shareholder can get. A shareholder cannot sell to someone that the seller knows or ought to know is going to loot the corporation, but other than that, it takes an agreement to which the shareholder is a party and of which the buyer has notice to restrict transferability of stock. § 4-27-627. If the shareholder agrees and the potential buyer has notice, however, any reasonable share transfer restriction will be upheld. § 4-27-627.

Corporations pay out income to shareholders in the form of distributions, generally in the form of dividends. § 4-27-640. No dividend may be paid if it would render the corporation insolvent, either in the sense of not being able to pay its bills as they come due, or having liabilities that exceed the remaining assets. § 4-27-640. Other than that, however, directors have wide discretion in determining if and when to declare dividends, unless the directors are acting in bad faith in refusing to declare dividends (as would be the case if they are trying to freeze out a minority shareholder).

Shareholders do not have a great deal of authority in a corporation, but the statutes do provide for annual meetings at which directors are to be elected. § 4-27-701. Shareholders may also call special meetings if holders of at least 10% of the outstanding shares entitled to vote so request. § 4-27-7 02. Meetings are not required if a majority of the shares entitled to vote agree to the action and sign a written consent. § 4-27-704. For actual meetings, the statute includes some degree of formality, setting out rules for determining the record ownership date, and how much notice of the meeting needs to be given. §§ 4-27-705, -707. The statutes also impose on the corporation the obligation to make available a shareholder list prior to any such meeting. § 4-27-721.

Proxy voting is specifically allowed, unless the Articles or Bylaws provide otherwise. § 4-27-722. Proxies are presumed to last no longer than 11 months unless a longer date is expressed, and are always revocable unless coupled with an interest. § 4-27-722.

In order to make sure that voting arrangements between shareholders are respected, the statutes allow both shareholder agreements and voting trusts. §§ 4-27-730 to - 731. Voting agreements are less formal, and are enforceable so long as they are signed and in writing, and have no common law defenses, for example, contract defenses or public policy objections such as sterilizing the board, oppressing the minority, or being entered into for a private benefit. § 4-27-731. In addition to those requirements, a voting trust must be filed with the corporation, must result in the legal ownership of the shares being transferred on the corporate records to the trustee, and must not last more than ten years. § 4-27-730.

However, most decisions in corporations are to be made by or under the authority of the board of directors. § 4-27-801. The only real exception to this is if a corporation with 50 or fewer shareholders elects to reserve certain power to shareholders (§ 4-27-801(c)), an option that does not happen all that frequently.

Directors are generally elected for one year terms (§§ 4-27-803, - 805), although if the board has at least nine members staggered terms of up to three years are permissible. § 4-27- 806. Directors can resign any time, and can be removed by shareholders at any time without cause unless the Articles provide that the directors may only be removed for cause. § 4-27-808. Vacancies on the board may be filled by the shareholders or remaining directors. § 4-27-810. Directors set their own compensation. § 4-27-811. Meetings, voting, quorum, notice and record keeping requirements are set out in the statute. §§ 4-27-820 to -824.

The statutory standard of care for directors seems to say that they must act in good faith, as an ordinary prudent person in like position, acting in a manner reasonably believed to be in the best interests of the corporation (§ 4-27-830), but in reality the business judgment rule protects most decisions made by directors, even if negligent. In fact, so long as directors make a business judgment in a manner that does not implicate bad faith, while being reasonably informed and avoiding a conflict of interest, they will not be liable unless the action is irrational (and as far as I can determine there are no cases in the real world finding irrationality absent findings of bad faith, failure to be informed, or a conflict of interest as well).

A conflict of interest is not "voidable" "solely" because of the conflict if it has been disclosed to and approved by disinterested directors (of which there must be at least two); or disclosed and approved by the disinterested shareholders; or it is fair. § 4-27-831. Under the applicable case law, however, unless the transaction is fair, the courts find that damages may be imposed, or that a self-interested contract may be struck down under common law obligations of good faith and fair dealing or the duty of care requirements, even if the conflict has been disclosed and the transaction technically approved by disinterested directors or shareholders. The effect of such approval seems to be only in changing who has the burden of proof as to fairness.

Indemnification of directors and officers is permissible, so long as the statutory requirements are met. § 4-27-850. If a director or officer is successful on the merits, indemnification is mandatory; if there is a finding of bad faith or liability to the company, indemnification is not allowed. § 4-27-850.

Advantages:
There is no form of business that is better understood than the corporation. The case law is by far the most developed, and both lawyers and accountants who practice in the area should have a good grasp on the rules applicable to this form of business. The statutes are complete, are fairly uniform, and are quite detailed. The rules set out a degree of formality that may be attractive to passive investors, as their rights are clearly spelled out. It is clearly the business form of choice for public entities. It offers limited liability for owners and

a high degree of protection for managers, even those who are expected to engage in risk taking ventures on behalf of the business.

Disadvantages:

The same specificity that may be desirable for some investors, may make this unwieldy for smaller operations that want less formality. The business is not eligible for partnership tax treatment, and subchapter S is available to a limited number of corporations, and is not as flexible as subchapter K in at least some regards. The corporate taxation, combined with high level of formality and inflexibility prevent this from being an ideal form of business for many start up operations.

CHAPTER II.   CONSIDERATIONS   IN CHOOSING BETWEEN   ORGANIZATIONAL OPTIONS

II.1.   Developing an Enterprise Profile

The first thing that you are likely to want to do when a client seeks your assistance in helping them choose and form an Arkansas business is get a general understanding of the business that is planned by your client. What kind of business are they planning to operate (not the form that they may be interested in, but the type of business activities in which they will be involved)? Different considerations may apply to companies providing services, manufacturing, new technology development, retail sales, etc. What stage are they at in their planning? Have they already begun operations? Have they already formed one kind of business and are considering a change in organizational form? This is the kind of general background information that will often be essential for you in helping to counsel your clients on their options.

II.1.1. What is the Nature of the Enterprise?

Obviously, you cannot be expected to be intimately familiar with the details of every possible type of business enterprise. Learning the general nature of the business to be undertaken by your clients may help you in explaining the limits of your expertise to your clients, may help you predict the time commitment you are making, and may raise other considerations for you.

First, there may be some kinds of operations that require expertise that you do not wish to develop or be associated with. Some kinds of businesses or business issues may not be covered by your professional malpractice carrier (for example if substantial securities issues will be raised). It is more likely, however, that you

43

will be asked to give advice about a particular kind of business that is subject to special regulations with which are you not very familiar, at least at the outset of the representation. These special regulations may limit the available form of business, who may own the business, who is eligible to participate in the management of the business, or may govern other operational aspects of the business that will dictate how it must be organized. Alternatively, there may be considerations implicate that federal regulations (such as the federal securities, copyright, patent, or franchise laws). In any of these instances you might need to do additional research to make sure that there are no rules that limit how your client's proposed business can be structured, or to make sure that you understand the rules that do exist. In some instances, you might even decide that the client would best be served by finding a different attorney to assist in the formation of the business. Alternatively, you might wish to associate with other counsel to handle specific issues (such as securities or patent work).

While conducting the preliminary investigation, if a client comes to you seeking advice about setting up a professional association, you might find that the businesses is required to be owned only by licensed members of the relevant profession. (This requirement might exist either because of the professional association statutes[6] or the statutes or regulations applicable to the particular profession under consideration[7]). A business involved in the distribution of alcoholic beverages will be subject to regulations promulgated by the Arkansas Alcohol Beverage Control Board, which will probably need to be reviewed before any formal advice is

---

[6]   The Arkansas Professional Corporation Act includes such a requirement. § 4-29-208.

[7]   For instance, businesses formed to provide public accountancy services are subject to such rules. See § 17-12-402.

given.[8] A technology-based business that will be dependent on federal grants may be subject to requirements embodied in the terms of the available grants.[9] Certain kinds of businesses may have special statutes governing their ownership or operation.[10] Franchises are subject to extensive federal regulation,[11] as are various kinds of financial institutions.[12]

---

[8]   One such regulation prohibits persons who have an ownership interest in one level of the distribution change from being an owner of any business at a different level of the distribution structure in this state. Regulations of the Arkansas Alcohol Beverage Control Board may be accessed online at http://www.dfa.arkansas.gov/offices/abc/rules/Pages/default.aspx (last visited July 1, 2011).

[9]   For example, federal Small Business Innovation Research (SBIR) grant recipients must be at least 51% American owned. Eligibility requirements for SBIR grant recipients can be found in Section III. Eligibility Requirements, PA-06-006: Small Business Innovation Research Program Parent Announcement, available online at http://grants.nih.gov/grants/guide/pa-files/PA-06-006.html#SectionIII (last visited July 1, 2011).

[10]   By way of example, an Arkansas Industrial Development Company can not have any one owner of more than 10% of the total outstanding equity. § 15-4-1211. In some states, statutes prevent out of state residents from being shareholders in corporations that own agricultural lands. An Arkansas business seeking to own agricultural land elsewhere might be subject to such restrictions. Kansas has such restrictions. See Kan. Stat. Ann. §§ 17-5903 to- 5904.

[11]   Federal law sets forth certain mandatory disclosures that must be made before a franchise is sold. This general mandate is set out in the Federal Trade Commission's Franchise Rule ("Disclosure Requirements and Prohibitions Concerning Franchising and Business Opportunity Ventures," 16 CFR 436). The required format is described in the Federal Trade Commission's Interpretive Guides ("Interpretive Guides to Franchising and Business Opportunity Ventures Trade Regulation Rule", 44 Federal Register 49966 (August 24, 1979), Bus Franchise Guide (CCH) ¶6206), or franchisors may utilize the state-ordained "Uniform Franchise Offering Circular" disclosure format (although this does not necessarily work in all states).

[12]   Federally insured banks and savings and loans (for instance) are subject to extensive federal regulation. See Federal Deposit Insurance Act (12 U.S.C. §§ 1811 et seq.).

Obviously, this is not a comprehensive listing of special requirements that can apply to every kind of business. It does, however, highlight the need to understand what kind of business is anticipated in order to help you conduct any specialized research that may be needed before you undertake the task of helping your client choose an appropriate organizational form.

There are some other facts about the enterprise that will also help you in representing your client competently.

II.1.2. Is a New or Existing Enterprise Involved?

This may be a factor of critical importance to you and your client. When you are asked to give legal advice about the best way to organize and operate a business, you must consider whether the business is new or is already in existence. If the business has already been set up as a corporation, partnership, or LLC, it may be perfectly possible to adapt the existing structures to meet the client's needs. Indeed, this may be the most efficient and cost-effective way of proceeding, even though you might have advised the client to consider a different form of enterprise if the business did not already exist. Moreover, tax considerations may make it impracticable to change organizational forms even if it will be difficult to adapt the current business form to meet the client's needs.

Take for example, a client who formed a small corporation several years ago to operate her business. She contributed certain property, including real estate, to the corporation in exchange for her shares. Now she wants to change the nature of the business and wants to determine whether another form of business enterprise might be more advantageous. While she may be correct in assuming that other forms of operation might be a better choice for her current operations, if she converts to a partnership or LLC, she could trigger a dissolution of the corporation for tax purposes. That would mean that if the property she contributed to the corporation has appreciated in value to a significant degree, she will have to report that gain as income upon conversion (because of the deemed dissolution required under our current tax code). The tax consequences are generally greatest when converting from a form of business that was taxed as a corporation to one that would be taxed as a partnership. In such a case, the consequences of converting may be sufficiently adverse that the disadvantages will outweigh any prospective advantages of changing the form of business.

On the other hand, a business that is taxed as a corporation can often easily convert to another form that is taxed as a corporation (whether automatically or by election), and a business that is taxed as a partnership can typically easily convert to another form of business that will be a tax partnership. In 2009, Arkansas amended its business organization statutes to facilitate conversion of business entities to a different operational form.[13] Under prior law, it was possible but often complicated for a business to change its form of business, with such changes often requiring multiple steps and the formation and merger of the various entities. Now, however, it is generally possible under state law for any form of business, by adopting a plan of conversion, to change from one form of business to another. Corporations may convert to another form of business and other forms of business can change to a corporation. § 4-27-1002. LLCs have the same privilege (and other organizations the privilege of becoming an LLC). § 4-32-1202. General partnerships and LLPs are governed by § 4-46-902, and limited partnerships and LLLPs are subject to § 4-47-1102. Under all of these statutes, the appropriate persons (those with management power and/or an ownership stake) must vote to approve the conversion, and appropriate articles of conversion must be filed with the Secretary of State. Remember,

---

[13]   The subject of conversions is dealt with in more detail in Chapter 7 of these materials.

however, that even though it is easy and simple to convert under state business law there may be tax considerations that are not addressed in the state statute, particularly if the conversion means that a business taxed as a corporation would, after the conversion, expect to be taxed as a partnership.

II.1.3. What is the Likely Duration of the Enterprise?

In counseling your client about optimal business structure, you will also want to consider the likely duration of the business. If it is essential that the business continue uninterrupted for extended periods of time (for example, if non-transferable licenses or leases are involved), a business that is subject to involuntary dissolution in too many situations would not be ideal. If your client anticipates a very quick public offering of ownership interests in the venture, this may also suggest preferable organizational choices. Even where conversion is relatively easy, if it is absolutely certain that another form will shortly be required, it makes sense to at least consider whether the ultimate form should simply be adopted from the outset.

II.1.4. What are the Likely Capital Needs of the Enterprise?

Another very important factor in choosing a form of business will be a basic understanding of the capital needs of the enterprise. In many cases, your clients will not be able to provide for all of the capital needs of their business. They may be anticipating additional investors in the foreseeable future, or they may anticipate borrowing funds. Alternatively, they may be seeking research grants from federal or state authorities. In any case, to the extent possible, the enterprise should be set up to easily accommodate foreseeable additional investment, whether it will take the form of debt, equity, or grants.

II.1.5. What are the Needs for Management Expertise?

The answer to this question is important because it may make one or more forms of business more or less appropriate. If a business requires special managerial expertise, it will be important to choose a business form that allows individuals having such expertise to actually perform the essential management functions. Allowing or requiring individual investors who lack that expertise to participate in management is likely to be inefficient and could ultimately be harmful or even fatal to the business. On the other hand, it will be much easier to protect minority investors if they have a say in at least some management decisions. Therefore, an understanding of the special management needs and experience of the various investors will be important in properly forming a business.

II.2. Who are the Investors?

Once you have done any specialized research required because of the type of business being contemplated, you will need to collect information about the anticipated participants in the venture. The individual or group of individuals who actually show up at your door seeking legal representation in connection with the formation of the business might be the sole participants, or there might be other investors for whom these individuals are acting as representatives. Either way, you will need to know about all of the current and planned investors.

You may want this information in order to evaluate whether you can or should represent all of the concerned parties at this stage, or whether you should advise particular individuals to seek outside counsel because they might have different interests at stake. But you will also need information about the various investors because this information will be relevant in helping you and your clients decide on what legal options are available, and which of those options are most likely to meet their needs.

One other point should be made at the outset. "Investor" can have different meanings depending on the context, and "investment" in an enterprise can take many forms. People can plan on investing cash, property, services, promises to pay money in the future, or promises to perform services in the future. For example they can make such investments hoping to become owners (i.e. "equity" investment), or creditors (an investment pursuant to which the business takes on debt, or an obligation to repay the creditor on a priority basis), or lessors (where property is rented to the business), or employees (where services are performed in exchange for compensation). All such persons can be said to be "investing" something in the business, and each may have a different stake in the success of the venture. However, when it comes to choosing between available forms of business enterprises, it is generally most important to understand who is intended to be an "owner" first, and then to understand the other players on the field.

II.2.1. Number of Investors

The easiest information to obtain is likely to be how many people are getting together to form the business. In order to obtain this information, depending on their level of sophistication and experience, you may have to explain to your clients the different types of investors and the roles they may play in the business.

At the outset, you need to know how many people are going to be involved in financing and operating the business as owners. How many people are going to contribute money, property, or services to the business? Be sure that you know whether all of these persons are expecting to become "owners," with the expectation of sharing in profits and management at some level, and potentially the willingness to share in losses (depending on the kind of business chosen). Then determine whether there are other persons who are expected to contribute to the business as creditors, with the expectation that they will not "own" or manage the business, but with the benefit of knowing that they will be repaid before the owners are allowed to take profits out of the business. Finally, make sure you know if the business contemplates other participants in the form of employees or otherwise.

One reason that you need to be concerned with the number of participants and their respective roles is that if there is the wrong number of investors who will be "owners," certain forms of business enterprise may be unavailable. For example, a sole proprietorship can have only one owner. If there are more than two owners involved, the business might be a partnership, a joint venture, or some other form of association, but it cannot be a sole proprietorship. Similarly, an S corporation can have no more than 100 equity investors (the number used to be much lower), and even the presence of creditors can raise problems if their investment looks like an ownership interest that is merely masquerading as debt. On the other hand, partnerships require at least two owners, and that is true regardless of what kind of partnership your clients are considering.

Even if the number of participants may not automatically rule out a significant number of options as a matter of law, the number of participants is still likely to have a significant impact on the optimal organizational structure. For example, if your client informs you that he has a string of friends and relatives who are each going to contribute relatively modest amounts of money for fractional interests in the enterprise, the presence of a large, diverse, and widely dispersed group of owners may make the general partnership, LLP, and member-managed LLC forms of business less attractive, and may make it more important to choose a form of enterprise that allows for delegated management authority with relatively little direct investor participation.

51

II.2.2. Types of Investors

In addition to ascertaining the number of investors, you will also need to understand what types of investors are being contemplated. This means understanding not only the type of investment (for example, determining whether the investment in intended to take the form of debt or equity, as discussed in the preceding section), but also the nature of the particular investor.

Most forms of business enterprise can have a number of different kinds of investors. Natural persons can invest in virtually every kind of business enterprise, and other forms of business entities, such as corporations, general and limited partnerships, and LLCs can also be investors in most other businesses. There are, however, some exceptions to this general rule. For example, only a natural individual can be a sole proprietor. Moreover, with few exceptions, only natural individuals can be shareholders (equity participants) in an S Corporation. In fact, only certain individuals can own shares in an S Corporation. Citizens of foreign countries are generally ineligible shareholders in such corporations. Corporate ownership might also disqualify businesses from certain funding sources.[14]

You must therefore be in a position to determine how many investors are planning on participating in the planned enterprise, and either who or what they are. Are they individuals? Are they legal persons such as corporations, partnerships, or LLCs? Are they

---

[14]   Federal grants in particular may restrict eligible recipients. For a description of basic eligibility requirements for SBIR grants as an example, see Section III. Eligibility Requirements, PA-06-006: Small Business Innovation Research Program Parent Announcement, available online at http://grants.nih.gov/grants/guide/pa-files/PA-06-006.html#SectionIII (last visited July 1, 2011).

American citizens? What is their permanent state of residence?[15]

II.3.   Identifying Investor Expectations/Objectives

Of course, identifying the investors is only the starting point of the necessary inquiries that you must make with regard to investors in a planned business in order to determine how best to advise clients. While knowing about the number and type of investors may help you rule out certain forms of business enterprise, by itself, such information will not provide you with much to go on in evaluating which of the available forms of business enterprise are most likely to meet the objectives of your clients, or whether it is possible, through careful planning, to mold some other form of enterprise so that it will also serve you clients' needs. In order to attempt these tasks, you will need to make a considered inquiry about the expectations and objectives of the investors, both as a group and individually.

II.3.1. Participation in Management

There is no right or wrong starting point for investigating the particular expectations and objectives of the various investors in a planned enterprise.   However, one of the most important considerations, at least from the perspective of many investors, is likely to be their right (and the rights of others) to participate in management decisions and the obligations that are associated with assuming such a role.

For example, some investors may feel perfectly comfortable with investing money in an enterprise and sitting back quietly,

---

[15]   Remember that for some kinds of business other questions will need to be asked as well. For example, in the case of a professional corporation, the owners and managers may need to be licensed members of the profession. Inquiries that are relevant only to certain categories of activities will not be covered in any detail in this book.

waiting for a return on that investment to materialize at some point in the future. Particularly since many investors in a new enterprise are likely to be close friends or family members of the primary entrepreneur, those investors may be quite willing to be passive, with little or no expectation that they will assume any management responsibilities in connection with their investment.

On the other hand, there may also be investors who expect a large say in how the business is to be run. For example, if two friends have an idea for going into business together, they may both expect to participate in decisions about how the business will operate. They may want an equal say in such decisions; they may wish to have some types of decisions that must be made jointly; they may have some kinds of decisions that could be made by either one of the two; and they may have some that must be made by a particular individual. An anticipated angel or venture capital investor is also likely to expect or demand a significant management role, and an organizational form that allows for such involvement may be very important, especially if one of the goals of the business is to be able to attract such investment.

Finally, there may be some investors who do not want the responsibility of making day-to-day decisions for the business, but will want to participate in major decisions, such as the decision to sell the entire business to someone else, or the decision to accept a new equity participant, or any decision to incur substantial indebtedness. Flexibility in structuring management rights and responsibilities may therefore also be important in some cases.

Of course, along with the right to participate in management often comes certain responsibilities. If there are investors who want a certain amount of control, but are absolutely insistent about limiting their personal responsibility and fiduciary duties owed to others in the enterprise, the time for you to learn about that is at the beginning, before the clients have incurred expenses associated with drafting documents and properly forming their business.

II.3.2. Personal Risk Comfort Level

The idea of owing limited duties to other participants in the venture goes hand in hand with other considerations related to the desire of business participants to minimize personal risk. While it is fair to say that almost all clients would prefer to minimize all risk all the time, in reality there are multiple components to how much risk investors are actually willing to assume in order to achieve their other goals, such as ultimate financial success of the venture.

First, clients need to be aware that there are different types of investments that can be made in a business. Investments can take the form of equity or debt, or a combination of the two. Loans to a business can be secured or unsecured, and may be supported by personal guarantees from some or all other participants as well. One essential inquiry is therefore to determine how much risk a particular investor is willing to assume with regard to whether the investment will be repaid.

In general, equity participants are paid last, after creditors of the business enterprise. Therefore, if your client has investors who are particularly concerned about not losing their investments, you may have to be concerned about structuring the investors' involvement so that they become creditors rather than shareholders (in the case of a corporation), partners (in the case of a partnership), or members (in the case of an LLC). If the investors are even more risk adverse, your client may have to consider the possibility of securing the debts with assets of the enterprise or with personal guarantees from other participants who are willing to execute such obligations.

In addition to this type of risk aversion, some investors will want to avoid liabilities to other participants in the venture. They may not want to be liable for negligent decisions, or failure to participate actively, or if they choose to compete with the business. Potential liability for breach of the duties of care and loyalty that are often associated with ownership of businesses where management rights are included as part of the ownership model may need to be discussed, defined, excluded, insured against, or otherwise considered when evaluating business options. Some forms of business may impose management responsibilities and fiduciary obligations on all owners, which might be unacceptable to some participants. General partners in particular always owe certain minimal obligations of care and loyalty, which can be defined but not eliminated. Similarly, in a corporation, a shareholder who insists on participation on the board of directors, may be unable to avoid certain responsibilities, even if the corporation is set up to provide indemnification for directors' liability to the broadest extent allowed by law. Therefore, knowing what obligations are acceptable to the proposed owners may help you advise your clients about optimal business structures.

Of course neither of these is the most obvious consideration when it comes to limiting liability of investors. Certain forms of enterprise are said to impose unlimited personal liability on owners (meaning that the owners' personal assets can be sought by the business's creditors to pay debts of the enterprise), while other forms offer "limited liability" to owners. This kind of limited liability has long been a hallmark of the corporate form of business enterprise. In recent years, however, other forms of business association have also developed that offer participants limited liability. The LLC offers members limited liability to the same extent that a corporation shields shareholders; the LLP protects all partners against personal liability for partnership obligations; the limited partnership, a form of business enterprise which has been around for a long time, also offers some participants (the limited partners) the benefits of limited liability; and the LLLP offers the general partners in a limited partnership the same protection limited partners are given.

This limitation of liability does not mean that the investor does not stand to lose his, her, or its capital contribution (another phrase for amount of equity invested in the business). Rather, it means that if there is insufficient equity in the business to pay all business creditors, the owners' personal assets cannot be seized in repayment of those business debts. Even this limitation is not absolute, as case law suggests that the so-called "veil" of limited liability can be pierced in certain circumstances.[16] In addition, the limitation of liability does not apply to liability for one's personal negligence or misconduct, and in the case of professional corporations, may not even protect completely against personal liability for the professional misconduct of other members of the firm if there was a duty to supervise or similar obligation owed to the client who has been harmed.

Even with these limitations, the attribute of limited liability may be one that seems very important to investors. It is, however, probably worth emphasizing that this kind of limited liability may not be as important as clients are likely to assume.

First, if virtually all of the investor's assets are going to be transferred to the business anyway, there is nothing to be lost in the event that a business creditor seeks to impose personal liability on the individual owners. For example, take the example of Mr. and Mrs. Brown, who have long been farmers. They are approaching retirement, and are contemplating transferring the family farm into some form of business entity as a mechanism for transferring interests in the farm to their children. It would not be at all unusual for such a transfer to take place as part of an estate plan for the elderly

---

[16]   For a fuller discussion of this issue, see Chapter 8 of these materials.

Browns. Of course, the Browns are likely to be quite adamant about not having personal liability for the debts of the farm. They are likely to be quite risk-adverse, and the prospect of personal liability may be very unappealing. In reality, however, if the Browns' personal assets consist of no more than the farm land and equipment, and if the land (including the family home) and equipment are transferred to the business entity, there is nothing left for a business creditor to take if the Browns are sued personally. Thus, the financial risk for the Browns is minimal even if the farm is transferred to a business entity that does not offer them the protections of limited liability.

There is another problem with allowing the attribute of limited liability to assume too much importance in the decision of what form of business enterprise to adopt. Most new businesses will require a certain level of debt in order to meet operating expenses, at the very least until the business is up and running. Commercial creditors, such as banks or other lending institutions, are extremely unlikely to lend funds to the business without the personal guarantee of the investors. Therefore, even though shareholders generally are not personally liable for debts of the corporation, partners are not liable for the debts of an LLP or LLLP, and members are not personally liable for debts of the LLC, if the creditors require personal guarantees, personal liability on such debts exists independent of the investor's status as shareholder or member. Much of the benefit of limited liability is therefore quite illusive.

However, if the business is one that might result in substantial tort liability, as might be the case if there is a risk of products liability claims or concerns about employee negligence, and at least some of the investors have substantial assets outside the business that they do not wish to risk losing in the event of business failure, an enterprise with limited liability will probably be preferred.

Keep in mind that this does not necessarily mean that a corporation is the best option, notwithstanding conventional wisdom that treats limited liability as a peculiarly corporate characteristic. Clients should be advised that there are several forms of business enterprise that offer limited liability to participants, and which, depending on other expectations and interests of the participants, may be more appropriate for them.

II.3.3. Distributions--When are Profits Paid Out, in What Amounts and to Whom?

Another concern that is likely to be critical to investors is the return on their investment. You will have to learn about how the various investors plan to split the earnings of the enterprise in order to advise clients about the various options available under Arkansas law. Does everyone intend to take a share of net profits? Is everyone going to be entitled to an equal share, or will each investor's share depend on the size of the investment? Is it the value of the contribution that will determine the right to participate, regardless of when contributions are made, or is it the number or shares, interests, or units owned (regardless of the value of consideration paid) that will govern rights to participate in the profits? Is a regular rate of return important? Who is to determine when distributions should be made, and in what amount? Are certain distributions mandatory or are other standards needed to protect the expectations of the investors?

These are the most obvious questions, but there are also some other, less obvious questions that may be critically important in choosing the right form of entity. As will be discussed in more detail later, there are different tax rules applicable to different forms of business enterprise. It can probably be assumed that everyone is interested in minimizing their tax obligations. Therefore, investors are likely to want to avoid choosing an enterprise that imposes double taxation on business income. (This is also a hallmark of the corporation, which is generally said to be subject to double taxation. In brief, double taxation occurs when income is taxed when earned by the business, and then again when the remaining profits, left after taxes have been paid, are distributed to the owners.) This may lead investors to prefer a form of enterprise that is taxed like a partnership. The drawback to this is that in a partnership, or any other enterprise that is taxed like a partnership, it is possible to be taxed on business earnings before they have been distributed (i.e. actually paid over to the owners).

The problem occurs like this. Suppose we have two businesses, one formed as a corporation between two individuals, and one formed as a partnership of two individuals. Both business have net earnings (earnings after operating expenses but before taxes) of $100,000 in a given year. The corporation pays corporate income tax on the $100,000. Whatever is left may be distributed, in whole or in part, to the shareholders, and the shareholders will have to pay personal income tax on the funds which are distributed to them. However, the shareholders will not be taxed on corporate earnings until and unless those sums are actually passed through to them. The partners in the other business are in a different situation.

The partnership also has net profits of $100,000. It pays no taxes on that amount. Rather, it files an informational return with the IRS for the year that the funds are earned. That return will show how the $100,000 in earnings are "allocated" to the various partners. If the two partners have an equal right to share in profits, each will be allocated $50,000 of income. The partners must immediately pay taxes on their allocated share of that income, even if the partnership does not distribute any of those funds to the partners. For example, if the partnership keeps the entire $100,000 and uses the money as cash reserves, the partners will have no cash in hand. Nonetheless, because they have been "allocated" $50,000 in income by the partnership, each partner will have to pay taxes on that amount. Partnership tax rules require that all income be allocated in the year that it is earned; tax cannot be deferred by having the partnership decline to allocate or distribute all of its income.

Therefore, a very important and less obvious question about appropriate and expected rates of return for investors is whether they are in a position to pay taxes on amounts that may be earned by the business (and allocated to the investors) but not actually distributed to the investors for their personal use. Note that even if investors are extremely reluctant or even completely unwilling to accept this risk, this does not mean that the form of business that will be taxed as a partnership will be unacceptable. Instead, it means that if a form of business that will be taxed as a partnership is chosen, you will know to take special care in drafting the distribution provisions of the enterprise's organizational documents to insure that distributions adequate to cover taxes are mandatory.

Even if your clients are looking at the corporate form of business, it is important to take into account whether your clients expect mandatory distributions, and if so, under what circumstances. Moreover, it will be important to learn up front if the investors expect that they will have a say in determining the timing and amount of distributions.

Note also some very important terminology. When profits are actually paid out, they are said to be distributed. For example, dividends that are paid to corporate shareholders are a form of corporate distribution. Similarly, when a partner receives his, her, or its share of partnership income, it is in the form of a distribution. The actual distribution is, however, different from the determination of how profits (or losses) are to be allocated. Because partners may be taxed on partnership profits before the funds are actually distributed, we also need to be able to talk about allocations of profits (and of losses) as well.

II.3.4. Profit Allocation

This is likely to be a critical issue for your clients. They are almost certainly going to be concerned with their share of enterprise profits. If you are forming a business for a number of clients, deciding on profit allocations may be very difficult, and may even necessitate separate clients retaining separate counsel.

In many cases, however, your clients will already have agreed on how profits are to be split. The clients may choose to split their profits equally, or proportionately based on an agreed valuation of their contributions to the enterprise, or in any other manner they wish. Once agreement has been reached, the only difficulty is making sure that the organizational documents reflect the agreement.

Do not assume that the default rules of the various organizational form you have chosen will automatically achieve the desired profit sharing arrangement. For example, in a corporation, absent careful drafting in the articles of incorporation, all shares will share equally in any corporate distribution. Therefore, in order to make sure that clients who select a corporation as the form for their business achieve their goals about profit sharing, it will be necessary to adjust the number of shares that each owns, or to adjust the rights and privileges of the stock to be held by each shareholder. In a partnership, absent agreement to the contrary, all partners are entitled to share equally in all profits. This means that, regardless of the relative value of the contributions of each partner, the sharing percentages will be equal unless the partnership agreement has been drafted to change this outcome. Arkansas LLCs work the same way under the default rules. In a limited partnership or LLLP, partners (both general and limited) are presumed to share income on the basis of the value of what they contributed for their ownership interests.

II.3.5. Allocating Losses

An issue that some entrepreneurs fail to consider is what to do with business losses. The possibility of business failure, or even a net operating loss during the start-up phase of the business, is all too often something that clients will not want to dwell upon. One of your jobs is to make sure that your clients consider what needs to happen if the business suffers losses.

One objective may be to make business losses deductible on individual investors' returns. Of course, if the investors do not have significant income against which to apply these losses, this may not be a significant objective at all. It is also possible that some investors will be better able to utilize losses against income if the losses are passed through to them. The need or desire for such special allocations of loss may limit the available business forms. In general, businesses that are taxed as partnerships have automatic pass through of losses, while associations taxable as corporations would only have pass through of losses if a special "S" election has been filed.[17]

One other issue with regard to the allocation of losses must be addressed. It is not at all uncommon for two or more persons to go into business together, with the understanding that some of the participants will provide cash or property to the business and other participants will provide services in exchange for their interest in the enterprise. Whenever you see investors who are contributing services rather than property, you may need to clarify the participants' understanding about what happens in the event of business failure.

---

[17]   The tax rules applicable to S corporations are discussed very briefly, and in overview form, in Chapter 3. The intricacies of such tax issues, however, are far beyond the scope of this book.

For example, unless there is an agreement to the contrary, partnership statutes provide that no partner is entitled to compensation for his or her services rendered to the partnership; these rules also provide that, absent agreement, profits and losses are to be allocated equally.[18] What happens in the following situation? Assume that there are two partners, Albert and Bertha. Further assume that Albert contributes $50,000 in cash to the partnership in return for a 50% partnership interest while Bertha contributes her services for a year in exchange for a 50% interest in the partnership. Finally, assume that at the end of the year the partnership has spent all $50,000 in cash that it had on hand to begin with, and is now bankrupt.

One might suppose that Albert has lost his $50,000 cash investment and Bertha has lost the value of her services. Neither would get a return on their investment. In actuality, however, unless there is an agreement to the contrary, partnership statutory law could be read as requiring that the loss of $50,000 be split equally, with Bertha being entitled to no credit or remuneration for her services. This would mean that Bertha would now owe the partnership $25,000, or half of the total loss. Her contribution would be allocated and distributed to Albert, making their "losses" equal.

As you can probably tell from the way that I have set up this hypothetical, it is entirely possible that this result would not reflect the expectations of Albert and Bertha, and it is therefore critical that you explore the issue of how losses are to be allocated in the event that one or more of your investors intends to

---

[18]   In Arkansas, these rules are codified at Ark. Code Ann. § 4-46-401. Subsection (h) specifies that partners are not entitled to payment for services to the partnership (absent agreement to the contrary, of course), and subsection (b) specifies that each partner is charged with losses in proportion to the partner's share in profits, which is presumed to be equal (again, unless the parties have agreed otherwise).

contribute services in exchange for his or her interest in the business. In fact, courts in other jurisdictions are split on the issue. Some courts have concluded it would be inequitable to require a partner in Bertha's position to have to make additional payments, and some would require her to do so. From your standpoint, by far the best result is to make sure your clients understand the risks, and to draft an agreement that specifies how services-only partners are to be treated.

In addition, there may be tax consequences associated with persons who make contributions in return for services. If the person is immediately entitled to a capital interest (i.e. an interest in the capital of the business) as a result of contributing services, there may be tax consequences to the investor, and gain may have to be recognized and reported. This is certainly an aspect of any proposed deal that should be explored with a client's tax advisors, before a business form is locked in.

II.3.6. Liquidation of Investment

A final consideration for many investors is likely to be how they can get rid of their investment. First and foremost, this issue encompasses the investors' ability to voluntarily or involuntarily dispose of their ownership interests to purchasers, creditors, heirs, or others. Some forms of business make such transfers very easy. In fact, if your clients choose a corporation, unless you draft a shareholder agreement or include in the corporation's organizational documents restrictions on the transferability of shares, the general rule is that shares are freely transferable. This means the shares can be sold at any time, to any one, for any price that the investor chooses. This may or may not be ideal from the business's standpoint.

On the other hand, other forms of business (including all partnerships and the LLC) set up default rules that make transfer of the ownership interest relatively difficult. Absent agreement to the contrary, in these forms of business, an owner may transfer his, her, or its economic interest (i.e. the right to distributions) but may not sell the right to be an owner (ie, to become either a partner or member) without agreement of all the other owners. This means that a transferee (whether by voluntary sale, foreclosure of a charging order on an ownership interest by a creditor of the owner, inheritance, divorce, gift, or otherwise) obtains only the right to the money and no rights to participate in management of the business. This may limit the value of the transferable interest, and may or may not be something that is desirable or acceptable in any given situation.

Regardless of whether a corporation or other form of business is chosen, the default rules mentioned here can be avoided by having the participants reach an agreement in advance. A shareholder agreement or articles, or even bylaws can contain share transfer restrictions that would be valid if reasonable and noted on the shares. A written operating agreement can allow free transferability or limited transferability of LLC membership interests (including management rights) with less than unanimous consent of all other members. Partnership agreements can do the same thing for partnerships. However, clients need to understand that the more they need to depart from the default rules, the more expensive it generally is to draft the appropriate documentation for their business. Transferability of interests may therefore affect the choice of which form of business entity is optimal, and can certainly influence how the organizational documents for the business are drafted.

In addition, it is important to ask questions about the nature of anticipated contributions (whether in the form of cash, property, or otherwise, and especially about the investor's tax basis in any contributed property) because this is also likely to impact them when it comes to withdrawing from participation.[19]

---

[19]   One other point about contributions. For historical reasons, the Arkansas state constitution includes a requirement that corporate stock may only be issued for "money or property actually received, or labor done." Ark. Const. Art. XIV, § 8; requirement also codified in corporate statutes at Ark. Code. Ann. § 4-27-621(b). Promissory notes and promises to perform services in the future are not acceptable consideration for the issuance of shares. Ownership interests in all other forms of business, however, may be issued for promissory notes or promises to perform services.

CHAPTER III. TAX IMPLICATIONS OF CHOICE OF ENTITY

III.1. INTRODUCTION TO TAXATION OF BUSINESS ENTITIES

III.1.1. Tax Status Versus State Law Business Label

As mentioned in the preceding chapters, under state law, a business operated for a profit can be organized as a sole proprietorship, a general or limited partnership, an LLP or LLLP, an LLC, or a corporation. For purposes of the Internal Revenue Code, the business may be treated in any of the following ways:

(1)   it may be classified as no more than an extension of the individual owner (as in the case of a sole proprietorship and possibly a single-member LLC);

(2)   it may be taxed as a partnership (in the case of general and limited partnerships organized under traditional partnership law, and most LLPs, LLLPs, and LLCs);

(3)   it may be taxed as a corporation under subchapter C of the Internal Revenue Code (the so-called "C Corporation"); or

(4)   it may be taxed as a corporation that has elected special tax status under subchapter S of the Internal Revenue Code (an "S Corporation").

Note that there are other taxable business forms, such as trusts and cooperatives, but these forms of business will not be discussed in detail here. Note, also, that the way in which an entity is classified under state statutes applicable to organization of businesses will not necessarily govern how the entity is classified for tax purposes.

Corporations are treated as separate entities under subchapter C of the Internal Revenue Code unless a special election has been made to have the corporation governed by subchapter S of the Internal Revenue Code. There are certain eligibility requirements that a corporation making an S election must meet but, in either event, an entity organized as a corporation under state law will be treated as a corporation for federal tax purposes and will be governed by either subchapter C or S. These rules will be discussed in a little more detail later in these materials.

Partnerships are taxed under subchapter K of the Internal Revenue Code, but the rules as to whether an entity is to be classified as a partnership for federal tax purposes are different from the rules governing partnership formation under state law. In general terms, if the partnership is a general or limited partnership formed under traditional partnership rules (such as the UPA or ULPA), it will be classified as a partnership for federal tax purposes unless the partners elect to have their business taxed as a corporation.

Until recently, the applicability of subchapter K to entities formed under newer statutes, such as the various LLP and LLLP statutes that exist in many states, was less clear, and the tax status of unincorporated associations such as LLCs was horribly complex. Recent changes to federal tax law have resolved most of these difficulties, and the current presumption for domestic companies is that most business entities other than corporations will be taxed as partnerships unless the owners specifically elect corporate tax status.[20]

---

[20]   These materials do not address entities formed outside the U.S. seeking to do business here.

III.1.2.   Very Broadly, Why it Matters

For many businesses, the taxable status of an enterprise will be very important. Not only will tax status determine whether net income of the enterprise will be subject to entity-level tax, it will also determine whether or not losses at the entity-level can be passed through to and utilized by the business's owners. Both of these considerations can be critical to maximizing investors' return on their investment.

III.1.3.   Default Rules About how a Business is Classified for Tax Purposes

It is therefore necessary to understand how an entity will be classified for federal tax purposes.

Prior to December 1996, unincorporated, multiple-owner business entities were generally evaluated for federal tax purposes under the so-called "corporate resemblance test" to determine whether they should be classified as associations taxable as corporations or partnerships for federal income tax purposes. The test was set out in Treas. Reg. § 301.7701-2, but originated in the case of Morrissey, et al. v. Commissioner, 296 U.S. 344 (1935). Under this test, very generally, the entity was to be treated as an "association" taxable as a corporation if its characteristics made it sufficiently similar to a corporation, and as a partnership if they did not.

Treasury regulations described the corporate resemblance test in terms of six primary corporate characteristics that a multiple-shareholder corporation would generally possess: (1) associates; (2) an objective to carry on business and divide the gains therefrom; (3) continuity of life; (4) centralization of management; (5) limited liability; and (6) free transferability of interests. Since the first two of these were characteristics that were shared by both corporations and partnerships, they were generally excluded from consideration when the options are corporate versus partnership tax treatment. Thus, the corporate resemblance test was applied by evaluating whether a particular unincorporated multiple-owner organization possessed more of the final four corporate characteristics than it lacked.

The regulations that codified the corporate resemblance test were in place when statutes authorizing most of the new forms of business were adopted. It is therefore not unusual to find provisions in the state laws that mirror certain of those tax regulations. State legislators wanted to make sure that the entities they were authorizing would be eligible for partnership tax status under the complicated corporate resemblance test, so the statutes often incorporated rather complicated language in an attempt to insure this result.

On December 18, 1996, the Treasury Department issued a detailed explanation of new regulations. In essence, under the new rules, a for-profit business organized under state law is presumed to be taxed as a partnership (if it has two or more owners) or disregarded for federal tax law purposes (if it has a single owner), UNLESS the business is: (1) required to be taxed as a corporation under some other provision of the Code; (2) the business is incorporated under state law; or (3) the business elects to be taxed as a corporation. These rules apply to domestic business organized after January 1, 1997.[21]

---

[21]   The presumptive tax classification is different for foreign entities, so care should be taken to review the treasury regulations starting with Treas. Reg. § 301.7701-1 (Classification of organizations for federal tax purposes) if you encounter such an entity and wish to understand its tax status.

These regulations are known as the "check the box" regulations because they presume that most domestic unincorporated business organizations will want to be taxed as partnerships under federal law, but if a contrary desire exists, all the entity has to do is fill out a form indicating a desire to be taxed as a corporation. This approach applies to all such organizations that have two or more associates and an objective to carry on business and divide the gains therefrom, unless the organization's classification is determined under another Code provision.

For example, an entity that is treated as a partnership, but is publicly traded and taxed as a corporation under IRC § 7704, would continue to be taxed as a corporation under these rules. Similarly, a taxable mortgage pool under IRC § 7701(i) would continue to be taxed as a corporation, and an entity that makes an election to be a real estate mortgage investment conduit (REMIC) under 860D(b) would continue to be taxed under the REMIC rules. This approach generally would not affect the existing rules for classifying trusts (other than trusts that are classified as associations or partnerships under Treas. Reg. §§ 301.7701-2 to-3).

Under this approach, all affirmative elections are prospective from the date the election is filed or a later date designated in the election. Retroactive elections are not permitted. The elections have to be executed by all members of the organization and are binding on all members, until superseded by a subsequent election.

These regulations include mechanisms for classifying organizations that do not make affirmative classification elections. Because the IRS and Treasury Department believe that domestic unincorporated business organizations typically are formed to obtain partnership classification, those organizations generally would be classified as partnerships for federal tax purposes unless the organization files an election to be classified as an association taxable as a corporation.

However, because the IRS and Treasury believe that the current classification of existing organizations should be altered only by affirmative election, those organizations that were in existence on or prior to the effective date of the revised regulations retain their prior classification unless an affirmative election to be classified differently is filed.

The following materials now turn to an examination of the consequences of being taxed as a partnership or as a corporation. You might recall that single owner unincorporated businesses are presumed to be disregarded for tax purposes, and the owner of such a business (whether it is a sole proprietorship or an LLC) is to report all taxable items (income, loss, etc.) on his or her personal tax return. If the owner desires to have the business taxed as a corporation, the check the box regulations would allow such an election to be made, but frankly it is difficult to understand when this would be desirable. A single owner corporation formed under state law is required to be taxed as a corporation, and no election to the contrary is permissible. Although it is therefore possible that business might fit one of three general categories (disregarded for tax purposes, a tax partnership, or an association taxable as a corporation), only the latter two options will be discussed here in any detail. Of those two, partnership taxation is discussed first.

III.2. SUPERFICIAL OVERVIEW OF PARTNERSHIP TAXATION

III.2.1.   The Problem of Terminology

In order to understand partnership taxation, it is first essential to understand certain basic terms. First, there is the notion that there are various kinds of "partnerships" under state law (and those may include general partnerships, LLPs, limited partnerships, and LLLPs), but also that there are "tax partnerships" for tax purposes that not only include all of the foregoing, but can also include multi-owner LLCs (even though an LLC is not a "partnership" under state law). Because this chapter is talking about tax partnerships rather than state law partnerships, it should be understood that the rules being discussed here might apply to any of these business forms, even if they are not technically "partnerships" under state law.

Another particularly confusing set of definitions involves the meaning of "allocations," "distributions," and "distributive share." For all practical purposes, "allocations" and "distributive share" mean the same thing; these words or phrases mean the proportion of items of gain, income, loss, deduction, or other economic interests that a particular tax partner is eventually entitled to under applicable law. "Distributions" occur when the partnership actually pays out something of value to the partners in respect of their partnership interests. These events need not, and often do not, occur simultaneously.

For example, assume that A, B, and C are equal partners in the ABC general partnership. A, B, and C may either have specifically agreed that they will be "equal" partners (i.e., sharing equally in all economic interests), or they may have allowed the statutory default rules to govern their business arrangement, because the default rule for general partnerships is that all partners share equally in profits and losses, absent agreement to the contrary.   In addition, for the purposes of this hypothetical, assume that the ABC general partnership earns $90,000 in a given year.   As a result of this, each partner's distributive share of that amount would be $30,000 (i.e., equal to that of every other partner). Note that this allocation has nothing to do with whether the partnership actually pays out any money to the partners at that time.   The payment to the partners (whenever it occurs) is a distribution, and may be either a liquidating distribution (upon a partner's withdrawal or the termination of the entire partnership), or an interim distribution (where all the partners continue to be associated with the partnership, and the partnership simply decides to pay out some amount of its available assets to the partners while the business continues). You must be able to understand and keep in mind the difference between allocations and distributions if you are to have any hope of understanding partnership tax rules.

Although there is nothing particularly complex or unique about this, in order to understand how partnership tax rules work, it is also essential to understand how tax partnerships and tax partners treat such things as contributions, profits, and losses.

First, contributions. A contribution is whatever a partner gives to the partnership in exchange for that person's partnership interest (i.e., what they pay for the privilege of becoming a partner). If a partner becomes a partner by purchase from another person, rather than directly from the partnership, the contribution of the original partner is generally treated as having been acquired along with the partnership interest.   Why does this matter? Because when a partner gets out of the partnership (either because he or she withdraws or dissociates for some other reason or because the entire partnership is winding up and everyone is being paid off), the first distribution to partners is deemed to be a return of the value of their contributions. Only after a return of the value of contributions will a partner be given a share of profits. (Interim distributions, on the other hand, are presumed to be out of profits. More about that in a moment.)

Second, profits and losses. Partnership law is particularly problematic in this area because the default rule about how profits and losses are shared (i.e., the rule which will apply in the absence of any agreement by the participants to the contrary) may seem counter-intuitive and are not the same for all kinds of businesses under state law that are subject to these partnership tax rules. For Arkansas general partnerships and LLPs, the default rule is that all partners are to share equally in the profits and losses of the enterprise (after the return of each partner's contribution).[22] For limited partnerships and LLLPs, the default rule is that amounts are to be shared "on the basis of value, as stated in the required records . . . of the contributions the limited partnership has received from each partner."[23] This is likely to be closer to what

---

[22]   This is, of course, subject to contrary agreement, but if the parties have not agreed otherwise, this is how amounts of income and gain will be allocated, and eventually, must be distributed. So, in the ABC general partnership, mentioned above, if A contributed $10,000 to the partnership, B contributed $20,000 to the partnership, and C contributed $30,000 to the partnership (and nothing is said about how profits are to be shared), in a year in which the partnership earns $90,000, A, B, and C share equally in those earnings. Even though C contributed half of the partnership's capital, she is entitled only to an equal one-third share of the amount earned. For persons used to thinking about corporations, and how earnings are split on the basis of how many shares of stock have been purchased, this may seem unfair. The solution is to make sure that the partnership agreement spells out the parties' intentions. This topic will be addressed in some detail in Chapter 4 of this book.

[23]   § 4-47-503 (sharing of distributions) and § 4-47-812(b) (disposition of assets). While this is likely to be somewhat closer to what people generally believe to be the manner in which earnings should be shared, there may be unhappiness if the original investors, who risked their capital at a far earlier and therefore less certain stage in the development of the business, find themselves unexpectedly sharing profits equally with later participants in the venture.

people generally think of as the way profits should be shared, but even this is somewhat different from the corporate model. The default rules for an Arkansas LLC model those applicable to a general partnership, and thus profits are presumed to be shared equally, absent agreement to the contrary.[24]

The reason that these concepts are so important to understanding partnership taxation is that tax partners are taxed based on how they are allocated profits and losses by the tax partnership. This is governed by the applicable statute, unless the parties have agreed otherwise (and even if the parties have agreed otherwise, in some cases the Tax Code will disregard an agreement and return to the default rules–as will be discussed in the materials that follow dealing with "special allocations").

With these definitions and concepts in mind, it is appropriate to consider, in very general terms, how partnership taxation works.

III.2.2.   Overview of Partnership Tax–Essential Concepts

Entity Versus Aggregate Treatment for Tax Partnerships

Partnership taxation is governed by subchapter K of the Internal Revenue Code (IRC or Code). Portions of subchapter K (notably IRC §§ 701 - 702) appear to adopt the aggregate approach with regard to the fundamental nature of partnership taxation-each partner as an individual calculates and pays taxes, and it takes the aggregate of all partners to pay taxes on the total amount of partnership income. On the other hand, other sections clearly treat

---

[24]   § 4-32-503.

the partnership as an entity, even though it does not itself pay any taxes. For example, § 703 of the Code adopts the entity approach with regard to determining the amount, character, and timing of certain events, and each partner is thereafter bound by the partnership's determination as to such matters. Items of income, gain, loss, and deduction for the partnership year are calculated at the partnership level based on this approach.

Taken together, these provisions essentially mean that the partnership is treated as a conduit through which items of income and loss flow to the partners and are then reported on the individual partners' tax returns. The partnership is required to file an informational return with the IRS (with each partner receiving a schedule itemizing amounts that the partner is required to individually report), but the partnership itself owes and pays no taxes. Taxes based on partnership income are imposed only on the partners, and only partners can use partnership losses to offset their income. The deductibility of losses is subject to a variety of rules that limit how much in the way of losses can be used and against what income those losses can be offset, particularly if the partner is not active in the partnership business or if the losses exceed the partner's basis or amount at risk in the business.

Time Frame in Which Taxes Are Imposed

One of the important aspects of partnership taxation (and one that some clients might not understand at the outset) is that tax is imposed on the partners in the year that the partnership earns income regardless of when that income may be payed out to the partners. The determination by the partnership that income has been earned by the partnership is binding on the partners. It does not matter whether the partnership distributes the income to the partners in that year; the tax is still due. Similarly, income tax is not imposed just because a distribution is made. IRC § 731. In general terms, in the case of partnership income, what has once been subject to tax will not be subject to a second layer of tax. Presumably, the tax will have been paid on any distributed funds in the year in which such funds were earned by the partnership, so if earnings are distributed later, no additional income tax is due.

General Operation of the Code–Calculation of Income

In considering subchapter K in general terms, it is worth noting that its provisions are organized around four types of transactions: (1) ordinary partnership operations (IRC §§ 701-709); (2) taxation associated with partners' contributions to a partnership (IRC §§ 721-724); (3) taxation of distributions from a partnership (IRC §§ 731-736); and (4) tax impact of transfers of partnership interests by the partners (IRC §§ 741-743). There are other provisions dealing with multiple kinds of specialized transactions, definitions, and large partnerships, but they will not be mentioned in any detail here. In addition, the tax impact of transfers of partnership interests by a partner to another is also outside the scope of these materials.

With regard to the provisions dealing with ordinary partnership operations, the Code treats a tax partnership as a separate entity for accounting purposes even though it is not itself subject to income taxes. IRC §§ 701-703, 706. For each taxable year, the partnership will calculate various items of income, gain, loss, and deduction. With certain minor changes, a partnership calculates income in the same way individuals do. A partnership does not offset foreign taxes, charitable contributions, or certain other items that instead are directly passed through to the partners and reported on the individual partner's returns. Nor is a partnership entitled to a personal exemption.

Taxable income is thus calculated at the partnership level, with certain items being stated separately if they may have differing effects on particular partners' taxable income. Such separately-stated items include capital gains and losses, dividends eligible for preferential rates, etc. The partnership's taxable income and these separately-stated items are then allocated among the partners, and this is all reported to the IRS. Each partner is responsible, in turn, for reporting his or her distributive share (as reported to him or her by the partnership), and paying any taxes that may be due on such amounts.

In order to understand all of this, it is critical that the basic terminology be understood. The terms "allocation" and "distributive share" refer not to actual distributions by the partnership to the partners, but rather to each partner's allocable share of partnership items (i.e., taxable income, and each separately-stated item on the partnership's informational tax return).

How Allocations are Made for Tax Purposes

The Code provides a means for determining how such allocations must be made. Generally speaking, amounts are allocated based on each partner's "interest" in the partnership. This is a determination that is made under state law. Remember that we are talking here about "tax partnerships," and therefore in Arkansas we may be looking at the UPA (1996), ULPA (2001), or the Arkansas LLC Act, depending on what kind of business format was chosen under state law. For general partnerships, LLPs, and LLCs, the presumption is that all amounts are to be shared equally; for limited partnerships and LLLPs, the presumption is that all amounts are to be shared in proportion to the agreed-upon value of contributions to the partnership. In all of these cases, however, the basic or default allocation is subject to the contrary agreement of the parties, and the partners or members might agree to allocate profits and losses on the basis of the number of ownership units or interests purchased, or in any other proportion that they desire. If such an agreement is made, IRC § 704(a) of the Code provides that the partnership agreement (which would include the operating agreement in the case of an LLC taxed as a partnership) will generally control such allocations, but under subsection (b) an allocation that is different from that partner's usual interest in the partnership will be disallowed if it does not have "substantial economic effect."

Obviously, this raises the question of when an agreed-upon allocation would be different from the partner's interest in the partnership. Recall again the hypothetical ABC General Partnership, composed of partners A, B, and C. Suppose that A, B, and C contribute property of equal value to the partnership, agree that they will have equal management rights in the partnership, and agree that they will share all items of income and loss equally. Clearly, this allocation would be in accordance with their usual interest and would not trigger application of the economic effect rules. Similarly, if they agreed that A will receive 10% of all items of income and loss, while B and C will each receive 45%, this would not involve any special allocation. Each item of gain and loss would generally be in accordance with their usual way of sharing in the economic aspects of the business. However, if we assume that A is a the child of B and C, and that A is in the lowest possible tax bracket while B and C are in a higher bracket, it might be tempting for the partners to agree that for the first three years of the partnership (while A is still in college), income will be "allocated" to A, even though distributions are to be shared 10%-45%-45%. This allocation of income to A would not be in accordance with the partners' usual interests in the partnership, and therefore would constitute a "special allocation." Once the partnership agreement includes a special allocation, the tax code requires that it have "substantial economic effect," or it will be disallowed for tax purposes.

Obviously, this raises the question of what it means for a special allocation to have "substantial economic effect." This is an incredibly complicated area of the law, and it is easier to explain the two parts of this test in concept rather than to try and utilize the actual treasury regulations. First, an allocation of income, loss, gain, etc., will have "economic effect" only if the tax impact of an allocation is matched by an economic impact. (In other words, if a particular partner reports income for tax purposes, eventually, that partner needs to realize that income in an economic sense as well. It cannot be distributed to anyone else. Similarly, if a partner reports a loss for tax purposes, the economic loss upon dissolution would actually have to be borne or paid by that partner.) The economic effect will be "substantial" if the tax effect is matched on a dollar for dollar basis with the economic impact.

More will be written about special allocations shortly, but this should be enough to provide you with basic background information about how partnership income is calculated and allocated. You should also now understand the basic rule that partnership losses also have to be allocated, generally in accordance with each partner's interest in the partnership, unless there is a special allocation that has "substantial economic effect."

Allocation of and Limitation of Deductibility of Losses

While clients are likely to be eager to focus on how profits are to be shared, they should also be encouraged to consider how losses should be allocated. This is true not only in the unhappy event of business failure, but also because there can be potentially significant benefits from the deductibility of business losses to offset other income. This attribute of tax partnerships can actually be a major benefit of partnership taxation. However, to prevent this benefit from being abused, the Code places certain limits on the deductibility of partnership losses, three of which will be addressed here. First, a partner may not deduct amounts in excess of that partner's basis in the partnership; second, a partner may only deduct amounts that are at risk; and third, if the partner does not "materially" participate in the activities of the partnership, passive activity losses may be deducted only against passive activity gains. To the extent that losses in excess of the allowable deductions are allocated to a particular partner, those losses are said to be "suspended," and may be carried forward until such time as there is sufficient basis, amounts at risk, or passive activity gains to allow utilization of the suspended loss. Each of these concepts probably calls for a little more in the way of explanation.

One of the most significant limitations on the deductibility of losses is that losses may only be deducted to the extent of the partner's outside basis. IRC § 704(d). Stated simply, if a partnership reports a loss to a partner, that partner's ability to take the loss is limited to the partner's tax basis in the partnership at the end of the tax year in which the loss is reported. Any disallowed loss is carried forward to later years. Obviously, to understand what this means, one has to be able to understand the concept of "basis."[25] Under IRC § 722, a partner's basis in the partnership is initially determined by considering that partner's investment in the partnership (i.e., the basis of any property and cash contributed in exchange for the partnership interest). Under IRC § 705(a), a partner's outside basis is adjusted upward for his distributive share of income and any additional capital contributions, and is adjusted

---

[25]   IRC §§ 705, 721-723 all deal with basis issues. Note, however, that they deal with basis from different perspectives. A partner's basis in his or her partnership interest (also referred to as "outside basis") is separate and distinct from the partnership's basis in its assets (often called "inside basis").

downward for his distributive share of partnership losses and any distributions from the partnership. IRC § 752 also provides that a partner's outside basis includes his or her share of partnership liabilities, meaning that if the partnership borrows funds the partner's share, such indebtedness can increase the outside basis available to absorb that partner's distribution share of losses. However, under IRC § 704(d), once a partner's outside basis has been reduced to zero, any further items of loss or deduction are suspended until his outside basis increases above zero.

A second limit on the deductibility of losses appears in the "at-risk" rules of IRC § 465, which limits deductions based on non-recourse debt. Generally speaking, a partner is considered "at risk" only to the extent that the partner has contributed funds or property having an adjusted basis equal to such activity, and is further considered at risk to the extent of amounts borrowed with respect to such activity. IRC § 465(b)(1). This mirrors the basis limitation described above. However, a particularly important consideration for all of the newer forms of business that provide limited liability to participants under state law is the further rule that in order to be "at risk," the participant must be personally liable for repayment of such amounts (IRC § 465(b)(2)), or has pledged property, other than the property used in such activity, as security for such borrowed amount. General partners in a traditional partnership are personally liable for at least their proportionate share of partnership debts, but in an LLP or LLLP, they would not be, absent a personal guarantee. Similarly, limited partners or LLC members would not be personally liable, absent agreement to the contrary. Thus, the at risk limitation can provide a significant limitation on the deductibility of losses from such forms of business (unless personal guarantees or pledges of personally owned assets are involved).

The third major limitation on the deductibility of losses is that partners may deduct losses from "passive activities" only against income from "passive activities." Basically, the passive activity rules mean that a tax-partner who is not materially involved in the partnership may deduct losses from the partnership only against income from passive activities (which would be income from this partnership or other passive activities). Any loss that is disallowed under the passive activity rules is treated as a deduction allocable to such activity in the next tax year. The rules that govern what is to be considered a passive activity are complicated, but basically ask the question of whether the facts and circumstances demonstrate that the partner materially participated in the partnership. The partner will be able to show this if he or she was involved in the operations of the activity on a regular, continuous, and substantial basis. IRC § 469(h)(1). Another way of stating these rules is that a taxpayer cannot deduct losses from business activities in which he or she does not materially participate unless he or she reports passive income on the tax return against which to offset the losses. Losses from passive activities may not be used to offset non-passive income.[26] Non-passive income includes such things as wages, salaries, portfolio, or investment income. This restrictive approach makes the passive activity rules a significant limitation on the deductibility of losses from tax partnerships.

---

[26]   Any suspended losses may, however, be utilized upon disposition of a partner's entire interest in the passive activity, but the tax consequences to individual partners are beyond the scope of these materials. Persons considering investment in a partnership are well advised to consult their tax advisors to assist them in understanding the particular impact taxes may have on them, before making the investment.

III.2.3.   "Capital Accounts"

The preceding discussion should make it clear that a tax partnership must keep track of the partnership's basis in each item of partnership property, so that gain and loss can be appropriately recognized, calculated, allocated, and reported. It is also important to keep track of each partner's basis in that partner's partnership interest, because this information will typically be necessary to determine how to allocate items of gain or loss.

From the partners' perspectives, it may be even more important to keep track of the fair market value of each partner's capital interest, because that is how they would normally expect their "share" of the partnership to be calculated in the event of dissolution. Typically, a partnership maintains capital accounts which reflect the value of each partner's interest in the partnership. In fact, UPA (1996) presumes that these "capital accounts" will be maintained as a basis for determining each partner's interest in a general partnership or LLP, but for accounting and tax purposes similar records will be needed for any tax partnership.

Obviously, the keeping of such records is much more an accounting than legal function. Still, in order to advise clients intelligently, and to understand the broad tax consequences associated with the various forms of business, it is critical the attorneys understand the general rules applicable to the maintenance of such "capital accounts."

Speaking very generally, the usual rule is that each partner's capital account starts when that partner contributes something of value to the partnership. When a partner contributes property to a partnership, his capital account is credited with the fair market (or "book") value of the contributed property, less any liabilities secured by the property.   Treas. Reg. § 1.704-

1(b)(2)(iv)(b). The tax basis of the contributed property does not affect the contributing partner's "book" capital account, since the partners' respective rights upon liquidation depend on the fair market value (not the tax basis) of partnership property. The partnership must keep track, however, of any differences between the tax basis and book value of contributed property for purposes of tax accounting.

The partnership is therefore required to maintain two sets of capital accounts-a tax capital account and a book capital account-whenever property is contributed with a tax basis different from its fair market value (or whenever book capital accounts are restated to reflect the fair market value of partnership property, which may be done at various times for various reasons). A partner's tax capital account is initially credited with the amount of cash contributed plus the tax basis of any other contributed property (net of liabilities secured by such property).

Undoubtedly, this is rather difficult to assimilate on such an abstract basis. A concrete example might help clarify the way these rules are intended to operate.

Consider again the example of ABC General Partnership, a newly-formed business in which A, B, and C each contribute property of equal value. In exchange for these contributions, they each receive an equal one third interest (which would be both the default rule and the usual expectation of business participants making equal contributions at the same time). Suppose further that A contributes $50,000 in cash; B contributes land with a basis of $15,000 and a value of $50,000; and C contributes securities with a basis of $75,000 and a value of $50,000. Immediately after the contribution, the partnership's balance sheet should show the following assets (left-hand side) and partners' capital (right-hand side).

	(1) Basis	(2) Value	(3) Basis	(4) Value
	[Assets]		[Capital]	
Cash	$50,000	$50,000	A $50,000	$50,000
Land	15,000	50,000	B 15,000	50,000
Securities	75,000	50,000	C 75,000	50,000
Total	$140,000	$150,000	$140,000	$150,000

Column 1 shows the partnership's basis in the assets that it holds. The partnership will have the same basis that the contributing partner had prior to contribution. IRC § 723. Column 2 represents the fair market or book value of the contributed assets in the hands of the partnership. This will also equal the fair market value of the assets at the time of contribution. For both LLCs and limited partnerships under Arkansas law, the parties are required to have an agreement about the actual or fair market value of property at the time of contribution. Column 3 is each partner's basis in his or her partnership interest. Note that the partners no longer have a direct interest in the contributed property, and that therefore they have basis in their respective partnership interests instead. This column also represents the tax capital accounts that will facilitate the partnership's determination of appropriate tax treatment for certain items of gain and loss. Finally, column 4 is the partners' book capital accounts. This column reflects both the partners' equal contributions and their equal rights to any liquidating distributions.

Note that the sum of the partners' book capital accounts ($150,000) is equal to the total book value of the partnership's assets (col. 2). The sum of the partners' outside basis (col. 3) equals the partnership's total inside basis (col. 1) (in both cases, the total is $140,000).

Over time, a partner's capital account will be adjusted (under rules similar to those found in IRC § 705(a)) to reflect partnership operations. Each partner's capital accounts will be increased by any additional contributions or allocations of income. This makes sense given that a partner's distributive share of income and any additional contributions increase his or her investment in the partnership. Similarly, each partner's distributive share of losses and any distributions reduce the partner's net investment in the partnership. These distributions will therefore result in corresponding reductions in the partners' capital accounts.

Note that under these rules, a partner's capital account (but not his or her outside basis) may be reduced below zero by his or her distributive share of losses or by distributions. In a general partnership (where the partners have personal liability for partnership debts), a deficit in a partner's book capital account normally represents the amount of cash that he or she would be obligated to contribute to the partnership upon liquidation. The value of partnership property, together with any partners' negative capital account balances, should equal the amount necessary to satisfy partnership liabilities and to pay out amounts equal to all other partners' positive capital account balances. In this way, all partners' final capital accounts should be zero after liquidation of the partnership. In a limited liability entity, there need not be an obligation to restore a negative capital account, and the parties are unlikely to wish to agree to have to do so, as this might compromise their limited liability.

Another important difference between capital accounts and outside basis shows up as a result of the treatment of partnership liabilities. When a partnership borrows funds, the resulting partnership liability is matched by a corresponding increase in the value of partnership assets (i.e., cash or purchased property); conversely, when a partnership repays borrowed amounts, the reduction in partnership liabilities is matched by a corresponding decrease in the value of partnership assets (i.e., the cash used to repay the debt). Since partnership borrowing and principal repayments have no effect on the partnership's net asset value (i.e., partners' equity), increases and decreases in partnership liabilities are not reflected in the partners' capital accounts. However, any increase or decrease in a partner's share of partnership liabilities does trigger a corresponding increase or decrease in his outside basis. This, in turn, may impact the allowable amounts that the partner may deduct under the basis rules described earlier in this chapter.

Section 752 of the Code adopts a pair of legal fictions to accomplish these outside basis adjustments. First, IRC § 752(a) treats an increase in partner's share of partnership liabilities as a deemed contribution of cash to the partnership, while IRC § 752(b) treats a decrease in his or her share of partnership liabilities as a deemed cash distribution to the partner. Put more simply, this means that each partner will be allocated a share of any debt incurred as a result of funds having been borrowed by the partnership. Each partner's basis account will be increased by that partner's share of the debt. When the debt is repaid, the partners' shares of the debt will be reduced, and the basis account will similarly be reduced.

Often, a partner's outside basis may be determined indirectly by adding his or her share of partnership liabilities to his or her tax capital account. The complete relationship between outside basis and book capital account is actually more complicated than this implies, because book capital accounts also reflect differences between the basis and fair market value of contributed property.

At this point, it is probably important to say something more about the terminology. In particular, attorneys should make sure that they understand the difference between cash flow and taxable income. The term "net cash flow" refers generally to the partnership's cash from operations available for distribution after paying (or setting aside reserves for) all necessary expenses. This need not be the same as partnership taxable income (or loss), since deductions for certain non-cash items (e.g., depreciation allowance) are taken into account in calculating the latter but not the former. Thus, net cash flow may be positive even though the partnership has a taxable loss for the year. From the partners' perspective, net cash flow is important because it may determine actual distributions, either under the partnership agreement or by agreement of the partners at the time when distributions are considered. Taxable income (or loss) is obviously important for other reasons.

Remember that a book capital account should reflect the fair market value of a partner's equity ownership interest in the partnership, or, in other words, it should show the value of the partner's share of the partnership assets, less the partner's share of partnership liabilities. This should then reveal what that partner would receive if the partnership were to liquidate with current assets and liabilities. The partnership's tax partner, or accountant, would therefore create a capital account for each partner that would include the value of any cash or property contributed by that partner, less any liabilities to which such property is subject. (For example, if a partner contributes $100,000 in cash, that partner's capital account balance will be $100,000. The same amount would be shown if the partner contributes a house worth $100,000. If the house is subject to a mortgage of $60,000, however, the net value of the contributed property is only $40,000, and that is the amount reflected in the book capital account.) The capital account would thereafter be increased every time that gain is *allocated* to the partner for tax purposes. Note that we are talking about "allocations" here, rather than distributions–the issue is not whether the partner has actually received the proceeds, but whether the partnership has "allocated" the amounts to him or her. When amounts are actually distributed (i.e., paid out), this serves to reduce the partner's capital account by the amount distributed. In addition, every time the partner has an item of loss allocated to him or her for tax purposes, those amounts must be subtracted from the capital account. So if a partner contributes $100,000 (cash), and in the first year of partnership operations that partner is allocated $20,000 in losses, the partner's capital account will drop to $80,000.

This is not, of course, anywhere near the whole story. The concept of capital accounts is substantially complicated by the fact that partnerships are required to keep one set of records reflecting fair market value of capital accounts and another reflecting the partner's basis in any contributed property. The partnership must keep track of the partners' basis for purposes of tax accounting. In addition, capital accounts are also affected by partnership debt (to the extent that the partners are personally liable for the debt). The purpose of this discussion is to enable you to understand and respond appropriately to advice from a tax expert about what a partnership agreement might need to say about the maintenance of capital accounts in a particular situation. It is not intended that this discussion will enable you to provide a running total of a partnership's capital accounts during its operational years, for either tax or accounting purposes. Rather, if the tax expert tells you in advance that your client's operational agreements need to provide for the maintenance of capital accounts, you should now be in a position to understand (more or less) what this advice means.

One reason it may be particularly important to understand what is involved with the maintenance of capital accounts has to do with how the partners might want to allocate particular items of gain and loss. As mentioned earlier, the Internal Revenue Code requires that certain items of gain and loss be allocated to particular partners. For example, whenever a partner contributes property in which the partner has a basis that is different from fair market value at the time of contribution, there is either built-in gain or built-in loss (depending on whether the fair market value is greater or less than the contributing partner's basis). Upon sale or other disposition of the contributed property, this built-in gain or loss must be allocated to the partner who contributed it to the partnership.

However, this is not the only situation in which a "special allocation" (i.e., an allocation that differs from the usual way in which those particular partners share items of gain, loss, etc.) may be desirable. One of the benefits of partnership taxation is that losses of the business will pass through to the owners and, subject to various rules and limitations, may be deducted by the owners against other income. To the extent that one partner may be in a better position to immediately utilize those losses to offset other income, it may be advantageous to allocate the initial losses to that partner, at least for tax purposes. The tax code specifically addresses the extent to which such voluntary special allocations will be respected. The rules, which are complicated, generally start from the requirement that the partnership maintain capital accounts, make distributions in accordance with such accounts, and handle negative account balances in specific ways.

The following section of these materials addresses this issue in more detail.

III.2.4.   Special Allocations and "Substantial Economic Effect"

It probably bears repeating that this is a very general overview of an extremely intricate and involved part of partnership taxation.   This discussion omits many of the subtleties and complexities that are necessary for a real understanding of special allocations.   Remember that the purpose of these materials is to give you a feeling for the basic tax considerations that are important in the choice to form a partnership, and to enable you to understand what a tax expert's advice means.

Generally speaking, state law allows great flexibility in establishing their rights and responsibilities with respect to management and operation of business that may be taxed as partnerships (this includes the general partnership, the LLP, the limited partnership, the LLLP, and the LLC).   The partnership or operating agreement can require unanimous consent of the owners to take certain actions, can allow a single person (who need not even be one of the owners) to have full management power, or can set up virtually any other conceivable scheme of management. Equal flexibility is allowed in setting up rules as to how profits and losses will be shared among the participants.   The state statutes provide default rules (i.e., rules that will govern in the absence of an agreement among the participants), but in general clients can choose from a virtually unlimited array of options as to how profits and losses might be shared.

Similarly, the Internal Revenue Code allows business participants in a tax partnership significant leeway in drafting the relevant agreements to control tax consequences. Not only can tax partners' sharing ratios generally be set up any way your clients might desire, they also often choose to allocate specified items of income, gain, loss, etc., differently from the way that other items of income, gain, loss, etc. are to be allocated.   For example, a partnership or operating agreement can allocate losses to certain owners to offset other income, and can allocate income differently from the way in which those losses are allocated. In other words, it is not necessary for partners to share in partnership income to the same extent that they share in partnership losses. This right to make special allocations is one of the attributes of partnership taxation that has allowed tax partnerships to operate as effective tax shelters.

Primarily to curb abusive allocations of gain and loss, the current partnership tax rules include complex regulations requiring that such "special allocations" have "substantial economic effect." Any allocation that fails to have substantial economic effect will be disregarded by the IRS for tax purposes, and the transactions will be recharacterized to reflect the economic substance of the underlying arrangement.   On the other hand, if the special allocation in a partnership agreement does have substantial economic effect, it will be binding on the IRS. You can insure that allocations will have substantial economic effect, if you know what you are doing.

In essence, the requirement of economic effect under the treasury regulations traditionally requires three things: (1) capital accounts (described in the preceding section of this chapter) must be maintained for each partner; (2) liquidating distributions must be made in accordance with capital accounts; and (3) partners must restore negative capital account balances.   In the case of a traditional general partnership, this means that capital accounts are required for tax purposes, general partners with positive account balances must share in liquidating distributions in proportion to those balances, and partners must have an unconditional obligation to restore any deficit in their capital accounts.

Since general partners traditionally had unlimited personal liability for partnership debts, this obligation to restore deficit accounts may not have been particularly onerous. For limited liability businesses, however, the obligation to restore any negative capital account may be extremely undesirable (as it could remove the benefit of limited liability), and so the regulations under IRC § 704 provides an alternative method of achieving economic effect. This alternative is known as the "qualified income offset."[27] In essence this alternative requires that the tax partnership follow the first two components of the ordinary substantial effect test (maintenance of capital accounts and liquidating distributions in accordance with the balances in such accounts), but instead of an unlimited obligation to restore deficits, a special allocation will still be respected if: (1) the allocation does not cause or increase a deficit balance (taking into consideration such things as planned distributions); and (2) in the event that a deficit does occur, future allocations of gain or income must be allocated to eliminate the deficit "as quickly as possible."

The actual language that one might expect to see in the business's operational documents is dictated by the language of the Code and regulations promulgated thereunder, and the purpose of this discussion is not to provide you with that level of detail. Rather, if a tax professional questions you (or the client does, perhaps upon the advise of his or her tax advisor), you will understand the issues relevant to special allocations, the general obligation to restore deficit accounts, and the concept of "qualified income offsets."

While this is complex and may seem overwhelming to an attorney who does not have a substantial background in tax, it might help to remember that the whole notion of substantial economic effect is only triggered when the agreement of the parties includes special allocations--that is, when tax partners are not allocated all items of income, gain, and loss in accordance with their usual economic interest in the partnership. This does not mean that any unequal allocation between the partners will trigger

---

[27]   Treas. Reg. § 1.704-1(b)(2)(ii)(d).

the regulations–it is only where individual items of gain and loss are treated differently than other items as to particular partners that the special allocation requirements come into play.

For example, consider again my ABC General Partnership. If A, B, and C agree to split everything equally, there has been no special allocation. If C is to get 60% of all items of gain and loss, and A and B are each to get 20%, there is still no special allocation because each partner will presumably share in their usual sharing ratio as to any item of gain or loss. On the other hand, if A, B, and C agree to share profits equally, but allocate all losses to C for the first two years, or the first $100,000 in losses to her, then they have made a special allocation of those losses because those losses would not be shared in the usual way that interests have been divided up in that partnership.

You may be wondering why anyone would ever voluntarily complicate things so much by choosing to agree to special allocations. The answer is that there may be substantial tax benefits to special allocations.

Consider again that ABC General Partnership. Suppose that C is a wealthy lawyer, with lots of income each year. She is the financier of the project, having contributed $60,000 to get the project off the ground. A and B have no money, and no other income, but they had the idea, and are providing the labor to make the partnership work. All three have agreed to share income equally. Suppose that it is expected that in the first year the partnership will have losses of $60,000 (or in other words, that the partnership will spend $60,000 more than it will make). How should that loss be allocated?

Under state law, if the partners do not otherwise agree, items of loss are shared in the same proportion as are items of income. In this case, that would mean that A, B, and C would share all items of loss equally since that is how they have agreed to share income. On these facts, they would each be allocated a $20,000 loss against other income. This might help C, who could use that loss to offset other income (subject to any passive activity loss limitations), but A and B have no basis in the partnership at this point, and therefore would not yet be able to utilize any of the losses allocated to them. Yes, they can carry the loss forward to future years, but it gets them no immediate tax benefit. On the other hand, C has basis sufficient to offset all of the losses. Does it therefore make sense for them to agree that the first $60,000 of loss will be allocated solely to C (with income still to be shared equally)? If the parties do this, it would be a special allocation. Under this agreement, assuming that the allocation has substantial economic effect as defined by the treasury regulations, C could shelter $60,000 worth of income for the first year of partnership operations, at no current cost to A or B. This is a special allocation with immediate tax benefits.

Note that the allocation may also have economic consequences. If the partnership loses $60,000 in year one-as predicted-and the partners elect to dissolve at that point in time, all of those losses have been allocated to C. Certainly under the default rules of UPA (1996), where partners are deemed to have a capital account pursuant to which liquidating distributions are to be made, this ought to mean that A and B will not have to share in the economic loss (beyond having lost the value of their services).

III.2.5. Recap of Partnership Taxation

To sum it up, multi-owner, unincorporated businesses under state law are presumed to be taxed as partnerships. This means that the business is required to calculate income and certain separately-stated items, to report those totals to the IRS, and to allocate them among the partners. Each partner is required to report his or her distributive share as reported to him or her by the partnership, and to pay taxes on such allocations. There is no tax imposed at the partnership level, and losses are also passed through to the partners.

Partners may deduct losses that have been allocated to them against other income, subject to the basis limitation, at risk rules, and passive activity rules incorporated into the Code.

To assist in understanding each partner's interest in the partnership at any given time, as well as for purposes of complying with tax requirements, tax partnerships are required to maintain capital accounts showing each partner's basis and economic interest in the partnership over time. Capital accounts start with the basis or value of amounts contributed, are increased both by additional contributions and allocations of income or gain, and are decreased by distributions and allocations of loss.

Allocations are made by the partnership based upon the partners' relative interests in the partnership, as determined by state law. State statutes generally provide rules that will control such allocations in the absence of agreement, but the parties are given wide latitude in making alternative arrangements. A contrary agreement about items of gain, loss, etc., will be respected if it has "substantial economic effect" under the federal tax regulations (which might require either an obligation to restore negative account balances, or more likely for the limited liability entities, a qualified income offset).

Individual circumstances of particular partners may complicate the application of partnership tax rules to them, but this should give a general overview of the way partnership taxation works from the perspective of the business.

III.3.   EQUALLY SUPERFICIAL OVERVIEW OF CORPORATE TAXATION

Corporate taxation works quite differently. As is the case with partnership taxation, it is not necessary for the business in question to actually be a "corporation" under state law in order for it to be an association taxable as a corporation. In fact, corporate taxation applies to any Arkansas business that is incorporated under state law, any business that is publicly traded or otherwise required to be taxed as a corporation under IRC § 7704, or any business that elects to be taxed as a corporation under the check the box regulations. An Arkansas corporation will always be taxed as a corporation, but other businesses also may find themselves subject to these rules.

Unlike tax partnerships, which are all governed by subchapter K of the Tax Code, associations taxable as corporations may be governed either by subchapter C or subchapter S of the Code. Subchapter S status requires an affirmative election, and is available only to corporations meeting certain requirements, so these materials will start with subchapter C.

III.3.1.   The Traditional C Corporation

A C corporation is simply a corporation that, for a particular taxable year, does not have in place an effective election to be taxed under subchapter S of the Internal Revenue Code. IRC § 1361(a)(2). The C does not refer to a close or closely held corporation-it refers to subchapter C of the Internal Revenue Code, which applies to and governs the taxation of all corporations that lack an effective S election.

In general terms, a C corporation is a separate taxable entity for federal income tax purposes. This means that a C corporation is required to calculate taxable income, and to pay a corporate level tax on that income. IRC § 11 (regular tax) and IRC § 55 (alternative minimum tax). The remaining income, after corporate taxes, may be taxed again at the shareholder level if and when the amounts are distributed as dividends. IRC § 301(a), (c). This is the "double-taxation" that has so long been negatively associated with corporate tax status. Corporate shareholders are entitled to a "dividends received" deduction ranging from 70% to 100% of the amount of the dividends received. IRC § 243. This is a long standing rule that prevents triple or quadruple taxation when there are multiple layers of corporate ownership involved.

In addition to double taxation, the C corporation has another significant potential drawback from a tax planning standpoint. Losses must be reported and taken at the corporate level; they are not available to offset other income at the shareholder level. In other words, corporate losses do not pass through to the shareholders. Since most start-up companies can expect substantial losses in their early years, this may be a significant drawback to the C corporation from the standpoint of investors, but such losses are not "wasted" just because a corporation does not have sufficient taxable income in any given year to offset against the losses. Corporate losses may be carried backwards and forwards for a number of years, to offset taxable income (and thereby reduce taxes owed) in those other years.

There is really no way to avoid this limitation losses in a C corporation cannot be conveniently passed through to shareholders through any planning device. However, the same is not necessarily true for the double layer of taxes imposed on corporate income.

In a closely-held C corporation, avoiding the potential double level of taxation is likely to be a constant planning concern. This is typically done by having the owners occupy a variety of relationships with the corporation, including: (1) equity owners; (2) creditors; (3) employees; (4) lessors; and (5) debtors. Distributions to the shareholders as employees, for example, will, within limits, generate a corporate deduction if they constitute a reasonable business expense. IRC § 162(a)(1). This analysis also applies to professional corporations. A professional C corporation is likely to qualify as a "personal service corporation." The incentive to plan and avoid the corporate level tax is even greater with respect to the personal service corporation. Every dollar of its taxable income is taxed at a flat rate, the highest corporate rate, and none of the taxable income receives the advantage of the lower corporate tax brackets. IRC § 11(b)(2). Participants do need to be aware that amounts paid out as compensation are subject to employment taxes as well as income taxes, which may make this alternative less desirable than it might otherwise be.

Another alternative to paying salaries to participants (and thereby avoiding the corporate level of income tax), is for participants to lend funds to the corporation, and receive their return on investment in the form of interest. Reasonable interest payments are also deductible by the corporation. The investor still has to pay taxes on amounts received, but this would not normally include the employment taxes imposed on compensation, and it does avoid the tax that might otherwise be imposed at the corporate level. So long as the amounts paid are reasonable in relation to the amounts lent and current interest rates, this kind of planning can have significant tax benefits.

Participants might also choose to lease property to their corporation and receive their return in the form of rent. Reasonable rent is also a deductible business expense and is not subject to employment taxes. Participants do have to worry about their payments being reclassified as disguised sales, which would result in a disallowance of the deduction at the corporate level, but there are guidelines that can help investors avoid this. However, a tax professional should certainly be consulted any time property is being leased from the tax corporation's owners, particularly if the total rentals will equal the actual sales value of property that depreciates over time, or if the rental contract includes a lump sum payout at the end of the term, or portions of each rental payment may be used against the eventual purchase of the property.

This information should demonstrate the two primary potential disadvantages of a C corporation–the difficulty in avoiding multiple levels of tax upon income, and the fact that losses do not pass through to investors. The tax advantages are that there is some power to control the timing and amount of taxable consequences to the individual owners (although the modern tax code imposes penalties for excess retained earnings if a corporation tries to defer the second level of tax on an excessive amount of corporate income), and that owners are not required to pay taxes on income from the corporation until it is paid out.

If a tax corporation is desirable for one reason or another, but it is essential that losses flow through to the participants, or there is no reasonable way to avoid what would be a double level of taxation on corporate income, the subchapter S election may provide relief, if the business in question satisfies the restrictions included in that portion of the Tax Code.

III.3.2.   The Subchapter S Election

An S corporation is simply an otherwise ordinary corporation or association taxable as a corporation that is eligible for and has elected to be taxed under subchapter S of the Internal Revenue Code. For state law purposes, it is formed like any other corporation, or any other form of business that could choose to be taxed as a corporation under the check the box rules. The ordinary state business statutes and regulations will apply. The only differences between S and other corporations come from rules and restrictions imposed by subchapter S of the Internal Revenue Code.

The benefit of electing subchapter S status is that an S corporation is a flow-through entity. In other words, there is no entity-level tax, and items of income and loss flow through to the shareholders and are taxed only at the shareholder level. In very, very general terms, an S corporation is taxed like a partnership, although there are some potentially significant differences that it would probably take a tax expert to understand and explain.

The disadvantages of an S corporation are that S corporations are considerably less flexible than C corporations and other forms of business that could be taxes as such. An S corporation can have no more than 100 owners (the number was originally much smaller; it has been raised several times in the past decades); the moment it is owned by more than 100 investors, the tax corporation loses its status as an S corporation and becomes taxable as a C corporation.

Moreover, with certain limited exceptions, only individuals can be owners of S corporations. Other corporations or partnerships are ineligible to invest in an S corporation. For a limited period of time, the estates of deceased shareholders may be investors, but they cannot own those interests indefinitely. Certainly, the plan should be to have only individual owners if the goal is to seek subchapter S status.

Finally, and probably most importantly, an S corporation can have only one class of shares (or ownership interests if it is another kind of business that has elected to be taxed as a corporation, and seeks S corporation status). It is not nomenclature or management rights that matter here; it is the economic rights that are important. Another way of stating this rule is that every ownership interest, unit of ownership, or share must have identical economic rights to every other interest, unit, or share. This does not mean that all participants must share equally, but instead that every ownership "interest" (however denominated and divided between the owners) must have the same economic rights as every other interest. This substantially limits the business's ability to structure different rates of return for different investors. The only way to regulate rates of return is to give different owners a different number of interests, units, or shares. Other than that, all interests, units, or shares must have equal rights to share in the profits and losses of the corporation.

In certain circumstances, the IRS and courts have even declared certain forms of debt to be disguised classes of equity investment which render the corporation ineligible to S corporation status. Share transfer restrictions may also run afoul of the restrictive S corporation rules.

Even though these restrictions are cumbersome, the S corporation is relatively popular, and for some businesses continues to be so even after the advent of LLCs and similar business entities that have been authorized under state law in recent years. These new forms of business allow for the business law benefit of limited liability for all owners while preserving pass-through taxation. Until LLCs, LLPs, and the like became widely available, the S corporation was the only alternative to the double-taxation imposed under subchapter C of the Internal Revenue Code if the business in question was organized so as to give all owners limited liability. Now these other limited liability businesses can have partnership tax status, but could also (at least theoretically, since it is difficult to see when they would want to) elect to be taxed as a corporation, and then make a subchapter S election.

III.4. CONCLUSIONS

Remember: this is a highly simplified and abbreviated discussion of business tax issues designed to introduce you to the basic nature of partnership and corporate taxation, so that you can understand many of the basic considerations that go into choosing this as a form of business organization. Even if you intend to limit your representation of business clients to non-tax matters, you need to be able to understand the advice and recommendations that your clients' tax advisors give. Furthermore, it will likely be your responsibility to actually draft any legal documents that are required. Therefore, you need to be able to draft documents in compliance with tax requirements, even if you do not need to know enough to choose between competing tax options on your own.

CHAPTER IV.   THE GENERAL PARTNERSHIP AND THE LLP

IV.1.   Statutes–A Bit of History for Context

In 1914, the National Conference of Commissioners on Uniform State Laws (NCCUSL) approved the Uniform Partnership Act, which was eventually adopted in every state except Louisiana. This act, widely referred to as the UPA, was modeled on traditional common law principles that had governed "partnerships" and "joint ventures," and it adopted a number of rules that eventually proved somewhat problematical. As was the case in many other jurisdictions, Arkansas made a number of modifications to its version of the UPA over the years, in an attempt to make the partnership form of business suit the needs of entrepreneurs in the state. Our general partnership statute at this time was codified at Ark. Code Ann. §§ 4-42-101 et seq (now repealed).

Gradually, an increasing number of commentators began to suggest that it was time to revisit the question of what the ideal state partnership statute should look like. NCCUSL undertook the reform project, and eventually promulgated a Revised Uniform Partnership Act (typically referred to as RUPA) in 1992. The timing was, in some respects, unfortunate. Limited Liability Partnership (LLP) legislation was sweeping the nation after having been "invented" by Texas in 1991.[28] The original version of RUPA, however, did not incorporate language authorizing or otherwise dealing with LLPs, and thus in some sense the new model legislation was outdated from the moment it was promulgated. Moreover, there were other criticisms of the revised

---

[28]   LLPs are discussed in greater detail later in this Chapter. See section IV.10.

act, which prompted NCCUSL to almost immediately being considering a number of amendments to its new and improved "uniform" act.

The first set of amendments to RUPA were approved by NCCUSL in 1993. These changes basically responded to a number of comments and suggestions, and at the same time the official name of the act was changed to the Uniform Partnership Act (1993). Additional amendments were adopted in 1994, and the new version of the act was officially called the Uniform Partnership Act (1994). In 1996, further changes were made to add provisions dealing with LLPs, and the name of this version of the uniform statute was changed to the Uniform Partnership Act (1996). Additional changes have been made in subsequent years, and it appears that more may be adopted in the future.

Given the speed and frequency with which the uniform act has been amended, the choice to change its nomenclature is quite understandable. "RUPA" may have been a convenient acronym for the Revised Uniform Partnership Act. Re-RUPA (for Revised, Revised Uniform Partnership Act) or Re-Re-RUPA (for three sets of revisions) certainly would not be. On the other hand, there is plenty of room for confusion when a state adopts the Uniform Partnership Act (1996) in a year other than 1996 and uses the official name of the act in the state statute. That is the situation in Arkansas.

General partnerships (and LLPs, which are discussed later in this chapter) in Arkansas are now governed by the Uniform Partnership Act (1996), which is codified at Ark. Code. Ann. §§ 4-46-101 et seq.[29] This statute was not actually adopted in Arkansas until 1999, and did not become applicable to existing

---

[29]   The name of the statute is specified in § 4-46-1202.

partnerships until 2005, which makes the "1996" in the title somewhat misleading. These materials adopt the official title (in abbreviated form) and will therefore refer to current Arkansas law as being the UPA (1996), but that does not mean that we began using the new statute in that year, and forms in use in this state prior to 1999 or even 2005 might well be based on a statute that has now been repealed and replaced by one with some significant changes.

In addition to substantive changes in the law, one change in the structure of the partnership statutes in Arkansas deserves mention. Under prior law, the statutes created a set of "default" rules, and these default rules would govern the partnership in the absence of agreement by the partners. Where a statutory default rule was subject to change by the partners, the statutory provision in question would specify that the default rule was subject to modification if the partners agreed otherwise. Most of the statutory default rules were, in fact, subject to contrary agreement. When NCCUSL promulgated UPA (1996), however, the structure of the statute reflected new drafting principles. Notably, the statute now collects in one section those provisions of the entire act that are NOT subject to the contrary agreement of the partners. A listing of the mandatory provisions (i.e., those that are not subject to modification by the parties) can be found at Ark. Code Ann. § 4-46-103. ALL of the other rules in the act may be modified, even if they appear at first glance to be mandatory. Thus, for example, § 4-46-401(b) says that "[e]ach partner is entitled to an equal share of the partnership profits . . . ." and makes no mention of the possibility that this can be changed. I still, as a law professor teaching in this area, occasionally get calls from laypersons who are attempting to do their own legal research, asking if this is really mandatory. Once one understands that this provision is not included in § 4-46-103, however, it should be clear (at least to lawyers) that the apparently mandatory language about equal sharing of profits is indeed subject to contrary agreement of the partners.

The remainder of this chapter considers various issues and substantive provisions applicable to general partnerships and LLPs in more detail. The textual material explains the law that is generally applicable to these businesses, and the citations are to the relevant statutory language that governs the particular issue being discussed.

IV.2. Formation and the Partnership Agreement

IV.2.1.   Proof of Formation

A partnership is often a very informal arrangement between two or more persons. § 4-46-202. No particular formalities are required to form a general partnership; nothing need be filed and, in fact, the statute does not even require a written partnership agreement. The association of two or more persons as co-owners to carry on a business for profit will form a partnership, even if this is not the intended legal consequence of such action. In fact, the sharing of profits by two or more persons is normally sufficient evidence that a partnership exists, and creates a presumption that the persons who share profits are partners. § 4-46-202(c)(3). As was the case under prior law, this rule that sharing of profits normally evidences a partnership is subject to being rebutted if it can be shown that the share of profits was given to repay a debt, to serve as compensation, as payment of rent, as an annuity or retirement or health benefit to a former partner, to pay interest on a loan, or for the sale of goodwill of the business. § 4-46-202(c)(3)(i)-(vi). Current law also maintains the long-standing rule that neither joint or co-ownership of properties nor sharing of gross returns by itself establishes the existence of a partnership. § 4-46-202(c)(1) - (2). It is the combination of co-ownership and operation of a business, that the Code dictates can normally be inferred from sharing of profits, that creates a partnership.

IV.2.2.   The Value of a Partnership Agreement (Preferably Written)

Because so little formality is required, it has not been at all uncommon for partnerships to have been formed without the assistance of counsel. Thus, it is not at all surprising that this legal relationship is often created in situations where the participants have not sat down and considered the way in which they really prefer that their business should operate. They may not discuss in advance simple issues such as what happens if there is a disagreement among the partners, the sharing of losses, continuation of the business upon withdrawal of one or more of the partners, or similar issues that might really matter to them. Even if they do consider these issues, they may not choose to write the terms of their agreement down, and this can cause no end of difficulty later.

Without assuming any bad faith, in the absence of a written partnership agreement, memories can fail, and in the event of a dispute some time down the road, the partners may simply not recall accurately what had been originally agreed to. Alternatively, one of the partners might have died, and the heirs and representatives might claim certain rights on behalf of the deceased partner with no knowledge of any unwritten agreement.

To minimize the possibility of such disputes and frankly, to encourage persons seeking to form a partnership to consider the potential issues relevant to operation of the business in a systematic fashion before there is any hint of dispute or disagreement, it is always advisable to have a written partnership agreement. This might increase the expenses associated with formation of the business, especially if a lawyer does all the drafting, but it can be invaluable later on in the life of the business.

In the absence of agreement, or if there is insufficient proof that the partners reached an agreement, the default rules of the statute will apply. Sometimes these rules will provide the outcome that the parties would have desired had they taken the time to reduce their agreement or understanding to writing, but sometimes, the default rules will provide results different from what the parties would have wanted.

A partnership agreement can cover a long list of topics, and if you are responsible for drafting one, you might want to consider the following substantive subjects (in addition to normal drafting considerations like an appropriate document name, table of contents, definitions section, date, signatures, etc.):

*Name of Partnership
>If the partnership in question is to be an LLP, there are name requirements that must be adhered to. In addition, remember that merely forming a business under Arkansas law does not register that name as a tradename or prevent its use in other jurisdictions.

*Names and Addresses of Partners
>No formalities are required to form a general partnership, and there is no requirement that general partners be listed anywhere. However, it is probably advisable to include a alphabetized list of general partners in the partnership agreement, and at least the last known mailing address for each. To avoid or minimize the necessity of amending the entire document every time the list of partners changes, it might be desirable to keep these names and addresses on attachments or exhibits to the main agreement.

*Partnership's Purpose

> Many partnership agreements list a purpose for the partnership, which may be either informational or limiting, depending on the nature of the partnership. It may also be appropriate to include in this section any limitations on partners' rights to engage in activities that might be seen as competing with the partnership.

*Addresses and Agent for Service of Process

> If the partnership chooses to register as an LLP, Arkansas requires that it have a designated office and an agent upon whom service of process may be had, together with an address for such person unless they are a commercial registered agent in this state. This need not be in the agreement itself, and because it is also subject to change, it might be desirable to include this in an exhibit, attachment, or other addendum, to make amendments simple to do.

* Initial Contribution of Partners

> In order to facilitate the proper maintenance of capital accounts, it is probably a good idea that any partnership maintain a list of the contributions and agreed-upon value of all non-cash contributions. Because partners may be added or may leave, this is also the kind of information that is advisable to include on exhibits or attachments. Ideally, for each partner, the agreement should include the date of the contribution, a legal description of the contribution, its agreed-upon value, and the effect of failure to comply with any terms of the agreement to contribute (particularly if a contribution takes the form of a promise to pay or perform services over time).

*Any Agreement about Additional Contributions

> The default rule in Arkansas is that partners are not required to make additional contributions beyond the amounts originally agreed to, so if the partners want to provide for additional contributions, the procedure for making or requiring additional contributions should be spelled out, along with effect of failure to make a required additional contribution.

*Allocation of Profits and Losses

> In an Arkansas general partnership, the presumption is that profits and losses are shared equally. This is a rule which may surprise some clients, and may frequently be different from what they want. Most investors will want and expect their return to be based on the value and timing of their contributions, and if this is the case, the partnership agreement should spell out how profits (and losses) are to be shared. Setting up the general partnership so that members get units or interests in exchange for their contributions, and that they share in profits and losses based on the number of units or interests purchased, may be more likely to coincide with clients' interests or real expectations. If the partnership is going to have special allocations, which happens when an allocation of a particular kind of gain or loss differs from the usual way in which allocations are made between the members, that should be spelled out as well, after consultation with a tax advisor, because there are very complicated rules applicable to special allocations

*Distributions

> The partnership agreement can spell out when distributions will be made, when they are required, who decides on timing and amount, if there are any limitations of

distributions, and also any rules applicable to advances, draws, or loans made in anticipation of distributions. In the absence of any specific provisions, the general partners would presumably have authority to decide on distributions as part of their general management authority.

*Salaries[30]

Partners who are also employees may want to have their salary arrangements approved in the partnership agreement or at least have the partnership agreement mention that partners who act as employees shall be entitled to receive salaries. If more information than this is to be included in the partnership agreement itself, the use of attachments or exhibits might be appropriate in order to facilitate any necessary amendments or updates. Lawyers should be aware that there may be tax consequences to having partners receive salaries, particularly in the case of persons who work as general partners but want to claim a share of non-wage income as owner of a limited partnership interest. This is also the kind of tax issue that should be discussed with a specialized tax advisor.

*Management and Control of Business

In a general partnership, the default rule is that all general partners share management authority, and every partner has one vote on every decision. In practice, especially with larger partnerships, this is likely to be inefficient, and alternative management structures are likely to be desirable. While the partnership agreement cannot take away partners' apparent authority to bind the business by

---

[30]   While partners can certainly serve as employees of the partnership, the default rule is that partners have no right to compensation for their efforts. § 4-46-401(h). This would be a very common thing to change in a partnership agreement.

acts that appear to be carrying on the business of the partnership in the ususal way, it can certainly allocate actual authority differently. A managing partner or committee may be chosen, or different groups (such as a compensation or executive committee) may be set up. The optimal structure will depend on the nature of the partnership and the clients' preferences. In addition to voting power, the agreement should establish any required formalities for decision-making because the statutes do not set out any particular procedural requirements, and clients will generally appreciate having such guidance. Notice, meeting, quorum, and voting requirements should be considered. The agreement should also specify what kinds of records of decisions should be made and kept. If there is an expectation that certain partners or classes of partners must spend a certain amount of time managing the business, this should also be in the agreement. This might also be an appropriate place to include authorization for or prohibition against outside or competing activities, depending on client needs and preferences.

*Fiduciary and Related Obligations

Under current Arkansas law, fiduciary duties are quite restricted. It is not that there is anything inherently wrong with simply having clients accept the default rules in this regard, but remember that one function of a partnership agreement is to collect the rules governing the partnership in one place. While attorneys have easy access to statutes, clients generally will not, so even if the clients intend on keeping the statutory default rules, it makes sense to spell out the scope of fiduciary obligations in the agreement. Of course, if the parties do not want to stay with the default rules, any modification, expansion, or explanation of those obligations should also be included in the agreement.

*Adding Partners

At some place, the agreement should address how new partners can be added to the partnership. The agreement should specify who must agree to the new partner and should set out any minimum qualifications before a new partner can be accepted. The impact of new partners should also be addressed, which means, for example, explaining how the addition of a new partner affects distribution or allocation of profits and losses, and voting rights. Note that this kind of information needs to address both partners who contribute directly to the partnership as well as those who are transferees of partnership interests seeking to be accepted as partners. If there are limits on the addition of new partners in either of these situations (for example, a requirement that before the partnership issue units or interests to new partners, existing partners must first be given the right to buy the units and thereby increase their partnership share) or on the right of existing partners to sell interests (such as an obligation to first offer their interest to other existing partners) this would need to be in the agreement. Limitations and conditions on when partners can be admitted, terms upon which payment can be accepted by the partnership, and the impact of new partners on partnership rights and obligations should all be spelled out.

*Rights of Transferees

Following or accompanying the discussion of new partners, the partnership agreement should include language discussing the rights of transferees who do not become partners. It would probably be convenient to explain their rights to distributions and allocations, their informational rights, and any other rights that they might have, in the partnership agreement. If there are differences in the rights of different classes of transferees, such as transferees as a matter of law (for example, as part of a divorce settlement or foreclosure of a charging order entered on a debt owed by a partner) or transferees who have in some way been agreed to by the other partners, that would also need to be explained.

*Withdrawal of Partners

The agreement should address both voluntary and involuntary withdrawal of partners. While the power of general partners to leave cannot be taken away, the partnership agreement can set out consequences for such withdrawal, and particularly whether and when a voluntarily withdrawing partner is required to be paid for his or her partnership interest immediately. The consequences of death or incapacity and its effect on the partnership should also be mentioned. Rights of heirs should be covered as well, both in terms of rights to the economic interest and conditions under which they may be named as substitute partners. Voluntary transfers, such as sale or gift of a partnership interest, should also be covered. If the other partners are to have a right of first refusal or an option to buy such partnership interests, this should be specified. If not included in another section, limits on the right of purchasers to become partners could be spelled out, even if the clients simply want to adopt default statutory rules. It is probably also important to consider involuntary transfers, such as those that might be ordered by a court in the event of divorce or bankruptcy. The rights of other partners or the partnership to buy out partnership interests in such a case could be set out.

*Termination of Partnership

> The agreement should spell out the circumstances under which the partnership will end. Events of dissolution, and the process of winding up (including who has the authority to arrange to dissolution and any rules as to how it should proceed) should also be addressed. The agreement might also explain how participants are to be compensated for arranging the winding up of the partnership business.

*Amendment of the Agreement

> This would include the process by which the agreement can be amended, the vote required, and whether amendments must be in a signed writing or may be proven by conduct or testimony about oral arrangements.

*Provisions Often Regarded as Boilerplate

> This could include a wide variety of topics. For example, it is now common to include an arbitration clause in partnership agreements, although this is, of course, completely optional with the client. Many partnership agreements address relatively routine things like who will be the tax matters partner, whether the books will be kept on the cash or accrual method, the fiscal year of the partnership, and where the partnership will bank. There may also be language stating that section headings are merely for convenience, that the plural includes the singular and vice versa unless the context clearly requires otherwise, and similar statements relevant to the interpretation of the document.

While not a comprehensive list of topics that might be covered in a partnership agreement, the preceding list at least gives an idea of what might be appropriately documented in a written agreement among the partners.

IV.2.3.   Mandatory Rules

It is worth emphasizing that there are a few provisions of the statute that are not subject to modification by the parties when forming a partnership. These mandatory rules are set out in one place in the statutes, although it requires some reference to other statutory provisions to understand precisely what may not be modified.[31]

One set of mandatory rules relates to filed statements. The partnership agreement may not modify the requirements as to execution, filing and recording of statements, nor the effect of such statements. § 4-46-103(b)(1), cross referencing § 4-46-105. While the partnership statute does not require that any document be filed, it does allow for statements of partnership authority (§ 4-46-303), statements of denial (§ 4-46-304), statements of dissociation (§ 4-46-704), statements of dissolution (§ 4-46-805), and (for LLPs) statements of qualification (§ 4-46-1001). A statement of qualification to become an LLP will be addressed at the end of this chapter, in the sections dealing with partnerships electing limited liability partnership status. The other documents mentioned here will be discussed in a little more detail in the next section of this chapter.

There is also a non-waivable provision that requires the partnership to provide partners and their agents access to its books and records. § 4-46-103(b)(2), cross referencing § 4-46-403(b). Books and records from the time in which such person was a partner are covered by this right. Although the partnership may

---

[31]   The "non-waivable" provisions of the partnership statute are collected at § 4-46-103, and there are cross-references in this provision to other sections of the Act dealing with duties of partners, the power of partners to dissociate, rules applicable to winding up, and rules governing LLPs. In addition, partners have no power to restrict the rights of third parties by modifying their partnership agreement.

impose reasonable charges for copies, the right to inspect and copy records during normal business hours may not be waived.

By far the most detailed non-waivable provisions relate to the kinds of duties that partners will owe the partnership and each other. § 4-46-103(b)(3) - (4). First, there are provisions relating to the duty of loyalty. § 4-46-103(b)(3). These obligations cannot be eliminated, although the partnership agreement may identify certain categories of activities that do not violate the duty of loyalty, so long as the modifications to the default rules are not "manifestly unreasonable." § 4-46-103(b)(3)(i). The partnership agreement may also give partners (either by unanimous vote or lesser vote specified in the partnership agreement) the right to ratify a transaction that would otherwise violate the duty of loyalty if there has been full disclosure of all material facts. § 4-46-103(b)(3)(ii). Absent these provisions, a partner owes the partnership and all other partners the duty to account to the partnership for any property, profit, or benefit derived by the partner in the conduct and winding up of the partnership business; to refrain from dealing with the partnership as or on behalf of an adverse party; and to refrain from competing with the partnership prior to its dissolution.

The next specific duty mentioned as being mandatory, to at least some extent, is the duty of care. § 4-46-103(b)(4). The partnership agreement may not unreasonably reduce each partner's duty to refrain from engaging in grossly negligent or reckless conduct, intentional misconduct, or a knowing violation of the law. § 4-46-404(c). (There is nothing in the statute that prevents a partnership agreement from imposing a higher duty of care, such as the duty to act as an ordinarily prudent person would.)

Finally, although the statue does not treat this as a fiduciary obligation, the default rule is that all partners must discharge their duties to the partnership and other partners under the statute and any partnership agreement and must exercise any rights "consistently with the obligation of good faith and fair dealing." § 4-46-103(5), cross referencing § 4-46-404(d). This obligation my not be eliminated, although the partnership agreement may include standards by which compliance with this responsibility may be measured, so long as the standards are not manifestly unreasonable. § 4-46-103(5).

In addition to mandatory responsibilities and duties owed by partners, the partnership agreement may not take away a partner's power to dissociate from the partnership by simply giving notice to the partnership of desire to do so. § 4-46-103(b)(6), cross referencing § 4-46-602(a). The partnership agreement may require that the notice be in writing (§ 4-46-103(b)(6)), and may provide that the partner will be liable for damages for breach of contract by withdrawing in violation of the agreement, but may not force anyone to stay on as partner. The possibility of damages for wrongful withdrawal is established in § 4-46-602(c).

Similarly, a partnership agreement can not take away the power of a court to expel a partner if the court determines that the partner engaged in wrongful conduct that adversely and materially affected the partnership business, or the partner willfully or persistently committed a material breach of the partnership agreement or a duty of loyalty or care, or the partnership engaged in conduct relating to the partnership which makes it not reasonably practicable to carry on the business in the partnership with the partner. § 4-46-103(b)(7), cross referencing § 4-46-601(5).

In addition, dissolution and winding up is mandatory if there is an event that makes it unlawful for all or substantially all of the partnership's business to be continued, unless that illegality is cured within 90 days. § 4-46-103(b)(8), cross referencing § 4-46-801(4). It is also mandatory if, on application of any partner, a court determines that the economic purpose of the partnership is likely to be unreasonably frustrated, another partner has engaged in conduct relating to the partnership which makes it not reasonably practicable to carry on the business of the partnership with that partner, or it is not otherwise reasonably practicable to carry on the partnership in conformity with the partnership agreement. § 4-46-801(5). Finally, dissolution is mandatory on application of a non-partner who has acquired a partner's transferable (economic) interest, if a court determines that it is equitable to wind up the partnership after expiration of the partnership's term; completion of the undertaking for which the partnership was formed, or at any time if the partnership was at will at time of the transfer of the transferable interest in the partnership. § 4-46-801(6).

The final category of non-waivable provisions of the act relates to the rights of third parties. § 4-46-103(b)(10). As one would expect, parties to a partnership agreement may not by their agreement change the statutory or common law rights of third parties who have not entered into that agreement. Thus, for example, when the statute gives partners apparent authority to act on behalf of the partnership, the partnership agreement may not take away the rights of third parties to rely on such authority. § 4-46-301(1). The rights of third parties are not enumerated in any one place in the partnership statute, but it is worth noting that wherever the rights of third parties are implicated, the partnership agreement may not ordinarily limit those rights.

IV.2.4.   Optional Documentation

As mentioned in the preceding section, the current partnership statute, unlike earlier versions of the partnership act, provides rules governing the filing of certain optional documents with the Secretary of State. These documents can affect the authority of partners in a partnership in certain defined ways. Any supplemental document to be filed by the partnership must be executed by at least two partners, and copies must be sent to every non-filing partner or person named as partner. A separate section governs the execution, filing, and recording of such statements. § 4-46-105. Other statements must be executed by a partner or person authorized by the statute. The Secretary of State is authorized to assess and collect a fee for filing these documents or for providing certified copies of any of these documents. § 4-46-105(f).

.

A statement of partnership authority (§ 4-46-303) may be used to expand a partner's authority, or limit the power of one or more partners to transfer real property if a certified copy of the original filing is recorded in the office for recording transfers of that real property. § 4-46-303(e). A statement of partnership authority may include limitations on other kinds of authority, but such limitations are not effective as to non-partners. § 4-46-303(f). A statement of authority must include the partnership's name; the address of its chief executive office and one in-state office (if the partnership has one); the names and mailing addresses of all partners or an agent's name and address (where the agent is required to maintain the names and addresses of all partners, and must make that information available upon a showing of good cause); the names of partners authorized to execute instruments transferring real property in the partnership's name; and may state authority or limitations on authority of partners. § 4-46-303(a). An affirmative grant of authority contained in a properly executed and filed statement of partnership authority is conclusive proof of authority in favor of a person who gives value without knowledge to the contrary, unless another filed statement contains a limitation on that authority. § 4-46-303(d)(1).

To provide notice of authority to transfer real estate, a certified copy of the statement of authority must be filed with the office for recording transfers of that real property. § 4-46-303(d)(2). A similarly filed certified copy of a statement of authority limiting authority to transfer real property is also effective as against non-partners. § 4-46-303(e). Statements of partnership authority expire by operations of law five years after filing of the document, or after the filing of its most recent amendment. § 4-46-303(g).

A partner or person named as a partner in a filed statement of partnership authority, or in the list maintained by an agent named in such a statement, may execute and file a statement of denial. § 4-46-304. Such a statement of denial acts as a limitation on that partner's expanded authority or on that partner's status as partner under the prior statement of authority. § 4-46-304. The statement of denial must include the name of the partnership, the name of the person filing the denial, and whatever fact that is being denied, including any grant of authority or status as a partner. § 4-46-304(1) - (3). If filed with the Secretary of State, a statement of denial limits the authority that is contained in a statement of partnership authority.

A dissociated partner or the partnership may file a statement of dissociation (§ 4-46-704), stating the partnership's name, the name and mailing address of the dissociated partner, that the partner has dissociated, and the effective date of that dissociation. § 4-46-704(a). Such a statement of dissociation limits any prior expansion of authority under a statement of partnership authority but is binding on non-partners only after 90 days. § 4-46-704(b) - (c).

To understand the statement of dissolution authorized by the UPA (1996), it is imperative to understand how the statute uses the word "dissolution." Under prior law, a partnership was "dissolved" any time any partner dissociated for any reason. That dissolution may have been only a technical dissolution, in the sense that the business was often continued by the remaining partners. However, because the partnership itself was an "association" of persons, the statutory definition of dissolution was the change in association triggered any time any one of the partners dissociated for any reason. Although the new statute does not specifically define dissolution, it does appear that it is now intended that dissolution is to be understood as the first step of the winding up and termination process. The statute talks about "dissolution and winding up"[32] or circumstances where the "partnership is dissolved, and its business must be wound up. . . ."[33] Thus, when the current statute speaks about the permitted statement of dissolution, we can presume that the partnership has begun the winding up process. In fact, the statute merely says that "after dissolution" any partner who has not wrongfully dissociated may file a statement of dissolution containing the partnership's name and a statement that the partnership has dissolved and is winding up. § 4-46-805. Once filed, a statement of partnership authority gives notice to non-partners of the dissolution 90 days after its filing, and at that time acts as a cancellation of any filed statement of partnership authority. § 4-46-805(b) - (c). To change authority of a partner to convey real estate, the dissolved partnership may execute a new statement of partnership authority (described above) to grant authority to transfer real estate in connection with the winding up of the partnership's business (and such a statement would be effective as to third parties even if the

---

[32]   For example, see § 4-46-801 (entitled "Events causing dissolution and winding up of partnership business"), § 4-46-603 (governing circumstances where dissociation "results in dissolution and winding up"), or § 4-46-701 (which governs situations where dissociation does not result "in dissolution and winding up") .

[33]   Section 4-46-801, for instance, begins by stating that "[a] partnership is dissolved, and its business must be wound up, only upon the occurence" of the events specified in that section.

transaction is not really appropriate for winding up). § 4-46-805(d).

IV.3. Management, Authority, and Fiduciary Duties

Absent these optional statements, which have no precedents under prior law, the general rules relating to management of the partnership and authority of the partners are essentially unchanged. Fiduciary duties of the partners have been modified, so this section will first address the default rules that mirror earlier law, and then address the nature of a partner's current responsibilities to the partnership and other partners.

Absent agreement to the contrary, all partners have "equal rights in the management and conduct of the partnership business." § 4-46-401(f). A difference in opinion about a matter in the ordinary course of partnership business requires a decision of a majority of the partners (with no requirement of a formal vote or meeting). § 4-46-401(j). Presumably this means that it takes a majority vote to change the way things have been operating in the ordinary course of business; if less than a majority want to change, things will continue as before. However, if the matter is outside the ordinary course of business or involves an amendment to the partnership agreement, all partners must consent. § 4-46-401(j). These rules relate to actual authority to manage the business, and do not affect the obligations of the partnership to third parties, if it turns out (for example) that a partner acts with the appearance of authority and a third party relies on that apparent authority.

Apparent authority of partners is one of those issues that is not readily subject to contrary agreement in the partnership agreement. The statute itself gives all partners agency power to take all acts that would be "apparently carrying on in the ordinary course the partnership business or business of the kind carried on by the partnership" unless the partner had no actual management authority to take that act <u>and</u> the person with whom the partner was dealing knew or had notification of the lack of authority. § 4-46-301(1). This apparent authority does not extend to acts outside that ordinary course of business, and such acts would require actual authority before the partnership would be bound by them. § 4-46-301(2).

These are perfectly consistent with the rules governing general partners' authority that have long been in place. Remember also that while apparent authority may not be modified by a partnership agreement, the partners' actual authority may be delegated any way that the partners desire. Management power can be given to a limited group of partners, one partner, hired managers who are not themselves partners at all, or distributed in any way that the partners agree. These types of arrangements are perfectly enforceable as to the partners' actual authority, and are binding on the partners themselves. However, a third person without knowledge of such changes is legally entitled to rely on the apparent agency power of partners to act in the partnership's ordinary course of business. This type of action would be binding on the partnership, but would also create personal liability on the part of the partner who exceeds his or her actual authority.

The fiduciary and other obligations of partners under Arkansas' current statute line up nicely with these rules, and with the way that obligations are generally imposed on persons with management responsibilities in other modern businesses. Traditionally, general partners owed each other almost unlimited fiduciary duties. Justice Cardozo once famously wrote that this was more than the "morals of the marketplace," and amounted to the duty to observe "the punctilio of an honesty the most sensitive."[34]   The modern general partnership statute, however, presumes a far more limited set of obligations. The default rules (which are subject to expansion by agreement of the parties, but the partnership agreement is limited in the extent to which it can reduce these obligations) set out only a restricted duty of loyalty and duty of care. § 4-46-404. By statute these are the "only" fiduciary obligations owed as a matter of law.

The statutory (default) duty of loyalty is limited to the following (which is excerpted directly from the statute):
A partner's duty of loyalty to the partnership and the other partners is limited to the following:

(1)   to account to the partnership and hold as trustee for it any property, profit, or benefit derived by the partner in the conduct and winding up of the partnership business or derived from a use by the partner of partnership property, including the appropriation of a partnership opportunity;

(2)   to refrain from dealing with the partnership in the conduct or winding up of the partnership business as or on behalf of a party having an interest adverse to the partnership; and

(3)   to refrain from competing with the partnership in the conduct of the partnership business before the dissolution of the partnership.

§ 4-46-404(b).

As mentioned earlier, it is possible to expand these rules by agreement, but the right of the partners to restrict or narrow these obligations is limited.   A partnership agreement may not "eliminate" the duty of loyalty, but "may identify specific types or categories of activities that do not violate the duty of loyalty, if not

---

[34]   Meinhard v. Salmon, 249 N.Y. 458, 164 N.E. 545 (1928).

manifestly unreasonable." § 4-46-103(3)(i). Although "manifestly unreasonable" is not clarified or defined in the statute, one would presume that this means that it would be difficult to challenge rational standards that are written into an agreement. In addition, by unanimous consent, or such lesser percentage or partners as may be specified in the partnership agreement, the partners may "authorize or ratify, after full disclosure of all material facts, a specific act or transaction that otherwise would violate the duty of loyalty." § 4-46-103(3)(ii).

The duty of care is similarly laid out in the statutes: "A partner's duty of care to the partnership and the other partners in the conduct and winding up of the partnership business is limited to refraining from engaging in grossly negligent or reckless conduct, intentional misconduct, or a knowing violation of law." § 4-46-404(c). While the level of care required from some or all of the partners may be increased if the parties so desire, it is not permissible to "unreasonably reduce" this obligation. § 4-46-103(4). Perhaps unfortunately, the statute does not attempt to define what "unreasonable" means in this context, but comment 6 to section 103 of the UPA (1997) (which contains similar language about the fiduciary duties of general partners in general partnerships) notes that "partnership agreements frequently contain provisions releasing a partner from liability for actions taken in good faith and in the honest belief that the actions are in the best interests of the partnership and indemnifying the partner against any liability incurred in connection with the business of the partnership if the partner acts in a good faith belief that he has authority to act." (Comment 6, § (1997)) The comment also notes that a different way to reach a similar result is to have a partnership agreement list various actions and explicitly provide that those particular activities are agreed "not to constitute gross negligence or willful misconduct." The drafters of the UPA specified that "[t]hese types of provisions are intended to come within the modifications authorized by subsection (b)(4). On the other hand, absolving partners of intentional misconduct is probably unreasonable. As with contractual standards of loyalty, determining the outer limit in reducing the standard of care is left to the courts." (10)

Although not technically set out as a fiduciary obligation, there is also a statutory duty to act in good faith. "A partner shall discharge the duties to the partnership and the other partners under this chapter or under the partnership agreement and exercise any rights consistently with the obligation of good faith and fair dealing." § 4-46-404(d). This obligation may not be eliminated, "but the partnership agreement may prescribe the standards by which the performance of the obligation is to be measured, if the standards are not manifestly unreasonable." § 4-46-103(5). The official comments to the UPA (1997) state that the drafters of the uniform act intended to borrow standards applicable under the Uniform Commercial Code, which the drafters concluded would generally allow specific limitations and waivers but not blanket waivers.[35] The validity of this approach has, however, not yet been tested in the courts.

---

[35]   Official comment 7 to UPA (1996) § 103 states: "The language of subsection (b)(5) is based on UCC Section 1-102(3). The partners can negotiate and draft specific contract provisions tailored to their particular needs (e.g., five days notice of a partners' meeting is adequate notice), but blanket waivers of the obligation are unenforceable." The drafters also cite a handful of cases dealing with the meaning of "manifestly unreasonable" in the context of commercial transactions. In PPG Indus., Inc. v. Shell Oil Co., 919 F.2d 17 (5th Cir.1990), the court deferred to the "sophisticated" parties' arrangements governing whether explosions were covered in a force majeure clause. In First Security Bank v. Mountain View Equip. Co., 112 Idaho 158, 730 P.2d 1078 (Ct.App.1986), aff'd, 112 Idaho 1078, 739 P.2d 377 (1987), the court allowed the parties to waive impairment of capital as a defense. In American Bank of Commerce v. Covolo, 88 N.M. 405, 540 P.2d 1294 (1975), the court enforced a contractual waiver under a guaranty agreement, even though the trial court found that the waiver would not have been commercially reasonable.

An important caveat to the default rules governing the duties owed by partners to each other also appears in the statutory language. As written, the statute specifically authorizes partners to further their own interests and to transact business with the partnership. "A partner does not violate a duty or obligation under this chapter or under the partnership agreement merely because the partner's conduct furthers the partner's own interest," (§ 4-46-404(e)), and "[a] partner may lend money to and transact other business with the partnership, and as to each loan or transaction the rights and obligations of the partner are the same as those of a person who is not a partner, subject to other applicable law." § 4-46-404(f). If, for any reason, the partners in a partnership do not desire these rules to apply to their business, the partnership agreement should clarify that such actions will not normally be permitted.

IV.4. Liability of Participants in a General Partnership

One of the hallmarks of the general partnership form of business is that partners are personally liable for the debts of the business. At one time, there was considerable confusion over the extent of this liability, stemming from the fact that the uniform statute made some kinds of liability joint and some kinds several only. Many states, including Arkansas, simply modified their version of the uniform act so that it was no longer uniform, but provided instead for joint and several liability in all circumstances. The modern uniform act dispenses with any distinction between joint liability and liability that is several only, and instead specifies that, absent certain defined circumstances, "all partners are liable jointly and severally for all obligations of the partnership unless otherwise agreed by the claimant or provided by law." § 4-46-306(a). The statutory exceptions to this liability are that "[a] person admitted as a partner into an existing partnership is not personally liable for any partnership obligation incurred before the person's admission as a partner" (§ 4-46-306(b)), and the personal liability rules do not apply if the general partnership in question has registered as an LLP. § 4-46-306(c).

This is the language that was adopted in Arkansas in 1999, when we enacted our version of the UPA (1996). The meaning of the statute was complicated in 2003, however, with our adoption of the Civil Justice Reform Act of 2003. Acts of 2003, Act 649, eff. March 25, 2003. As part of the Civil Justice Reform Act, which was designed to reform our state's tort laws, the legislature redefined the meaning of "joint and several liability." In the section entitled "Modification of Joint and Several Liability" our statute now provides that "[i]n any action for personal injury, medical injury, property damage, or wrongful death, the liability of each defendant for compensatory or punitive damages shall be several only and shall not be joint." § 16-55-201(a). This is further explained to make it clear that "[e]ach defendant shall be liable only for the amount of damages allocated to that defendant in direct proportion to that defendant's percentage of fault". § 16-55-201(b)(1). In addition, there must be a" separate several judgment . . . rendered against that defendant for that amount." § 16-55-201(b)(2). Even the mathematical calculation is statutorily explained: "To determine the amount of judgment to be entered against each defendant, the court shall multiply the total amount of damages recoverable by the plaintiff with regard to each defendant by the percentage of each defendant's fault" (§ 16-55-201(c)(1)), and this "shall be the maximum recoverable against that defendant." § 16-55-201(c)(2).

This new provision raises the question of whether Arkansas has now returned to a system where some partnership liability is joint and some is several, or whether the specific partnership language regarding partnership debts "trumps" the more recent tort reform effort. No other state has done what we have done: adopt the language of the UPA (1996) and then a few short years thereafter adopt a tort reform measure essentially seeking to eliminate the very liability provided for under the partnership statute. There is, perhaps not surprisingly, no reported decision in this state specifically addressing what these statutes mean in concert.

The issue here is the extent of a partner's liability for a partnership obligation, so the first inquiry would have to be under what circumstances is the partnership itself liable for "personal injury, medical injury, property damage, or wrongful death," any of which would have to have been caused by an agent of the partnership in order for the partnership itself to be liable. Arkansas' partnership statute provides that the "partnership is liable for loss or injury caused to a person, or for a penalty incurred, as a result of a wrongful act or omission, or other actionable conduct, of a partner acting in the ordinary course of business of the partnership or with authority of the partnership." § 4-46-305(a). Does this make a partnership liable, without any fault of the partnership, for "personal injury, medical injury, property damage, or wrongful death" caused by partners or authorized agents of the partnership? Under both the partnership statute and traditional notions of respondeat superior, the answer would clearly be yes. Does the Civil Justice Reform Act of 2003 (Ark. Acts of 2003, Act 649, eff. March 25, 2003) change this?

While it is somewhat hard to believe that the legislature specifically intended this consequence, or even considered it, the wording of the more recent legislation appears absolute. The Civil Justice Reform Act says that "[e]ach defendant shall be liable only for the amount of damages allocated to that defendant in direct proportion to that defendant's percentage of fault." § 16-55-201(b)(1). This appears to eliminate vicarious liability (i.e., liability without fault) for torts involving "personal injury, medical injury, property damage, or wrongful death." Logically, this would mean that not only are partners not to be held liable for the misconduct of others, but that the partnership itself should not be liable.

On the other hand, in a recent decision, the Arkansas Court of Appeals determined that the Civil Justice Reform Act did not affect respondeat superior liability for trespass and conversion so long as the tortious conduct was within the scope of employment.[36] The opinion is brief, contains little in the way of reasoning or analysis, and does not explain if the court believed that the tort reform legislation was not intended to affect respondeat superior theories rather than joint misconduct, or if "trespass and conversion" somehow does not involve "property damage." There is no subsequent history to this case, so its eventual impact on the law in this state is uncertain. Certainly the opinion did not consider partnership law specifically.

As to how the Arkansas courts will eventually interpret our partnership and tort reform statutes, only time will tell. Until such opinions have been rendered, it would be wise to at least advise clients that they might be personally liable for tortious misconduct of their fellow partners and partnership agents, even if recent tort reform legislation gives them an arguable defense in the event that someone seeks to impose such liability upon them. A safer alternative may be the LLP, which not only protects against liability for torts of others, but also offers individual partners statutory protection against liability for contractual obligations of the partnership.[37]

---

[36]   Shamlin v. Quadrangle Enerprises, Inc., 101 Ark.App. 164, 272 S.W.3d 128 (Ark. App. 2008).

[37]   See section IV.10. of this Chapter.

IV.5. Sharing of Profits and Losses; Distributions

IV.5.1.   Profits and Losses Generally

Another issue that is likely to be of considerable importance to clients is the sharing of profits. In conjunction with this, even if they are not particularly excited about thinking about the possibility of losses, they should be asked to consider how they wish to allocate and share losses, as well.

In the absence of an agreement between the partners, the default rule is that "[e]ach partner is entitled to an equal share of the partnership profits and is chargeable with a share of the partnership losses in proportion to the partner's share of the profits." § 4-46-401(b). Thus, if nothing at all is said, every partner will share equally in all profits and will also share losses equally. If the agreement changes the way in which profits are to be shared and is silent about losses, then the losses would be presumed to be allocated in the same way that the agreement specifies for the sharing of profits.

IV.5.2.   The Services-Only Partner

There are some issues with regard to these rules that probably need a little more explanation. The first is the question of what happens (if the parties do not have a clear agreement) if some partners contribute tangible items and others contribute services in exchange for their partnership interests. The presumption is that regardless of the relative values of these contributions, partners are presumed to share equally in profits and losses. So what happens if, after a year, the partnership is to dissolve and all of the tangible value contributed to the partnership has been lost? Do the partners go their separate ways, the services-only partner being deemed to have lost the value of his or her services?   One might presume that this is the likely intent of the parties, but the statute does not draw the line so clearly.

The UPA (1996) specifies that (absent agreement to the contrary) "[a] partner is not entitled to remuneration for services performed for the partnership, except for reasonable compensation for services rendered in winding up the business of the partnership." § 4-46-401(h).   So if no wages are to be paid to the services-only partner, what has he or she lost?   How has he or she shared equally in the partnership's losses?

Courts that have faced the issue of whether a services-only partner should be compelled to contribute to partnership losses to "equalize" losses have not reached consistent results in interpreting what the prior statute meant.   The language of the current and earlier versions of the statute seems clear—a services-only partner should be compelled to pay in amounts sufficient to share equally in any capital loss.[38]   However, there are several cases reaching the opposite result, primarily on grounds that to compel a services-only partner to contribute more in addition to losing the value of services is contrary to logic and notions of fairness.[39]   This means that an attorney assisting a client with a partnership agreement must take special care to provide for the

---

[38]   For cases applying state statutes as written, consider Parker v. N. Mixing Co., 756 P.2d 881, 890 (Alaska 1988) (Alaska statutes); Seguin v. Boyd, 654 P.2d 808, 812 (Ariz. Ct. App. 1982) (Arizona statutes); Richert v. Handly, 330 P.2d 1079, 1081 (Wash. 1958) (using the provisions of the Uniform Partnership Act). That this is clearly the import of the statutory language has also been noted by commentators. If you are looking for more detailed analysis of this issue, I suggest looking at Val D. Ricks, Service Partner Capital Agreements: The Leading Cases and a Response to Critics, 12 U. Penn. J. Bus. L. 1 (2009)

[39]   On this side of the equation, the most recent leading case is Becker v. Killarney 532 N.E.2d 931 (Ill. App. Ct. 1988), but the most well-known is probably Kovacik v. Reed, 315 P.2d 314 (Cal. 1957). The oldest of the reported cases reaching this result is Heran v. Hall, 40 Ky. (1 B. Mon.) 159 (1840).

appropriate sharing of losses, particularly if one partner is providing services in lieu of a capital contribution. Note also that there are potential tax consequences that may flow from a decision to have one or more partners contribute services only. For this reason, it is always advisable to have your clients consult a tax advisor if contributions of services are contemplated.

IV.5.3. Distributions

In addition to providing clear rules about how profits (and losses) are to be allocated between the partners, when drafting provisions about the sharing of profits, it is also important to make sure that clients understand how those profits are likely to be distributed (i.e., paid out). Again, the statutes provide some default rules if the parties do not agree in advance about how distributions are to be determined. The first of these is that "[a] partner has no right to receive, and may not be required to accept, a distribution in kind." § 4-46-402. In most partnerships, this arrangement might be perfectly acceptable, but consider a partnership where one person is contributing cash and the other a patent or a unique property that has no readily ascertainable value. If, before partnership operations really begin, the partnership dissolves and must be wound up, the partner contributing the unique property might expect that it would be returned to him or her. Or, alternatively, the partner who put up the cash in contemplation of development of the unique property might expect that he or she would get back the cash, and the property would be returned to the other partner. The default rules simply do not work this way, and if this does not serve the partners' interests, the partnership agreement should be drafted to reflect their needs.

The default rules that govern the timing of distributions are a little more complicated, although there is not much disagreement about how they work. In accordance with the requirements of partnership tax law, every partner in a general partnership:

> ... is deemed to have an account that is:
>
> (1)　credited with an amount equal to the money plus the value of any other property, net of the amount of any liabilities, the partner contributes to the partnership and the partner's share of the partnership profits; and
>
> (2)　charged with an amount equal to the money plus the value of any other property, net of the amount of any liabilities, distributed by the partnership to the partner and the partner/s share of the partnership losses.

§ 4-46-401(a).

This provision relates to distributions because the default rules on settlement of accounts upon liquidation and winding up specify that "[e]ach partner is entitled to a settlement of all partnership accounts upon winding up the partnership business. In settling accounts among the partners, profits and losses that result from the liquidation of the partnership assets must be credited and charged to the partners' accounts. The partnership shall make a distribution to a partner in an amount equal to any excess of the credits over the charges in the partner's account." § 4-46-807(b). This is the only default rule about a required distribution. There are no statutorily presumed interim distributions.

Thus, in order to have interim distributions (which one presumes would be desired in any profitable partnership where there are earnings in excess of expenses), the partners must agree to the distribution. Either the partnership agreement can specify how and when distributions are to be made, or the default rules about the kind of agreement that is required can apply. Under the default rules, if interim distributions are the ordinary course of the partnership's business, they may be decided by a majority of the partners, but if there is no ordinary course of business regarding distributions, such a distribution would require consent of all the partners. § 4-46-401(j). The partnership agreement may fail to address distributions specifically, but may allocate management authority to one or more partners or other persons, and presumably decisions about distributions would be within the scope of such a grant. It is not outside the realm of possibility, however, than an unusual distribution could be challenged as being outside the ordinary course of business, and thus invalid without unanimous approval. In most circumstances is it probably preferable to spell out the authority to declare interim distributions in a partnership agreement. Ideally, the authority to decide upon both the amount and timing of distributions should probably be addressed.

Two other points are worth making about partnership distributions. Recall from chapter 3 that tax partners are taxed when income is allocated to them; not when distributions are made (so long as the partner has sufficient basis in his or her partnership account to offset the amount that is distributed). This means that partners may find themselves facing the obligation to pay taxes on income that they have not received and have no "right" to receive. This may be quite unpalatable to many clients or potential investors. To alleviate the burden of having to pay taxes in the absence of a distribution sufficient to offset such obligation, it is not uncommon for partnership agreements to have a mandatory distribution provision sufficient to offset taxes. Such a provision might read something like this:

> For each fiscal year, to the extent that the partnership has operating income sufficient to make such payments and to retain in its net reserves an amount equal to at least $____, each partner shall be entitled to receive within 90 days after the end of such fiscal year a tax distribution equal to the product of (a) the net profits for that fiscal

year, if any, allocated to that partner and (b) the sum of (i) the highest marginal rate of federal income tax applicable to ordinary income for individuals for that fiscal year plus (ii) the highest marginal rate of state income tax applicable to ordinary income for individuals residing in Arkansas for that fiscal year, in each case determined without regard to phase-outs, alternative taxes and the like, and without regard to any other tax attribute of the individual partner. Such tax distribution is an advance to help partners to pay their taxes resulting from partnership operations and is not intended to indemnify partners against their taxes on partnership income.

This is NOT a perfect tax distribution provision and does not cover every conceivable circumstance. It is to be expected that your clients will have special needs, and you should consider a variety of factors in tailoring the partnership language to meet their needs. You may wish to pay special attention to such issues as: how mandatory these distributions should be; whether the distribution should be sufficient to pay minimum or maximum tax liability whether and to what extent it should include potential liability for state taxes and if so which state; whether local taxes should be considered; whether prior losses allocated to a partner should be considered in setting minimum distributions; whether interest needs to be paid on the distributions and if so when and at what rates; the timing of the mandatory distribution; whether it would be better to calculate the distribution based on net taxable income allocated rather than net profits (which might be especially important if there is built-in gain associated with property contributed to the partnership by one or more partners); whether there needs to be quarterly advances to cover estimated tax payments; effect of tax credits allocated by the partnership; whether the provision should continue in effect if the partnership has gone into liquidation; the impact of subsequent tax audits, etc.

Each deal is different, and how you choose to address mandatory distributions to offset taxes should be rethought for every partnership agreement you draft.

A second drafting issue that is likely to come up involves the timing of distributions. You might recall that partners generally pay taxes on amounts that are allocated to them and do not pay taxes when amounts are distributed to them; this is true, however, only to the extent that the partner's basis in his or her partnership account is sufficient to offset the distribution. 26 U.S.C.A. § 731. This works very well if every partner waits until after each year's allocation of income in order to receive distributions, because when a partner pays taxes on his or her allocative share, that partner's basis increases, so that subsequent distributions of that pre-taxed income are not taxed. In the case of an investment partnership, it might be perfectly acceptable to have annual distributions. On the other hand, consider what would happen if your clients intend to work for the partnership, and to make their living from those efforts. They are likely to want regular payments, so that they can pay their regularly occurring bills (just like the rest of us).

The drafting solution to the problem of partners who want regular distributions before the end of the partnership's fiscal year is typically found in the inclusion of drawing accounts. Funds withdrawn from the partnership through such drawing accounts may be referred to as "draws" or "advances," and generally serve the same purpose as a type of salary. You will certainly want to explain to your clients that amounts withdrawn in this manner are best thought of as an advance, or perhaps a periodic reduction of accumulated profits. These draws, unlike salaries of non-partner employees, which continue to be a partnership obligation even absent profitability, depend on the profits earned by the partnership.

Suppose your clients want you to draft a partnership agreement covering their existing business, which has a fairly stable income. They want the agreement to provide that most of the profits are to be paid out to the partners on a regular basis. Although your clients need most of the partnership income to be available to them in regular installments, they prefer to be a little conservative about how much they take out. They are not at all adverse to an end-of-year bonus, but want to limit the likelihood of having to repay amounts to the partnership at the end of the year. A drawing account that meets these objectives can be established with language like this:

A drawing account shall be established and maintained for each partner. On the first business day of each month, the account shall be credited with 1/13 of that partner's share of the prior year's net profits. On the first business day of each month, each partner shall have the right to withdraw up to 100% of the amount in such partner's drawing account. At the end of the partnership's fiscal year, each partner's drawing account shall be credited with the additional amount, if any, equal to such partner's share of profits for that year reduced by the sum of the amounts previously credited to his or her drawing account. If, however, such partner's share of profits for that year is less than the amounts credited during the year, the account shall immediately be reduced by the amount by which amounts previously credited exceed such partner's share of profits. At the end of each fiscal year, each partner shall receive the amount, if any, equal to the share of profits for that year reduced by the sum of the amounts withdrawn from such partner's drawing account during the year. If, however, any partner's share of profits for that year is less than the amounts withdrawn during the year, such partner shall promptly repay the difference to the partnership. A credit balance in a partner's drawing account shall be considered a debt of the partnership to that partner, payable upon demand, and a deficit balance therein shall be a debt of that partner to the partnership, payable upon demand. Except with the prior unanimous written consent of the other partners, no partner shall make withdrawals from his drawing account that will result in a deficit balance.

Again, this language will not work in all circumstances. For new partnerships, it will not make sense to talk about allocated amounts equal to the prior year's net profits. Instead, they may allocate a percentage of that month's earnings. In addition, 1/13 of the prior year's earnings may be too conservative or too risky for some clients. Some clients may want the right but not the obligation to make withdrawals, and may want to discuss whether interest should be paid on amounts that are not withdrawn. Some clients will prefer the partnership agreement to cover withdrawals in excess of the current drawing account amounts. The goal is to draft language that suits your client's needs, and that will vary considerably from deal to deal.

IV.6. Partnership Interests

IV.6.1.   Nature of Partnership Interests

Before speaking about the nature of partnership interests, it is probably wise to have a word about terminology. "Partnership property" generally refers to property owned by the partnership, while a "partnership interest" is a partner's ownership interest in the partnership. Property is partnership property if it is acquired by the partnership (§ 4-46-203), and this happens if property is acquired in the name of the partnership, transferred to the partnership in its name, is acquired by one or more partners "with an indication in the instrument transferring title to the property of the person's capacity as a partner or of the existence of a partnership" even without an indication of the partnership's name, or is transferred to one or more partners in their capacity as partners, if the name of the partnership is indicated in the instrument transferring title. § 4-46-204. If property is "purchased with partnership assets," it is presumed to be partnership property even if the documents transferring title do not comply with these rules. § 4-46-204(c). On the other hand, even if property is used by the partnership, if it was acquired in the name of one or more partners without indication of the acquiror's capacity as partner or the existence of partnership, it is presumed to be the partner's property unless partnership assets were used to acquire it. § 4-46-204(d).

A person's status as partner does not make such person a co-owner of partnership property, and in fact a partner "has no interest in partnership property which can be transferred, either voluntarily or involuntarily." § 4-46-501. This can be changed by agreement, of course, but the typical default rule is that "[t]he only transferable interest of a partner in the partnership is the partner's share of the profits and losses of the partnership and the partner's right to receive distributions. The interest is personal property." § 4-46-502. A person's partnership interest includes not only the transferable interest, but also "all management and other rights." § 4-46-101(9).

How does someone become a partner? There are two alternatives: either the person can make a contribution to the partnership at its formation or thereafter and be accepted as partner; or an existing partner can sell his or her transferable interest (in whole or in part) and the other partners can agree to accept the transferee as a partner. Under the default rules, both of these alternatives require unanimous consent of all other partners, but the process does work in exactly the same way, so each of these alternatives will be discussed separately.

147

IV.6.2.   Issuance of New Interests (Becoming a Partner)

Persons may become partners by making a contribution directly to the partnership, so long as all other partners accept them as such. (The requirement of unanimous agreement is a default rule which is subject to contrary agreement of the parties.) Initially, a partnership is formed only when persons associate as co-owners to run a business for a profit. § 4-406-202(a). In order for this to happen, all of the participants must obviously agree to the co-ownership and association. Absent agreement to the contrary, admission of new members subsequent to the initial formation also requires unanimous consent, as there are no default rules that would require acceptance of a new member. The unanimous consent may be given at the time the new partner seeks to be admitted, or authority to authorize the admission of new partners may be delegated in advance, in the partnership agreement. In the latter case, the consent of the other partners would be found in their agreement to the terms of the partnership agreement.

IV.6.3.   Sales and Voluntary Transfers of Interests by Existing Partners

The other way that a person can become a partner is by buying a partnership interest from an existing partner, and being accepted as partner. The statute makes it abundantly clear that the purchase of a partner's partnership interest alone will not make the purchaser a partner. In fact, unless the partnership agreement changes it, the "only transferable interest of a partner in the partnership is the partner's share of the profits and losses of the partnership and the partner's right to receive distributions." § 4-46-502. The transfer of a partner's transferable interest, while permissible (in the absence of an agreed-upon restriction that is known to the purported transferee), neither causes the transferor partner to stop being a partner nor "as against the other partners or the partnership, entitle[s] the transferee, during the continuance of the partnership, to participate in the management or conduct of the partnership business, to require access to information concerning partnership transactions, or to inspect or copy the partnership books or records." § 4-46-503(a)(3). The only rights of such a transferee are:

(1)   to receive, in accordance with the transfer, distributions to which the transferor would otherwise be entitled;

(2)   to receive upon the dissolution and winding up of the partnership business, in accordance with the transfer, the net amount otherwise distributable to the transferor; and

(3)   to seek . . . a judicial determination that it is equitable to wind up the partnership business.

§ 4-46-503(b).

To make it quite clear that the original partner retains his or her status as partner even following transfer of all of his or her transferable interest, the statute specifically states that "[u]pon transfer, the transferor retains the rights and duties of a partner other than the interest in distributions transferred." § 4-46-503(d). Thus the transferor continues as a partner, unless the partnership agreement provides otherwise or the transferor is expelled by the remaining partners. The statutory default rules give the remaining partners the right, by unanimous vote, to agree to expel a partner if "there has been a transfer of all or substantially all of that partner's transferable interest in the partnership, other than a transfer for security purposes, or a court order charging the partner's interest, which has not been foreclosed." § 4-46-601(4)(ii). The partnership agreement can change this default rule, either by eliminating the right to expel a transferring partner, or (more likely) by reducing the vote required, or by specifying that even the sale of less than all or substantially all of a partner's transferable interest can give the other partners the right to expel a transferee.

IV.6.4.   Creditors and Charging Orders

The preceding two subsections have dealt with voluntary transfers. It is also possible that a third party can gain the rights of a transferee without the voluntary participation of the transferor. If a partner or a partner's transferee becomes a judgment debtor, the judgment creditor may apply to a court for a charging order against the transferable interest of the debtor to satisfy the judgment. § 4-46-504(a). Under this provision the court has the option of appointing a receiver of the share of the distributions and has authority to make other orders and directions that the circumstances may require. Once obtained, a charging order operates as a lien on the judgment debtor's transferable interest, and so long as the debt remains unpaid, the court may order foreclosure of such transferable interest, with the purchaser at a foreclosure sale gaining the rights and status of transferee. § 4-46-504(b). At any time prior to foreclosure, the interest charged may be redeemed by the debtor, by any other partner using personally-owned property, or by the partnership with partnership property, with unanimous consent of all partners other than the judgment debtor. § 4-46-504(c). This charging order (and its possible foreclosures) is the exclusive remedy for a judgment creditor of a partner to satisfy the judgment out of the partner's partnership interest. § 4-46-504(e).

While the partnership agreement cannot affect the right of third parties, and therefore cannot take away a judgment creditor's right to obtain a charging order or to foreclose upon that interest, the partnership agreement can change the rights or even impose an obligation upon the other partners or the partnership with regard to redemption of a charged interest.

IV.7. Leaving the Partnership (Dissociation)

IV.7.1.   Effect on the Partnership

Dissociation of a partner from a general partnership traditionally meant that the partnership had to "dissolve" because the association itself necessarily had to change if even a single partner left for any reason. Under our current partnership statute, however, dissociation is separated from dissolution more clearly, and there are two possibilities if a partner dissociates from a partnership (i.e., stops being a partner) for any reason. The first possibility is that this dissociation will result in a dissolution and winding up of the partnership, in which case certain rights and obligations are triggered under the statute, and certain procedures must be followed in order to liquidate the business. The second alternative is that the partner leaves, but the business of the partnership is continued. This kind of dissociation triggers a second set of rights and obligations, and does not involve liquidation of the business at all. Because there are two discrete paths that are possible following dissociation under our current partnership statute, the following materials will first outline what events cause dissociation and then what events cause the dissolution and winding up of the partnership. In both cases, the materials start with the events that are listed in the statute as default events (i.e., rules that will apply in the absence of agreement by the partners). In both cases, most of the default rules are subject to modification by the partnership, but there is a small core of events that cannot be changed by agreement of the parties.

IV.7.2.   Events that Cause Dissociation

The UPA (1996) very clearly lists the events that will, absent agreement to the contrary, cause a partner to dissociate from the partnership. With some paraphrasing, the following list includes the events that result in a partner ceasing to be associated with the partnership as partner under the statutory default rules:

(1)   the partnership receives notice that the partner wants to withdraw either immediately or at a later date specified by the withdrawing partner;

(2)   the partnership agreement sets out an event that will cause dissociation, and the event happens;

(3)   the partner is expelled pursuant to the partnership agreement;

(4)   the partner is expelled by the unanimous vote of the other partners if:

    (i)   it is unlawful to carry on the partnership business with that partner;

    (ii)   there has been a transfer of all or substantially all of that partner's transferable interest in the partnership, other than a transfer for security purposes, or a court order charging the partner's interest, which has not been foreclosed;

    (iii)   a corporate partner files a certificate of dissolution or the equivalent and does not revoke the certificate or file for reinstatement within 90 days after the partnership notifies a corporate partner that it will be expelled; or

    (iv)   a partnership that is a partner has been dissolved and its business is being wound up;

(5)   a court expels a partner upon application by the

partnership or another partner on a finding that:

(i)   the partner engaged in wrongful conduct that adversely and materially affected the partnership business;

(ii)   the partner willfully or persistently committed a material breach of the partnership agreement or of a fiduciary duty owed to the partnership or the other partners; or

(iii)   the partner engaged in conduct relating to the partnership business which makes it not reasonably practicable to carry on the business in partnership with the partner;

(6)   the partner becomes a debtor in a bankruptcy or engages in other conduct specified in the statute evidencing insolvency;

(7)   in the case of a partner who is an individual, that partner's death or incapacity; or

(8)   the ending or termination of a non-individual partner.

§ 4-46-601.

The partners may agree at any time to eliminate, modify or waive most of these events of dissociation. Such agreement may appear either in advance in the partnership agreement or at the time of the event that would ordinarily trigger dissociation. The partners may also agree to include other events that will trigger dissociation. Both of these kinds of agreements would take the unanimous consent of all partners. The UPA (1996) does provide that the right of a court to expel a partner under these provisions may not be varied, and specifies that legal power to withdraw as a partner cannot be taken away (although the agreement may require written notice of intent to withdraw). § 4-46-103(6) - (7).

IV.7.3. Events that Cause Winding Up of the Partnership

The UPA (1996) also specifies a somewhat shorter list of events that will result in the dissolution and winding up of the partnership business. § 4-46-801. This list is subject to modification by the partners, but absent contrary agreement, the statute sets out a list of events upon which a partnership is to be dissolved and wound up.

In order to understand the statutory list, as a preliminary matter, it is probably worth noting the difference between a partnership at will and a partnership for a term or particular undertaking. The statute does not define these concepts, although the official comment to the definitions section of the Uniform Act explains that a partnership for a term is one in which the partners have agreed to remain partners until at least the expiration of a definite term. A particular undertaking implies that the partners have agreed to continue as partners until a "particular venture whose time is indefinite but certain to occur" has been completed.[40]

If the partnership is at will, any partner who has not previously dissociated for another reason (such as being expelled) can give notice to the partnership, and that will trigger the dissolution and winding up process. § 4-46-801(1). If the partnership has been formed for a particular term or express undertaking, dissolution and winding up occurs: when the term expires or the undertaking is complete; if all partners agree to wind up the business; or if a majority of the remaining vote to dissolve and wind up within 90 days after a partner wrongfully dissociates,

---

[40]   See comments to UPA (1997) § 101, and various cases from other jurisdictions cited in the comments.

dies, becomes bankrupt, or (for a non-individual partner) is dissolved or being terminated as described in the statute. § 4-46-801(2). Regardless of whether the partnership is at will or for a particular term or express undertaking, the partners may agree in the partnership agreement that any other event will trigger dissolution and winding up. § 4-46-801(3). In addition, unless there is a cure within 90 days of notice to the partners, a partnership is to be dissolved and wound up if anything happens that would make it "unlawful for all or substantially all of the business of the partnership to be continued." § 4-46-801(4). Any partner may apply for dissolution upon a judicial determination that:

> (i)   the economic purpose of the partnership is likely to be unreasonably frustrated;
>
> (ii)   another partner has engaged in conduct relating to the partnership business which makes it not reasonably practicable to carry on the business in partnership with that partner; or
>
> (iii) it is not otherwise reasonably practicable to carry on the partnership business in conformity with the partnership agreement.

§ 4-46-801(5).

A court may also require dissolution and winding up if it is equitable to make such an order and a transferee can show either that the partnership was for a particular term that has expired, an express undertaking that has been completed, or that it was a partnership at will at the time the transfer occurred. § 4-46-801(6).

Most of these events are subject to modification by the partners, although the partners cannot by agreement change the requirement that a partnership be wound up if it becomes illegal to carry on the partnership's business in a way that is not remedied within 90 days, or if there is a petition for judicial dissolution (either from a partner or transferee) that meets the above standards. § 4-46-103(8). The other events can be removed from this list, or modified (for example by adding provisions allowing cure or waiver by some or all of the remaining partners), and other events requiring dissolution may be added. These are the kind of possibilities that clients should be counseled to consider when the issue of how to handle dissolution is being discussed.

Now that the triggers for each of these two paths have been set out, the question becomes what happens under each alternative. The next section of this chapter addresses in some detail what happens if the business is to be continued, and the section after that deals with how a partnership is to be wound up if that path is required.

IV.8. Continuation of the Partnership Business when a Partner Dissociates

IV.8.1. The Process

If one or more partners leaves the partnership (i.e., dissociates for any reason), but the business of the partnership is continued, certain default rules come into play. In this case, the purpose of the partnership does not change, and the authority of the non-withdrawing partners to carry on partnership business does not change. The withdrawing partner's right to participate in management and conduct of the partnership business terminates (§ 4-46-603(b)(1)), and the fiduciary duties owed by the withdrawing partner are sharply curtailed. § 4-46-603(b)(2) - (3). The duty to refrain from competing with the partnership terminates upon dissociation, and the other duties of loyalty continue only with regard to matters arising before dissociation. The duty of care also applies only to matters arising before the partner's dissociation.

In very general terms, if this path is followed, the partners who are continuing in the business continue as before, and the dissociated partner's interest and obligations to the partnership end. To make that fair to the dissociating partner, the default rules provide that the dissociating partner must be bought out. § 4-46-701(a).

IV.8.2.   Buying out a Withdrawing Partner

Absent agreement to the contrary, the buyout price for a withdrawing partner is the amount that would have been paid to the partner if the business had in fact been wound up, and "on the date of dissociation, the assets of the partnership were sold at a price equal to the greater of the liquidation value or the value based on a sale of the entire business as a going concern without the dissociated partner and the partnership were wound up as of that date. Interest must be paid from the date of dissociation to the date of payment." § 4-46-701(b). Amounts owed by the dissociating partner (whether or not presently due), including any damages if the dissociation was wrongful, are to be offset against the buyout price. § 4-46-701(c). The partnership must also indemnify a dissociated partner who is being bought out in this manner "against all partnership liabilities" except those caused if the dissociated partners acts to bind the partnership and causes damages after dissociation. § 4-46-701(d). The statute contemplates a 120 day period in which the parties are to attempt to agree on the buyout price, and the default rule is that payment of as much as the partnership agrees on must be made in that time frame. § 4-46-701(e).

Because the partnership does not actually liquidate its assets, unless the partnership agreement has been drafted very carefully to cover this contingency, there is always the potential for disagreement between the partners who are continuing the partnership business and the dissociated partner(s) about the appropriate buyout amount. The statute sets out rules that will govern if this happens. In essence, if no agreement is reached within 120 of the dissociation, the partnership is to pay the dissociated partner in cash the amount it estimates is due (including interest, less any offsets). § 4-46-701(e). The payment must be accompanied by the following documentation from the partnership:

(1)   a statement of partnership assets and liabilities as of the date of dissociation;

(2)   the latest available partnership balance sheet and income statement, if any;

(3)   an explanation of how the estimated amount of the payment was calculated; and

(4)   written notice that the payment is in full satisfaction of the obligation to purchase unless, within one hundred twenty (120) days after the written notice, the dissociated partner commences an action to determine the buyout price, any offsets . . . or other terms of the obligation to purchase.

§ 4-46-701(g).

A dissociating partner has the right to challenge the payment in court within 120 of receiving the payment or one year after demand for payment if no payment is made. § 4-46-701(h). If the dispute does go before a judge, the statute gives the court authority to assess costs, expenses, and attorney's fees against any party that the court determines to have acted arbitrarily, vexatiously, or not in good faith. § 4-46-701(i).

Obviously, these default rules could cause great hardship to a partnership. A single partner could essentially hold the partnership hostage to his or her will by threatening to withdraw in a manner that would trigger the obligation to buy him or her out at a very inconvenient time for the business. Damages might be very difficult or even impossible to prove. The possibility of creating a different set of operating rules to govern in the event that a partner dissociates is therefore one that most clients should be encouraged to consider.

One way to change these default rules is to establish a particular term or definite undertaking for the partnership. If the partnership agreement provides either of these alternatives, the default rules for buying out a dissociating partner change. In these instances, the wrongfully dissociating partner is normally entitled to be paid the buyout price only upon expiration of the term or completion of the undertaking, although the price must be reasonably secured and must bear interest. The wrongfully dissociating partner can sue for earlier payment, but has the burden of establishing to the court's satisfaction that "earlier payment will not cause undue hardship to the business of the partnership." § 4-46-701(h). If a deferred payout is chosen, the parties must either agree to the price, or the partnership may tender its written offer of payment amount and terms (including security for payment). § 4-46-701(f). If the dissociating partner does not like the amount offered, he or she has 120 days to initiate an action challenging the amount. If no offer is made, the dissociating partner may make demand for one, and has a full year after making such demand in which to initiate litigation to set a buyout price. § 4-46-701(h). Costs, expenses, and attorney's fees may be assessed against any party found to have acted arbitrarily, vexatiously, or not in good faith. § 4-46-701(I).

Obviously, there are other ways to modify these default rules. Partners are generally free to provide for a deferred buyout in all instances (even if the partnership is technically at will), or to set a predetermined buyout price and interest rates, or to set a presumption that the buyout price is to be paid over time.

Liquidated damages for premature withdrawal may also be established to minimize the risk that partnership operations will be compromised by the obligation to buyout a withdrawing partner at an inconvenient time.

IV.8.3.   Wrongfully Withdrawing Partners

Additional potential complications occur if the business of the partnership is continued following a wrongful withdrawal. The UPA (1996) specifies that a partner's dissociation from an at will partnership is to be considered "wrongful" only if it is a breach of an express provision of the partnership agreement. § 4-46-602(b)(1). In the case of a partnership for a definite term or particular undertaking (i.e., a partnership in which the partners have agreed not to withdraw before a certain period of time has expired or until a particular condition has been satisfied), dissociation is wrongful if it occurs before the term is complete or before the undertaking has been fulfilled and any one or more of the following is true:

(1)   the dissociation is a by the partner's express will and is not within 90 days after another partner has dissociated wrongfully, or by reason of death, incapacity, bankruptcy or termination (for non-individual partners);

(2)   the dissociation is as a result of judicial expulsion;

(3)   the dissociation is because of bankruptcy; or

(4)   in the case of a non-individual partner, it has willfully dissolved or terminated.

§ 4-46-602(b)(2).

Under the default rules, a wrongfully withdrawing partner must still be bought out if the remaining partners intend to continue partnership operations, but the partnership is entitled to reduce the buyout price by any damages caused by the dissociation. § 4-46-701(c), referencing damages allowed under § 4-46-602(c). And, as mentioned earlier, if the partner who wrongfully withdraws from a partnership for a term or particular undertaking before that has been completed is not typically entitled to payment of the price until expiration of the term or completion of the undertaking. § 4-46-701(h).

IV.9. Winding up a General Partnership

IV.9.1.   The Process

If, instead of continuing the business, there is a dissociation by one or more partners followed by a dissolution and winding up of the partnership, the default rules change. First, the authority of all of the partners changes. Once dissolution has begun, the purpose of the partnership ceases to be carrying on the business for a profit and instead becomes winding up. § 4-46-802(a). If all the partners, with the exception of any partners who have withdrawn "wrongfully," agree, the dissolution may be stopped, and the partnership operations will resume "as if dissolution had never occurred," although the rights of third parties are not to be affected by this election. § 4-46-802(b). In this case, the default rules described above in section IV.8. would kick in.

Assuming, however, that there is no subsequent agreement to resume partnership operations, all partners other than those who have wrongfully dissociated may participate in the winding up, although a court may choose to supervise the winding up if any partner, partner's representative, or transferee shows good cause as to why such supervision is appropriate. § 4-46-803(a). If there are no surviving partners, the legal representative of the last surviving partner may wind up the business. § 4-46-803(b). The persons conducting the winding up "may preserve the partnership business or property as a going concern for a reasonable time, prosecute and defend actions and proceedings, whether civil, criminal, or administrative, settle and close the partnership's business, dispose of and transfer the partnership's property, discharge the partnership's liabilities, distribute the assets of the partnership . . . settle disputes by mediation or arbitration, and perform other necessary acts." § 4-46-803(c). The actual authority to act is, however, limited to acts that are "appropriate for winding up the partnership business," although the partnership will be bound by acts that would have bound the partnership under the doctrines of apparent authority "if the other party to the transaction did not have notice of the dissolution." § 4-46-804.

You might recall from earlier portions of this chapter that the partnership has the option of filing a statement of dissolution, which acts to put third parties on notice of the dissolution 90 days after it is filed. § 4-46-805. Even if no such statement is filed, a partner with knowledge of the dissolution who acts outside his or her actual authority to wind up the business is liable to the partnership for any damage caused by an act that is not appropriate to winding up the partnership business. § 4-46-806.

In the actual winding up, the assets of the partnership (including the partner's contributions) first "must be applied to discharge its obligations to creditors, including, to the extent permitted by law, partners who are creditors." § 4-46-807(a). After creditors have been repaid in full, the surplus is to be paid (in cash) to the partners in accordance with each partner's capital accounts. If the partner's account shows an excess of the credits over charges in the partner's account, the partnership will make a payment to the partner. If, on the other hand, a partner's account shows more charges than credits, that partner is to contribute the deficit back to the partnership (unless the partner has no personal liability for such losses). § 4-46-807(b). If one or more partners fail to make a required contribution, the other partners must contribute "in the proportions in which those partners share partnership losses" the total amounts necessary to satisfy the partnership debts. § 4-46-807(c). A partner who makes such an excess payment has the right to recover against the non-contributing partner. If, at a future date, additional obligations come to light, "each partner shall contribute, in the proportion in which the partner shares partnership losses, the amount necessary to satisfy" such obligations. § 4-46-807(d). The estate of a deceased partner is liable for a partner's obligations under this provision (§ 4-46-807(e)), and the obligations to contribute may also be enforced by "[a]n assignee for the benefit of creditors of a partnership or a partner, or a person appointed by a court to represent creditors of a partnership or a partner." § 4-46-807(f).

The rights of third persons such as creditors may not be compromised or affected by the terms of the partnership agreement, and this substantially limits the ability of the partners to modify these rules. Some of the provisions may be modified, such as the order in which partners are repaid. Alternatively, rather than simply giving some partners priority over others, the partnership agreement could require that contributions be repaid by the partnership before profits are shared among the partners. The easiest way to modify these rules, however, is to change the way in which profits and losses are allocated to the partners, because that will have a direct impact on how amounts are finally distributed to the partners.

IV.9.2.   Wrongful Withdrawal

A wrongfully withdrawing partner loses the right to waive winding up once it has been initiated (§ 4-46-802(b)), and the right to participate in the winding up process. § 4-46-803(a). A wrongfully withdrawing partner retains the power to bind the partnership by appearing to act in the ordinary course of the partnership's business (§ 4-46-804(2)), although any partner who has not wrongfully dissociated can file a statement of dissolution that will act as a limitation on all partners' authority 90 days after it is filed. § 4-46-805. A wrongfully withdrawing partner is personally liable to the partnership if he or she does cause the partnership to incur a liability that is not appropriate. § 4-46-806(b).

The other major consequence of withdrawing wrongfully in a manner that triggers winding up of the partnership business is that the withdrawing partner becomes liable to the partnership and to the other partners for damages caused by the wrongful dissociation. § 4-46-602(c). Typically such amounts would be charged to the partner so that the amounts otherwise due to be distributed to the partner upon termination of the business would be reduced.

Once the creditors have been paid off, and any excess paid out to partners in accordance with these rules, the partnership will have terminated. If new claims arise within the applicable statute of limitations, the partners will be personally liable and can be sued for their share of such obligations. Recall that while the partnership statute purports to make such liability joint and several (§ 4-46-306(a)), tort reform efforts in the state have confused this issue.[41] Partners may be able to limit their liability, at least in the case of tort claims, based on their percentage of fault.[42]

---

[41]   Civil Justice Reform Act of 2003, Acts of 2003, Act 649, eff. March 25, 2003, with the provision that reads "[e]ach defendant shall be liable only for the amount of damages allocated to that defendant in direct proportion to that defendant's percentage of fault" being codified at § 16-55-201(b)(1).

[42]   For a fuller discussion of this issue, see section IV.4 of this Chapter.

To avoid the risk of such unexpected liability, the general partnership statues in Arkansas (and now every other state, as well) allow a general partnership to elect to become a limited liability partnership (LLP), in which partners do not have such liability for debts of the business, at least not merely because of their status as partners.

IV.10.   Electing to Become an LLP

As should be apparent from the foregoing materials, one of the central characteristics of the traditional general partnership is that all partners are personally liable for debts of the business. That liability is also one of the enduring reasons why the general partnership form of business has been disfavored. The solution to this problem was legislative, and involves the option for a general partnership to "register," "elect," or "qualify" as a limited liability partnership, or LLP.

IV.10.1.   What is an LLP

Probably the simplest way of looking at the question of "what is an LLP" is to realize that an LLP is simply a general partnership in which the partners have elected to have limited liability for business debts. All of the owners of the business are still general partners; they still have the same management rights and fiduciary obligations that they would have had in any general partnership; they still retain the power to bind the partnership by acts that appear to be carrying on the ordinary business of the partnership; they still share profits and losses in the same way; they still retain the same ability to withdraw from the business even if that breaches the partnership agreement; and the same rules govern dissolution and winding up of the business. The only substantive change is that by electing LLP status, the partners gain limited liability for debts of the business.

Note that this protection against personal liability is not the same as saying that partners in an LLP have absolutely no liability for debts associated with the business. The actual language of the statute is that "[a]n obligation of a partnership incurred while the partnership is a limited liability partnership, whether arising in contract, tort, or otherwise, is solely the obligation of the partnership. A partner is not personally liable, directly or indirectly, by way of contribution or otherwise, for such a partnership obligation solely by reason of being or so acting as a partner." § 4-46-306(c). This language makes it possible for partners in an LLP to be found personally liable if the obligation is not solely that of the partnership, such as where a partner has made an enforceable promise to contribute to the partnership, guarantees a debt of the partnership, is liable because of personal conduct (for example, is the actual tortfeasor, or signs a contract without properly disclosing the existence or identity of the partnership as principal), or if the courts elect to disregard the veil of limited liability under the doctrine of piercing the veil.[43]

This is, however, exactly the same type of limited liability that has long been enjoyed by corporate shareholders and limited partners, and is generally shared by members in limited liability companies (LLCs). Thus, the benefit of electing LLP status is that the partners are no longer personally liable for debts of the partnership merely because of their status as partners, putting them on a par with limited liability investors in other forms of enterprise.

In order to accomplish this, the partners must make the appropriate filing, pay the required fees, adopt a name that reflects the partnership's status as an LLP, and file annual reports with the

---

[43]   For a fuller discussion of piercing the veil of limited liability, see Chapter 8 of these materials.

appropriate state authorities. Although the statutes are relatively straightforward, it is worth considering the required steps to elect LLP status in a little more detail.

IV.10.2.   How to Elect

The first step in electing LLP status in Arkansas is to have the required vote or approval of partners. The statute says that the vote required is "the vote necessary to amend the partnership agreement except, in the case of a partnership agreement that expressly considers contribution obligations, the vote necessary to amend those provisions." § 4-46-1001(b). Normally, a partnership agreement can be amended only by unanimous consent, unless the agreement itself specifies otherwise. § 4-46-401(j). The statute talks in terms of consent, not a vote, so persons concerned about the degree of formality with which such actions are to be taken should be counseled that the partnership agreement might need to address such issues as notice, quorum requirements, proxies, and record-keeping.

Once the required consent has been obtained, the partnership must file a statement of qualification (§ 4-46-1001(c)) containing the following information:

(1)   the partnership's name, which itself must comply with certain statutory requirements;[44]

(2)   the street address of the partnership's chief executive office and, if that is located outside the state, there must also be a street address for an office in this State, unless the partnership has no such office in Arkansas;

---

[44]   In order to qualify as an LLP, the name of the partnership "must end with 'Registered Limited Liability Partnership,' 'Limited Liability Partnership,' 'R.L.L.P.,' 'L.L.P.,' 'RLLP,' or 'LLP'." § 4-46-1002.

(3)   if there is no office in this State, the information required by § 4-20-105(a)[45];

(4)   a statement that the partnership elects to be a limited liability partnership; and

(5)   if the partnership wishes to defer the effective date of the election to become an LLP (presumably a very rare occurrence), a deferred effective date for the qualification.

A statement of qualification is treated like other statements under the UPA (1996), and must be executed, filed, and treated in accordance with the rules generally applicable to such documents. A statement of qualification must therefore be signed by at least two partners, and they must sign under penalties of perjury. § 4-46-105©. Unless the partnership agreement provides otherwise, a copy of the filed statement must be sent to every partner who has not executed the document. §§ 4-46-105(e) - 103(b)(1). On the other hand, failure to send the copy does not limit the statement's effectiveness as to third parties. Thus, as to creditors and non-partners, once a statement is filed, that is sufficient to establish "that a partnership has satisfied all conditions precedent to the qualification of the partnership as a limited liability partnership." § 4-46-1001(g). The consequences if the filing was in fact unauthorized, are discussed in section IV.10.4.

Unless a deferred effective date is specified in the statement of qualification, the partnership becomes an LLP on the date the statement is filed. § 4-46-1001(e). That status remains in effect, even if there are other changes in the partnership, until the statement is canceled by the partners or revoked by the Secretary

---

[45]   This is a cross reference to a provision in the Model Registered Agents Act, and that provision requires the entity to name a registered agent, and unless the agent is a commercial registered agent, the address at which the agent can be served.

of State. (Cancellation is governed by § 4-46-105(d), and revocation is explained in § 4-46-1003.) Errors in the statement, or subsequent changes to the information within the statement do not affect the status of the partnership as an LLP or the liability of the partners. § 4-46-1001(f).

Cancellation of the statement of qualification requires filing of a statement of cancellation, either by the persons who were authorized to file the statement of qualification in the first place, or by such other persons as might be specified in the partnership agreement. § 4-46-105(d). The statement of cancellation must name the partnership, identify the statement, and state the substance of the change. There is a $15 fee for filing a statement of cancellation (§ 4-46-1207), and it is effective when filed or upon a deferred date if one is included in the statement. § 4-46-1001(h). Although provided for in the statutes, it is difficult to conceive of reasons why such cancellation would be necessary or desirable.

IV.10.3.   Annual Reports

Once a general partnership has qualified as an LLP, it becomes subject to annual reporting requirements. The annual report is to be filed with the Secretary of State between January 1 and April 1 of each year following the calendar year in which the partnership qualifies as an LLP. § 4-46-1003(b). The report is required to include the following information:

(1)   the name of the limited liability partnership and the state or other jurisdiction under whose laws the foreign limited liability partnership is formed;

(2)   the current street address of the partnership's chief executive office and, if different, the current street address of an office in this State, if any; and

(3)   if there is no current office in this State, the

information required by § 4-20-105(a). § 4-46-1003(a). [46]

A $15 fee is imposed for the filing of this report. § 4-46-1207.

If an LLP fails to file the required report or pay the necessary fee, the Secretary of State may give the partnership 60 days' written notice that the partnership's LLP status is subject to being administratively revoked. § 4-46-1003(c). The notice must be mailed to the partnership's chief executive office as specified in its most recent statement of qualification or annual report, and must give the partnership notice that its LLP's status will be revoked as of a specified date unless the report is filed and/or the fee is paid. If the report is filed and/or the fee paid before the specified date, the status will not be revoked. If the revocation is effective, it is not an event of dissolution for the partnership; it merely affects the partnership's status as LLP. § 4-46-1003(d).

In addition, even if the LLP's status is administratively revoked for failure to file the required report or pay the fee, the partnership may apply for reinstatement within two years after the effective date of revocation. § 4-46-1003(e). The application must include the partnership's name, and must state that the revocation was in error or that the ground for revocation has been corrected. A reinstatement relates back to the date of revocation, so that for all practical purposes the partnership's status as LLP continues "as if the revocation had never occurred." § 4-46-1003(f). This relation back doctrine is designed to prevent gaps in a reinstated LLP's liability shield, but it is only available if the application for reinstatement is made within two years of the administrative

---

[46]   Subsection (c) of this provision cross-references the Model Registered Agents Act, and includes the requirement that the LLP's annual report identify a registered agent, and under some circumstances, an address for the agent as well.

revocation of LLP status.

IV.10.4.   Unauthorized Election

One other issue is possible when it comes to the filing of an election to become an LLP. Unless the partnership agreement provides otherwise, it takes consent of all partners in order to actually authorize the filing of a statement of qualification to become an LLP. However, the statement need be signed only by two of the partners, so it is at least theoretically possible that not all partners agreed to the election. Suppose a creditor can prove that one or more partners did not consent. Would this impact the legal effectiveness of the election? Even if partnership creditors might not have standing to raise such issues, are there scenarios where it might be important for other partners to be able to contest a statement of qualification?

The statutes are actually fairly clear with regard to the impact of a statement of qualification on third parties. Even if there are errors in the form, the mere filing of the statement of qualification suffices to give the partnership LLP status and creates a liability shield for the partners. This is in accord with the analysis provided in the official written comments to the Uniform Act, which state that the partnership's LLP status "is intended to be conclusive with regard to third parties dealing with the partnership."[47] The commentary continues: "[A] properly executed and filed statement of qualification conclusively establishes the limited liability shield described in Section 306©. If the partners executing and filing the statement exceed their authority, the internal abuse of authority has no effect on the liability shield with regard to third parties."

---

[47]   This is taken from the official commentary to Uniform Partnership Act (1997) §1001(f).

On the other hand, the comment also says that internal abuses of authority were not intended to bind partners. The commentary explicitly states that "[p]artners may challenge the abuse of authority for purposes of establishing the liability of the culpable partners." Thus, for example, if an unauthorized statement is filed, and this negatively impacts the partnerships' ability to borrow funds or otherwise creates problems for other partners, there should be redress by and between the partners. While the comments to the official Uniform Acts are not part of the enacted statutes, they clearly show what was intended by the language, and because they help make sense of the actual wording, should be quite persuasive if a problem does arise involving this type of issue.

And, of course, the unauthorized partners who sign the statement of qualification falsely indicating that the election has been authorized might be liable for perjury.

CHAPTER V.   LIMITED PARTNERSHIPS & LLLPs

V.1.   Formation and the Partnership Agreement

V.1.1   A Word about the Arkansas Statutes

In 2007, the Arkansas Legislature adopted the Uniform Limited Partnership Act (2001).[48] The date in the official name of the statute refers not to the date of enactment or effective date of the legislation, but rather the date on which NCCUSL promulgated the version of the Uniform statute upon which the Arkansas bill and legislation was based. This book will refer to the current limited partnership statute as ULPA (2001).

Prior to 2007, Arkansas had a number of different statutes governing limited partnerships. In 1953, Arkansas adopted the initial Uniform Limited Partnership Act (ULPA),[49] and that statute applied to all limited partnerships in this state until 1979. In 1979, Arkansas adopted a version of the Revised Uniform Limited Partnership Act (RULPA),[50] although ULPA continued to regulate pre-existing limited partnerships. In 1991, RULPA was substantially amended and the official name of the Arkansas limited partnership statute became   the Revised Limited Partnership Act (1991) (sometimes called RULPA (1991)). At

---

[48]   Ark. Acts of 2007, Act 15, effective Sept. 1, 2007. This Act is codified at Ark. Code §§ 4-47-101 et seq.. As is the case with other chapters of this book, references in the text to specific statutory provisions will be to this Chapter of the Arkansas Code.

[49]   This Act was codified at Ark. Code §§ 4-44-101 et seq.

[50]   This Act was codified at Ark. Code §§ 4-43-101 et seq., and the official name of this statute in Arkansas was the "Revised Limited Partnership Act of 1991." The "1991" in the official name of the act referred to the date of enactment in this state, not the date upon which the uniform statute had been promulgated by NCCUSL.

that time, ULPA was also officially repealed. In 2007, when ULPA (2001) was enacted, RLPA (1991) was also repealed.

The history of these statutes would not be of particular note, except that the evolution of limited partnership law has been gradual, rather than the sudden change that the state saw in the case of general partnerships. Because there are numerous older forms that are familiar and known to many Arkansas practitioners, and because many lawyers were trained under older statutes, it is important to make sure that current statutes are being applied and relied on, rather than historically accurate but now outdated understandings about the nature of the limited partnership as a form of business organization. This is particularly important when it comes to the permissible roles of limited partners in the management of a limited parntership's business.[51]

V.1.2   Forming a Limited Partnership

A domestic limited partnership can be formed only upon the filing of a certificate of limited partnership. § 4-47-201(a). The certificate must include an appropriate name for the partnership (§ 4-47-201(a)(1)), the street and mailing addresses of the limited partnership's initial designated office (§ 4-47-201(a)(2)), the name and address of the entity's agent for service of process as required by the Model Registered Agents Act (§ 4-20-105); the name, street and mailing address of each general partner (Ark. Code § 4-47-201(a)(3)); and a statement as to whether the limited partnership is a limited liability limited partnership (§ 4-47-201(a)(4)). If the limited partnership comes into existence by virtue of a merger, consolidation or similar form of reorganization, additional information might be required. § 4-47-201(a)(5), cross

---

[51]   This will be dealt with in more detail in Section V.3.2 of this Chapter.

referencing subchapter 11 of ULPA (2001).

In order to be an appropriate name, unless the limited partnership has registered as a limited liability limited partnership (LLLP), it "must contain the phrase "limited partnership" or the abbreviation "L.P." or "LP" and may not contain the phrase "limited liability limited partnership" or the abbreviation "LLLP" or "L.L.L.P."." § 4-47-108(b). Unlike some of the earlier Arkansas statutes, modern rules allow the limited partnership to include the name of any partner, including a limited partner. § 4-47-108(a).

It is also possible for the certificate of limited partnership to contain optional information if the organizers so desire, but there are certain statutory rules that may not be modified either in the certificate or any outside agreement. A limited partnership may not vary its statutory power to sue or be sued in its own name, and may not have any language that would attempt to do so in its organizational documents. § 4-47-110(b)(1). A limited partnership cannot change the governing law applicable to it, which for domestic entities is set as the law of the state of Arkansas, at least as to "relations among the partners . . . and between the partners and the limited partnership and the liability of partners as partners for an obligation of the limited partnership." § 4-47-106. It may not change the rules applicable to how documents to be filed with the secretary of state must be executed (§ 4-47-204), or change the information that must be maintained at the limited partnership's designated office (§ 4-47-111), or unreasonably restrict the rights of partners to have access to information as specified in the statutes (§§ 4-47-304 & 407).[52] The certificate may not eliminate the partners' duty of loyalty or the obligation of good faith and fair

---

[52]   These rights are discussed in more detail in section V.6.2 of this Chapter.

dealing, or unreasonably reduce the duty of care.[53] The certificate cannot take away the power of a person to dissociate as a general partner,[54] or change the power of a court to order dissolution (§ 4-47-802). The partnership must be wound up in accordance with the process set out in the statutes.[55] § 4-47-803. Partners' rights to bring direct or derivative actions may not be unreasonably restricted. §§ 4-47-1001 to 1005. Partners' rights to approve conversions or mergers of their limited partnership may not be restricted, nor may their right to consent to conversion of a limited liability limited partnership back to a limited partnership. § 4-47-110(b)(12). Finally, the certificate may not restrict the rights of persons other than partners or transferees. § 4-47-110(b)(13).

Unless a delayed effective date is stated in the certificate, and assuming there has been substantial compliance with the filing requirements, a limited partnership is formed when the Secretary of State files its certificate of limited partnership." § 4-47-201(c). The meaning of "substantial compliance" in this context has not been litigation, but the Secretary of State's office is usually quite particular in filing documents, so that the issue may never arise.

---

[53] These duties are set out in Ark. Code §§ 4-47-408(b) (duty of loyalty); 408(c) (duty of care); and 305(b) and 408(d) (obligation of good faith and fair dealing). These obligations of partners are discussed in more detail in sections V.2.3 (as to general partners) and V.3.3 (as to limited partners).

[54] The rights of a partner to dissociate from a limited partnership as a general partner are set out in Ark. Code § 4-47-604(a), and are discussed further in Section V.7.1 of this Chapter. The one limitation on the power to withdraw that is permitted is that the certificate may require the notice of withdrawal to be "in a record," which means that it is in a writing or other tangible or electronic form that "is retrievable in a perceivable form." Ark. Code § 4-47-102(17).

[55] The process for winding up is explained in more detail in section V.9 of this Chapter.

V.1.3   Continued Existence

Once a limited partnership has been formed, it will continued in existence until it is dissolved and its business has been wound up. Although the parties are free to state a date or other event upon which dissolution will occur in the certificate of limited partnership, this is not the usual way in which things are done. Usually, the partnership agreement or some other record maintained at the partnership's designated office will list the time or events upon which the partnership is to be wound up and dissolved. § 4-47-111(9)(D). While some limited partnerships are formed so that they expire automatically after the passage of a specified period of time, most do not. Most are designed to continue until the partners themselves do something that results in the termination of the business. However, in order to continue in good standing until such agreed-upon events occur, a limited partnership must comply with certain statutory requirements.

The first such requirement is that certain information must be maintained at the limited partnership's designated office. § 4-47-111. Technically speaking, failure to maintain this information is not listed as an event that triggers automatic dissolution or gives rise to grounds for either administrative[56] or judicial dissolution.[57] On the other hand, failure to observe formalities has long been one of the traditional considerations relied upon by courts when they are called upon to consider

---

[56]   Administrative dissolution may be ordered by the Secretary of State if the limited partnership fails, after 60 days' notice, to pay any fees, taxes or penalties due to the Secretary of State or fails to deliver its annual report to the Secretary of State. Ark. Code § 4-47-809.

[57]   Judicial dissolution may be ordered with a partner so requests and can show that it is not reasonably practicable to carry on the activities of the limited partnership in compliance with the requirements of the partnership agreement. Ark. Code § 4-47-802.

whether to pierce the veil of limited liability.[58] If the veil is pierced, all of the owners of a business may find themselves as liable as if the business did not exist.

The second on-going requirement for a limited partnership is that the business must maintain both an office and agent for service of process, in accordance with the requirements of the Model Registered Agents Act. § 4-47-114, referencing §§ 4-20-101 et seq. In addition, the certificate of limited partnership is to be amended to reflect certain changes in the required information. Any time a new general partner is added, an amendment signed by the new general partners is required. § 4-47-202(b)(1) (signing requirement in § 4-47-204(a)(5)(B)). An amendment is also required whenever a general partner dissociates from the limited partnership, and this must be signed by the dissociated partner, or a guardian or executor if the partner is deceased or incapacitated, unless the partner has previously filed a certificate of dissociation. § 4-47-204(a)(5)(C). An amendment is also required if someone is appointed to wind up the business of the partnership, and this amendment must be signed by the person appointed to this role. § 4-47-202(b)(3) (Signing requirements are set out in § 4-47-204(a)(4)). These requirements operate the same way as the obligation to maintain information at the partnership's office–failure to do so may be important in case of an attempt to pierce the veil, but should not by itself trigger dissolution or termination of the business.

---

[58]   Piercing the veil refers to the situation where a court, usually upon application by a creditor of the business, agrees that the business owners have failed to sufficiently respect the separate legal identity of the business under circumstances that make it equitable to allow the creditor to disregard the existence of the business as well. Thus, a creditor of the business may be allowed to disregard the normal rules that limit the personal liability of business owners, if the elements for piercing can be shown. The entire doctrine of piercing, and its application to the various forms of business available in Arkansas, is discussed in more detail in Chapter 8 of this book.

Finally, a limited partnership is required to file an annual report with the Secretary of State. § 4-47-210. This report must include the limited partnership's name, the street and mailing address of its designated office, information about its current agent for service of process as required by the Model Registered Agents Act. § 4-47-210(a). The first annual report is due between January 1 and May 1 of the year following the calendar year in which the limited partnership was formed and in the same time period of each subsequent calendar year. § 4-47-210(b). A filing fee of $15 must accompany this report.[59] Failure to comply with this annual filing requirement may result in administrative dissolution of the limited partnership,[60] and in fact there are a number of cases in which the Arkansas Secretary of State has done this.

V.1.4   The Partnership Agreement

The foregoing material explains how a limited partnership can be formed in Arkansas, and the minimal steps required as a matter of statutory law to avoid administrative dissolution, and to minimize the risk of piercing for failure to comply with normal formalities. Note that the statutes do not require any formal

---

[59]   The Arkansas Secretary of State website clearly indicates that this fee is charged any time a limited partnership files its annual report. (See on-line information applicable to Arkansas Domestic Limited Partnerships at ahttp://www.sos.arkansas.gov/business_entity_fees_forms_pro.htmlt, searched as of February 2011.)   The only explicit authority for such a fee appears to be § 4-47-1302(a)(1) which authorizes a $15 fee for "[a]ny other document required or permitted to be filed by this chapter." The only reason for confusion is that this is the section that, by its title, applies to fees for limited liability limited partnerships. The previous section, governing fees for limited partnerships, does not include the catch-all fee for documents that are not listed.

[60]   As mentioned earlier, the Secretary of State has authority to administratively dissolve any limited partnership that fails, after 60 days' notice, to pay any fees, taxes or penalties due to the Secretary of State or fails to deliver its annual report to the Secretary of State. § 4-47-809.

partnership agreement, oral or written. While certain information must be kept in written or other tangible form (referred to in the statutes as a "record") at the limited partnership's designated office, the statute itself provides a sufficient framework for a limited partnership so that no partnership agreement is technically necessary if the partners want to adopt all of the default rules set out in the statutes. In most cases, however, it is a very good idea to have a written partnership agreement.

First, even if the partners are happy with all the default rules, it is generally convenient to have one simple place where the partners can look up those rules. While the lawyers may have easy access to the statutes, the partnership's actual partners are not likely to have such information readily available. To minimize delays and questions if problems or disputes arise, it is nice to have a simple, readily accessible written document that covers the terms of the business arrangement. Second, most of the information that must be kept by the partnership (like the names and addresses of the general and limited partners, their contributions, the events of dissolution) is information that typically would be incorporated into a partnership agreement. Since that information must be kept anyway, it makes sense to do so in an integrated document that covers the other issues in which the partners are likely to be interested. Third, even if the partners say they do not need a written agreement, it is always easier to have a written document to avoid later arguments about whether there was an oral agreement or understanding covering some issue upon which the partners no longer agree. And finally, it is rarely safe to assume that clients fully understand all the default rules that would apply to a limited partnership if no agreement is entered into, until and unless those rules have been explained to them. To avoid later concerns about whether you, as an attorney, adequately explained the clients' rights and positions, it is generally advisable to put the information in writing, and again, once that is done, having it in a partnership agreement just makes sense.

A partnership agreement can cover a long list of topics, and if you are responsible for drafting one, you might want to consider the following substantive subjects (in addition to normal drafting considerations like an appropriate document name, table of contents, definitions section, date, signatures, etc.):

*Name of Partnership

Keep in mind the requirements under Arkansas law for naming a limited partnership, and remember that merely forming a business under Arkansas law does not register that name as a tradename or prevent its use in other jurisdictions.

*Names and Addresses of Partners

Under Arkansas law, you will want to have this divided into general and limited partners, and you will need both the street and mailing address of each partner. To avoid or minimize the necessity of amending the entire document every time the list of partners changes, it might be desirable to keep these lists as attachments or exhibits to the main agreement.

*Partnership's Purpose

Many partnership agreements list a purpose for the partnership, which may be either informational or limiting, depending on the nature of the partnership. Particularly if the limited partners want to restrict the power of general partners to conduct business other than that related to a particular purpose, this may be an important provision. It may also be appropriate to include in this section any limitations on partners' rights to engage in activities that might be seen as competing with the partnership.

*Addresses and Agent for Service of Process

Arkansas requires that every limited partnership have a designated office and an agent upon whom service of process may be had, together with an address for such person unless they are a commercial registered agent in this state. This need not be in the agreement itself, and because it is also subject to change, it might be desirable to include this in an exhibit, attachment, or other addendum, to make amendments simple to do. One reason for including this in the agreement is to help remind non-lawyer partners that when the information relative to service of process changes, it is a good idea to not only amend the agreement but also to update the required filings as well.

* Initial Contribution of partners

Arkansas law also requires that the partnership maintain a list of the contributions and agreed-upon value of all non-cash contributions at the designated office for the limited partnership. Because partners may be added or may leave, this is also the kind of information that it might be advisable to include on exhibits or attachments. Ideally, for each partner, the agreement should include the date of the contribution, a legal description of the contribution, its agreed-upon value, and the effect of failure to comply with any terms of the agreement to contribute (particularly if a contribution takes the form of a promise to pay or perform services over time).

*Any Agreement about Additional Contributions

The default rule in Arkansas is that partners are not required to make additional contributions beyond the amounts originally agreed to, so if the partners want to provide for additional contributions, the procedure for making or requiring additional contributions should be spelled out, along with effect of failure to make a required additional contribution.

*Allocation of Profits and Losses

In an Arkansas limited partnership, the presumption is that profits and losses are shared based upon the agreed-upon value of contributions, which is a rule that may have at least superficial appeal to clients. However, contributions made at different times during the life of a business may have different levels of risk, and this fact might not be within the contemplation of organizers. If they do consider this, they might desire that the "cost" of buying into a partnership should change over time, just as the cost of buying stock in a corporation will. Setting up a limited partnership so that partners get units or interests in exchange for their contributions, and that they share in profits and losses based on the number of units or interests purchased, may be more likely to coincide with clients' interests or real expectations. If the partnership is going to have special allocations, which happens when an allocation of a particular kind of gain or loss differs from the usual way in which allocations are made between the partners, that should be spelled out as well, after consultation with a tax advisor because there are very complicated rules applicable to special allocations.

*Distributions

The partnership agreement can spell out when distributions will be made, when they are required, who decides on timing and amount, if there are any limitations of distributions, and also any rules applicable to advances draws or loans made in anticipation of distributions. In the absence of any specific provisions, the general partners would presumably have authority to decide on distributions as part of their general management authority.

*Salaries[61]

Partners who are also employees may want to have their salary arrangements approved in the partnership agreement or at least have the partnership agreement mention that partners who act as employees shall be entitled to receive salaries. If more information than this is to be included in the partnership agreement itself, the use of attachments or exhibits might be appropriate in order to facilitate any necessary amendments or updates. Lawyers should be aware that there may be tax consequences to having partners receive salaries, particularly in the case of persons who work as general partners but want to claim a share of non-wage income as owner of a limited partnership interest. This is also the kind of tax issue that should be discussed with a specialized tax advisor.

*Management and Control of Business

In a limited partnership, the default rule is that all general partners share management authority while limited partners have virtually none, except over things like amendments to the partnership agreement. Older forms should not be relied upon for language governing the role of partners in the management of the business, because the current statute no longer penalizes limited partners who elect to participate in managing the partnership's business. This change means that careful consideration should be given to how the clients in any given situation prefer to allocate

---

[61]   While partners (either limited or general) can certainly serve as employees of the limited partnership, the default rule is that general partners (who would normally have all of the responsibility for managing the limited partnership) have no right to compensation for their efforts. Ark. Code § 4-47-406(f). This would be a very common thing to change in a partnership agreement.

management power and responsibilities. Limited partners may be especially interested in provisions relating to their rights to be notified or rights to participate in decision making. In addition, the agreement should establish any required formalities for decision-making because the statutes do not set out any particular procedural requirements, and clients will generally appreciate having such guidance. Notice, meeting, quorum, and voting requirements should be considered. The agreement should also specify what kinds of records of decisions should be made and kept. If there is an expectation that certain partners or classes of partner must spend a certain amount of time managing the business, this should also be in the agreement. This might also be an appropriate place to include authorization for or prohibition against outside or competing activities, depending on client needs and preferences.

*Fiduciary and Related Obligations

Under current Arkansas law, fiduciary duties are generally limited to general partners, and they are quite restricted. It is not that there is anything inherently wrong with simply having clients accept the default rules in this regard, but remember that one function of a partnership agreement is to collect the rules governing the partnership in one place. While attorneys have easy access to statutes, clients generally won't, so even if the clients intend on keeping the statutory default rules, it makes sense to spell out the scope of fiduciary obligations in the agreement. Of course, if the parties do not want to stay with the default rules, any modification, expansion, or explanation of those obligations should also be included in the agreement.

*Adding Partners

At some place, the agreement should address how new partners, both general and limited, can be added to the partnership. The agreement should specify who must agree to the new partner and should set out any minimum qualifications before a new partner can be accepted. The impact of new partners should also be addressed, which means, for example, explaining how the addition of a new partner affects distribution or allocation of profits and losses, and voting rights. Note that this kind of information needs to address both the admission of general and limited partners, and also needs to cover partners who contribute directly to the partnership as well as those who are transferees of partnership interests seeking to be accepted as partners. If there are limits on the addition of new partners in either of these situations (for example, a requirement that before the partnership issue units or interests to new partners, existing partners must first be given the right to buy the units and thereby increase their partnership share) or on the right of existing partners to sell interests (such as an obligation to first offer their interest to other existing partners) this would need to be in the agreement. Limitations and conditions on when partners can be admitted, terms upon which payment can be accepted by the partnership, and the impact of new partners on partnership rights and obligations should all be spelled out.

*Rights of Transferees

Following or accompanying the discussion of new partners, the partnership agreement should include language discussing the rights of transferees who do not become partners. It would probably be convenient to explain their rights to distributions and allocations, their informational rights, and any other rights that they might have, in the partnership agreement. If there are differences in the rights of different classes of transferees, such as transferees as a matter of law (for example, as part of a divorce settlement or foreclosure of a charging order entered on a debt owed by a partner) or transferees who have in some way been agreed to by the other partners, that would also need to be explained.

*Withdrawal of Partners

The agreement should address both voluntary and involuntary withdrawal of partners, whether general or limited. The consequences of death or incapacity, and its effect on the partnership should also be mentioned. Rights of heirs should be covered as well, both in terms of rights to the economic interest and conditions under which they may be named as substitute partners. Voluntary transfers, such as sale or gift of a partnership interest, should also be covered. If the other partners are to have a right of first refusal or an option to buy such partnership interests, this should be specified. If not included in another section, limits on the right of purchasers to become partners could be spelled out, even if the clients simply want to adopt default statutory rules. It is probably also important to consider involuntary transfers, such as those that might be ordered by a court in the event of divorce or bankruptcy. The rights of other partners or the partnership to buy out partnership interests in such a case could be set out.

*Termination of Partnership

The agreement should spell out the circumstances under which the partnership will end. In fact, the Arkansas statute requires limited partnerships to keep a record of the events requiring dissolution at the partnership's designated office, so it makes sense to include that in the partnership agreement. Events of dissolution, and the process of winding up (including who has the authority to arrange to dissolution and any rules as to how it should proceed) should also be addressed. The agreement might also explain how participants are to be compensated for arranging the winding up of the partnership business.

*Amendment of the Agreement

This would include the process by which the agreement can be amended, the vote required and whether amendments must be in a signed writing or may be proven by conduct or testimony about oral arrangements.

*Provisions often regarded as Boilerplate

This could include a wide variety of topics. For example, it is now common to include an arbitration clause in partnership agreements, although this is, of course, completely optional with the client. Many partnership agreements address relatively routine things like who will be the tax matters partner, whether the books will be kept on the cash or accrual method, the fiscal year of the partnership, and where the partnership will bank. There may also be language stating that section headings are merely for convenience, that the plural includes the singular and vice versa unless the context clearly requires otherwise, and similar statements relevant to the interpretation of the document.

While not a comprehensive list of topics that might be covered in a partnership agreement, the preceding list at least gives an idea of what might be appropriately documented in a written agreement among the partners.

The next sections of this chapter cover the rules governing most of these topics in more detail. For each topic, there is a consideration of any mandatory rules found in the statutes, the general default rules (which will govern the partnership unless a contrary agreement has been reached), and a discussion of any particularly difficult issues that may be likely to arise with regard to the issue under consideration.

V.2   The General Partners

In very general terms, general partners in a limited partnership are much like their counterparts in a traditional general partnership. Absent agreement to the contrary, they are the ones with the actual and apparent authority to bind the partnership; they owe the only fiduciary duties that exist automatically rather than requiring additional agreement of the partners; and they retain personal liability for debts of the limited partnership. Even though these rules track the same provisions applicable in the case of general partnerships, it is probably worth making sure that the appropriate statutory authority is understood. Arkansas' current limited partnership statute does not incorporate by reference any of the provisions directly from our general partnership statute, as used to be the case, but rather restates the rules, sometimes in slightly different language from that appears in the Uniform Partnership Act (1996).

V.2.1.   Becoming a General Partner

A person becomes a general partner as provided in the partnership agreement or upon the unanimous consent of all partners, or upon consent of limited partners owning at least a majority of the rights to receive distributions as of the time the consent is to be effective, if the consent happens within 90 days after dissociation of what would have been the last remaining

189

general partner. § 4-47-401. Once someone is added as a general partner, the certificate of limited partnership must be amended to show the new general partner as well as that person's street and mailing address (§ 4-47-202(b)(1)), and the amendment must be signed by the new general partner (§ 4-47-204(a)(3)). New general partners can also be added as provided by agreement in the case of a merger or conversion, but these topics will be dealt with later.[62]

V.2.2.   Management and Authority

Arkansas' current limited partnership act sets out two kinds of authority for general partners: (1) apparent authority (which seemingly cannot be modified in the partnership agreement); and (2) actual authority to manage (which is subject to the contrary agreement of the partners).

Just as is the case with a general partnership, general partners in a limited partnership are agents of the business, and acts by general partners "including the signing of a record in the partnership's name, for apparently carrying on in the ordinary course the limited partnership's activities or activities of the kind carried on by the limited partnership binds the limited partnership." § 4-47-402(a). The only way to limit this apparent authority is to remove that partner's actual authority to bind the limited partnership and to see that the third party with whom the general partner is dealing knows, receives a notification or has notice (as such terms are defined in ULPA (2001)) of that limitation on authority.[63]   Hand in hand with these rules is a

---

[62]   See Chapter 7 of this book.

[63]   The provision of ULPA (2001) dealing with knowledge and notice says that a person has notice if they know of the fact, has received notification of it, or has reason to know it exists from all of the facts known to such person at the time in question. A person notifies another by taking steps reasonably required to inform the

statutory provision making it clear that apparent authority does not apply if the act of the general partner was "not apparently for carrying on in the ordinary course the limited partnership's activities or activities of the kind carried on by the limited partnership." § 4-47-402(b).

As for actual authority of the general partners, the statutory provisions set out default rules, but these are subject to the contrary agreement of the partners if a different arrangement or allocation of responsibility is desired. Absent such agreement, however, "[e]ach general partner has equal rights in the management and conduct of the limited partnership's activities." § 4-47-406(a). Any matter relating to the ordinary business of the limited partnership "may be exclusively decided by the general partner or, if there is more than one general partner, by a majority of the general partners." § 4-47-406(a). Note that this is majority by number, not in interest, with each general partner normally having a single vote, unless the partnership agreement provides otherwise.

On the other hand, there are certain issues that require the unanimous approval of all partners, including limited partners, unless the partnership agreement establishes a different approval process. Included in the list of actions that require unanimous consent are decisions to amend the partnership agreement, amend the certificate of limited partnership to add or delete an election to be a limited liability limited partnership, or to sell or otherwise dispose of all or substantially all of the partnership's assets, other than in the ordinary course of business. § 4-47-406(b). Not only are the partners free to change the approval required for these

---

other person in ordinary course, and receives a notification if the notification comes to that person's attention or is delivered at the person's place of business or similar location. For full details about what constitutes notice and notification under ULPA (2001) see § 4-47-103.

actions, they can also add to the list of items requiring unanimous or greater than majority approval of the general partners.

There are also a number of decisions that, under the default rules, require consent of partners (sometimes general and limited, sometimes limited alone) owning a majority in interest of the rights to receive distributions as such partners. For example, it takes the vote of a majority in interest of all partners to dissolve a limited partnership after withdrawal of a general partner. § 4-47-801(3)(A). It takes a majority in interest of limited partners to continue the limited partnership and add a new general partner if the last general partner withdraws. § 4-47-801(3)(B). It also takes the consent of a majority in interest of limited partners to appoint someone to wind up the partnership's business following dissolution if there is no general partner remaining. § 4-47-803(c).

In order to enable general partners to make appropriate decisions for the partnership, the statute gives them relatively extensive rights to information. A general partner can inspect and copy any of the information required to be kept at the partnership's designated office without needing to have any particular purpose for seeking that information. § 4-47-407. The information that must be kept at the partnership's office includes copies of:

(1)   a current, alphabetized list of all general partners and their street and mailing address, and a separate one for all limited partners;

(2)   the initial certificate of limited partnership, all amendments and restatements, and signed copies of any documents authorizing the signing of those documents;

(3)   any filed articles of conversion or merger;

(4)   all federal, state, and local income tax returns and reports for the three most recent years;

(5)   any written partnership agreement or any such agreement in a tangible record, together with all amendments;

(6)   any financial statement of the partnership for the three most recent years;

(7)   the three most recent annual reports of the partnership as delivered to the Secretary of State;

(8)   three years worth of any voting records for partnership votes kept by the limited partnership; and

(9)   (if not in the partnership agreement) a record of the amount of cash, and a description and statement of the agreed value of anything else contributed and agreed to be contributed by each partner; a statement explaining any additional contributions agreed to be made by each partner; for anyone who is both a limited and general partner, a description of what transferable interest in owned in each capacity; and a list of all events upon which the partnership is to be dissolved and wound up.

§ 4-47-111. In addition to essentially unlimited access to these categories of information, a general partner can also obtain, at a reasonable location chosen by the limited partnership, "any other records maintained by the limited partnership regarding the limited partnership's activities and financial condition." § 4-47-407(a)(2). On 10 days' written notice made in good faith, even a former partner can obtain this information, so long as it pertains to a period in which the person was a general partner. §§ 4-47-407(c)(1) - (2).

Even without demand, the other partners and the partnership are required to provide general partners with "any information concerning the limited partnership's activities and activities reasonably required for the proper exercise of the general partner's rights and duties under the partnership agreement or this chapter." § 4-47-407(b)(1). If a request for information is made, a general partner shall also be furnished with "any other information concerning the limited partnership's activities, except to the extent the demand or the information demanded is unreasonable or otherwise improper under the circumstances." § 4-47-407(b)(2).

While the partnership agreement may not change the information that must be kept at the partnership's designated office or "unreasonably restrict" a general partner's right to information (§ 4-47-110(b)(4)), the partners may impose reasonable restrictions on the use of information provided to general partners (§ 4-47-407(f)), or may reasonably limit its availability (§ 4-47-110(b)(4)). Dissociated general partners may also be charged reasonable copying costs. § 4-47-407(g).

A general partner also has the right, under appropriate circumstances, to bring direct or derivative actions against the limited partnership or other partners, for legal or equitable relief, "to enforce the rights and otherwise protect the interests of the partner." § 4-47-1001(a). This does not require action of all or even a majority of the general partners, and instead is a right given to each of the partners, individually. A general partner wishing to bring such an action must plead and prove "an actual or threatened injury that is not solely the result of an injury suffered or threatened to be suffered by the limited partnership." § 4-47-1001(b). Before bringing a derivative action, the partner must "first make [ ] a demand on the general partners, requesting that they cause the limited partnership to bring an action to enforce the right" and either the general partners must fail to bring the action in a reasonable time or the demand must be futile. § 4-47-1002. This language applies to an individual general partner as well as to a limited partner seeking to initiate such an action. A derivative complaint must also "state with particularity: (1) the date and content of plaintiff's demand and the general partners' response . . . or (2) why demand should be excused as futile." § 4-47-1004. The person bringing the suit must have been a partner at the time the action is commenced as well as at the time the conduct giving rise to the claim occurred, or the plaintiff's status as partner must have "devolved upon the person by operation of law or pursuant to the terms of the partnership agreement from a person that was a partner at the time of the conduct." § 4-47-1003.

V.2.3.   Fiduciary and Similar Obligations

As is the case for general partners in a general partnership, general partners in a limited partnership do owe certain fiduciary obligations to the partnership and the other partners. Traditionally, the scope of these obligations was borrowed from general partnership law, which imposed an extremely high level of responsibility on such persons.[64] The current statute continues to track the rules applicable to general partners in general partnerships, but the default rules have changed so that general partners now owe only narrowly defined fiduciary duties under either kind of partnership.

A general partner owes both a duty of loyalty and a duty of care to the limited partnership and the other partners. The level of care owed can be raised by agreement, but this is one of the few places where the statute does not give completely unfettered freedom to amend the default rules. Generally speaking, it is difficult to significantly reduce the obligations owed, but this restriction should not be too burdensome on persons desiring to organize a limited partnership since the default rules are limited.

---

[64]   For a discussion of the fiduciary duties that were traditionally owed by general partners in general partnerships, see Chapter 4, section IV.3.

Absent agreement to the contrary, a general partner's duty of loyalty is limited to the following three components:

(1)   to account to the limited partnership and hold as trustee for it any property, profit, or benefit derived by the general partner in the conduct and winding up of the limited partnership's activities or derived from a use by the general partner of limited partnership property, including the appropriation of a limited partnership opportunity;

(2)   to refrain from dealing with the limited partnership in the conduct or winding up of the limited partnership's activities as or on behalf of a party having an interest adverse to the limited partnership; and

(3)   to refrain from competing with the limited partnership in the conduct or winding up of the limited partnership's activities.

§ 4-47-408(b).

The statute does not permit these duties to be eliminated, but the partners may agree to identify certain types or categories of activities that will not violate the duty of loyalty (so long as the agreement is not "manifestly unreasonable"), and the partnership agreement may also set out a number or percentage of partners who may authorize or ratify a specific act or transaction that would otherwise violate the duty, so long as there is full disclosure before the authorization or ratification. § 4-47-110(b)(5).

A general partner also owes a duty of care to the limited partnership and other partners, but it is limited to "refraining from engaging in grossly negligent or reckless conduct, intentional misconduct, or a knowing violation of law." § 4-47-408(c). This obligation, which is already fairly significantly limited, may not be "unreasonably" reduced in the partnership agreement. §

4-47-110(b)(6). As of the date these materials were prepared, there were no reported opinions in Arkansas defining what constitutes "unreasonably" reducing this duty of care.

Even the comments to the uniform acts offer little in the way of guidance about what the drafters intended. The official comments to section 110 of ULPA (2001) do not address this language specifically, and comment 6 to section 103 of the UPA (1997) (which contains similar language about the fiduciary duties of general partners in general partnerships) merely notes that "partnership agreements frequently contain provisions releasing a partner from liability for actions taken in good faith and in the honest belief that the actions are in the best interests of the partnership and indemnifying the partner against any liability incurred in connection with the business of the partnership if the partner acts in a good faith belief that he has authority to act." The comment also notes that a different way to reach a similar result is to have a partnership agreement list various actions and explicitly provide that those particular activities are agreed "not to constitute gross negligence or willful misconduct." The drafters of the UPA specified that "[t]hese types of provisions are intended to come within the modifications authorized by subsection (b)(4). On the other hand, absolving partners of intentional misconduct is probably unreasonable. As with contractual standards of loyalty, determining the outer limit in reducing the standard of care is left to the courts."

In addition to these fiduciary obligations, Arkansas statutes also specify that in discharging the duties owed either under the statute or any applicable partnership agreement, a general partner must act "consistently with the obligation of good of good faith and fair dealing." § 4-47-408(d). This is not precisely a fiduciary duty in and of itself, but does provide a standard that should apply when evaluating a general partner's actions. As with the fiduciary duties, the statute provides that the partners may not agree to "eliminate" the obligation of good faith and fair dealing, although it is possible for the partnership agreement to establish "standards by which the performance of the obligation is to be measured, if the standards are not manifestly unreasonable." § 4-47-110(b)(7). Again, the partnership statute does not define what "manifestly unreasonable" means in the context, but the official comments to the UPA (1997) (which technically applies to general partnerships, but uses the same language with respect to obligations of general partners) state that the drafters of the uniform act intended to borrow standards applicable under the Uniform Commercial Code, which the drafters concluded would generally allow specific limitations and waivers but not blanket waivers.[65] The validity of this approach has, however, not yet been tested in the courts.

The final provision in the Arkansas statutes that is relevant to understanding the duties owed by general partners, specifies only that "[a] general partner does not violate a duty or obligation under this chapter or under the partnership agreement merely because the general partner's conduct furthers the general partner's own interests." § 4-47-408(e). If this rule is contrary to what the parties prefer, his may be changed in the partnership agreement.

---

[65]   Official comment 7 to UPA (1996) § 103 states: "The language of subsection (b)(5) is based on UCC Section 1-102(3). The partners can negotiate and draft specific contract provisions tailored to their particular needs (e.g., five days notice of a partners' meeting is adequate notice), but blanket waivers of the obligation are unenforceable." The drafters also cite a handful of cases dealing with the meaning of "manifestly unreasonable" in the context of commercial transactions. In PPG Indus., Inc. v. Shell Oil Co., 919 F.2d 17 (5th Cir.1990), the court deferred to the "sophisticated" parties' arrangements governing whether explosions were covered in a force majeure clause. In First Security Bank v. Mountain View Equip. Co., 112 Idaho 158, 730 P.2d 1078 (Ct.App.1986), aff'd, 112 Idaho 1078, 739 P.2d 377 (1987), the court allowed the parties to waive impairment of capital as a defense. In American Bank of Commerce v. Covolo, 88 N.M. 405, 540 P.2d 1294 (1975), the court enforced a contractual waiver under a guaranty agreement, even though the trial court found that the waiver would not have been commercially reasonable.

V.2.4.   **Personal Liability**

General partners in an Arkansas limited partnership also retain the same sort of unlimited personal liability that applies to general partners in general partnerships. The statute provides that, with limited exceptions, "all general partners are liable jointly and severally for all obligations of the limited partnership unless otherwise agreed by the claimant or provided by law." § 4-47-404(a). The exceptions are for situations in which a general partner joins an existing limited partnership and there are pre-existing partnership obligations (§ 4-47-404(b)), or when the obligation is incurred while the partnership is a limited liability limited partnership (LLLP) (§ 4-47-404(c)).

Note that this language about joint and several liability raises the same issue that applies to general partners in Arkansas general partnerships.[66] To recap briefly, Arkansas adopted the Civil Justice Reform Act of 2003[67] as part of a system of tort reform. Included in this Act is a provision that purports to redefine "joint and several liability." That section, which is entitled "Modification of joint and several liability," states that "[i]n any action for personal injury, medical injury, property damage, or wrongful death, the liability of each defendant for compensatory or punitive damages shall be several only and shall not be joint." § 16-55-201(a). This is further explained to make it clear that "[e]ach defendant shall be liable only for the amount of damages allocated to that defendant in direct proportion to that defendant's percentage of fault". § 16-55-201(b)(1). In addition, there must be a "separate several judgment ... rendered against that defendant for that amount." § 16-55-201 (b)(2). Even the mathematical

---

[66]   See Chapter 4, section IV.4.

[67]   Acts of 2003, Act 649, eff. March 25, 2003.

calculation is statutorily explained: "To determine the amount of judgment to be entered against each defendant, the court shall multiply the total amount of damages recoverable by the plaintiff with regard to each defendant by the percentage of each defendant's fault" (§ 16-55-201(c)(1)), and this "shall be the maximum recoverable against that defendant." § 16-55-201(c)(2).

Although the Arkansas limited partnership act (ULPA (2001)) was adopted after our tort reform statute, we are still faced with the issue of whether Arkansas law makes some partnership liability joint and some several, or whether the specific partnership language regarding partners' liability "trumps" the tort reform effort. The issue is slightly different than it is for our general partnership statute, because the current Arkansas general partnership statute was adopted before the tort reform act. Our limited partnership statute, with essentially identical language, was adopted subsequent to the tort reform. To date, there are no reported cases in Arkansas resolving this potential conflict.

The limited partnership statute also specifies how such liability may be enforced, by authorizing claimants to either join general partners in an action against the limited partnership or to bring a separate action against them. § 4-47-405(a). The act also states that a judgment against the limited partnership is not, by itself, a judgment against the general partner, and that in order to satisfy a debt owed by the partnership out of a general partner's personal assets, there must be a judgment against the general partner as well. § 4-47-405(b). If the judgment is based on a claim against the limited partnership, one or more of the following requirements must be met in order to obtain a judgment against a general partner: (1) a judgment against the limited partnership has been entered and a writ of execution remains unsatisfied in whole or part; (2) the limited partnership is in bankruptcy; (3) the general partner has agreed that the creditor need not exhaust the assets of the limited partnership; (4) the court has granted an order permitting recovery against the general partner because the limited partnership's assets are clearly insufficient, it would be excessively burdensome to require the creditor to seek recovery against the limited partnership, or there are grounds in equity for such order; or (5) there are other grounds besides the debt against the limited partnership for recovery against the partner. § 4-47-405(c).

Finally, although not directly relevant to the issue of a general partner's liability, it should also be noted that the limited partnership itself is liable for actionable conduct by a general partner if the general partner was acting in the "ordinary course of activities of the limited partnership" or as authorized by the partnership. § 4-47-403(a). In addition, the limited partnership is liable if a general partner, while acting in the course of the partnership's activities or with authority, "receives or causes the limited partnership to receive money or property of a person not a partner, and the money or property is misapplied." § 4-47-403(b).

V.3.   The Limited Partners

General partnerships do not involve anyone with a role equivalent to that played by limited partners in a limited partnership. All equity owners in a general partnership have the same rights and responsibilities, at least under the default rules. Despite the fact that limited partners are also "owners" of the business, however, the default rules give them a very limited role to play in the management of a limited partnership, and the default rules also impose correspondingly limited responsibilities and liability.

Limited partners do not have any statutory right or power to manage or bind the partnership. They can be given actual authority, but that takes agreement of the general partners. The statutes also provides that they do not have any apparent authority to bind the business by virtue of their status as limited partners. Similarly, limited partners owe no fiduciary duties as limited partners. They have rights to certain information, but in general the partnership agreement should set out any rights that the limited partners want to have. Finally, limited partners are also, by statute, insulated from being liable for debts of the business solely by virtue of their role as limited partners.

Obviously, the limited liability of limited partners is one of the most important attributes of the limited partnership, and there are special rules for what happens if a person erroneously believes him or herself to be a limited partner. The statute both permits such a person to remedy the error or withdraw from the partnership, and provides rules about the extent of such a person's liability to third parties and how that liability may be limited.

Because limited partners are so different from general partners, each of theses topics deserves a more detailed exploration.

V.3.1.   Default Power and Authority

Limited partners do not have any statutory right or power to manage or bind the partnership. § 4-47-302. They can, however, be given actual authority by agreement. One way in which this might be accomplished is to give the limited partners such power in the partnership agreement. Either all limited partners can all be given authority, or one or more limited partners can be singled out for such responsibility. Alternatively, limited partners can be given actual authority to act on behalf of the partnership in the same way that authority would be given to any agent. This would take a manifestation of consent from the general partners, or from whomever has the power to delegate the limited partnership's authority to others.

Unlike general partners, limited partners do not have any apparent authority to bind the business by virtue of their status as limited partners. Moreover, because this is a concept that affects the rights of third parties, it is not a rule that may be changed by agreement of the partners. § 4-47-110(b)(13). They can still possess apparent authority, but it must arise in accordance with ordinary rules of agency law.[68]

V.3.2.   The Historical Problem of Control

The preceding section of these materials may raise concern for anyone familiar with the law that traditionally applied to limited partnerships. It has always been true that a partnership agreement "could" give limited partners substantial authority over the business, or that an individual limited partner might be able to exercise effective control of the limited partnership. Traditionally, however, there were some potentially very negative consequences if limited partners chose to exercise such control over management functions. Specifically, all of the earlier limited partnership statutes included rules that made limited partners potentially personally liable if they exercised too much control over partnership operations.

---

[68] For a discussion of the creation of apparent authority generally, see § 2.03, Restatement (3rd) Agency, and the official comments and notes. This section explains the "[a]pparent authority is the power held by an agent or other actor to affect a principal's legal relations with third parties when a third party reasonably believes the actor has authority to act on behalf of the principal and that belief is traceable to the principal's manifestations."

The original Uniform Limited Partnership Act (ULPA) was promulgated by the National Conference of Commissioners of Uniform State Laws (NCCUSL) in 1916, and was quickly adopted in most states. Section 7 of that act provided that a limited partner would "not become liable as a general partner unless, in addition to the exercise of his rights and powers as a limited partner, he takes part in the control of the business." This rule reflected the prevailing understanding that limited partners were to be "passive" investors, and if that status changed, so could the extent of their personal liability. Early cases involving limited partnership clearly adopted this rule.

In 1976, NCCUSL proposed an updated version of the statute, which became widely known as RULPA (standing for the new act's official name, which was the Revised Uniform Limited Partnership Act). Section 303 of the 1976 version of RULPA provided that "a limited partner is not liable for the obligations of a limited partnership unless he [or she] is also a general partner or, in addition to the exercise of his [or her] rights and powers as a limited partner, he [or she] takes part in the control of the business." The same section continued as follows: "However, if the limited partner's participation in the control of the business is not substantially the same as the exercise of the powers of a general partner, he [or she] is liable only to persons who transact business with the limited partnership with actual knowledge of his participation in control." This at least allowed limited partners to exercise some control so long as third parties were not aware of the activities and the limited partners did not exercise the same level of control as general partners.

Even prior to this loosening of statutory standards, lawyers had developed creative but complicated strategies to allow limited partners to retain limited liability but exercise practical control over the business. Typically, an individual would form a corporation, and that corporation would become the general partner of a new limited partnership. The individual, in his or her individual capacity, would become the limited partner. The corporation, naturally, could only act through its officers, directors, and employees–and the same individual would often be the person filling these roles. Courts generally concluded that so long as the arrangements were disclosed to third persons, acting as an agent of the corporate general partner would not result in the loss of such person's limited liability as a limited partner.

In part because states were slow to adopt the 1976 version of RULPA, NCCUSL wound up suggesting substantial changes to the act and promulgated an improved and updated version of RULPA in 1986. Arkansas was one of the majority of states that quickly adopted the "improved" version of RULPA.[69] This act specified that "a limited partner is not liable for the obligations of a limited partnership unless he is also a general partner or, in addition to the exercise of his rights and powers as a limited partner, he participates in the control of the business. However, if the limited partner participates in the control of the business, he is liable only to persons who transact business with the limited partnership reasonably believing, based upon the limited partner's conduct, that the limited partner is a general partner."[70] This language was accompanied by a relatively lengthy list of permitted activities which would not amount to participation in control, including acting as agent or employee of a general partner that was an entity, consulting with or advising a general partner, acting as guarantor for the partership, bringing derivative suits, attending partnership meetings, proposing a number of different specific

---

[69]   That statute was codified at Ark. Code Ann. §§ 4-43-101 et seq. The section dealing with limited liability of limited partners was § 4-43-303. These provisions were repealed in 2007.

[70]   Ark. Code Ann. § 4-43-303(a) (repealed).

matters listed in the statute, etc.[71]

When NCCUSL proposed ULPA (2001), a conscious decision was made to simply allow limited partners to participate in control directly without risking their limited liability. This decision resulted in language specifying that "[a] limited partner is not personally liable . . . for an obligation of the limited partnership solely by reason of being a limited partner, even if the limited partner participates in the management and control of the limited partnership." § 4-47-303.

There are two reasons for the extended history discussion here. First, it is important to understand how to update older forms and materials and how to apply older case law to the issue of when limited partners can now safely participate in control. Second, although Arkansas has adopted the most modern version of the uniform limited partnership act, many other states have not. In fact, as of the date these materials were being prepared, a majority of states continue to have the statutory rule that "excessive" participation in management may result in a limited partner being held personally liable. Although Arkansas' limited partnership statute has a conflict of laws provision suggesting that the law of the state of formation is to govern "the liability of partners as partners for an obligation of the limited partnership" (§ 4-47-106), this may not be the rule in another state, and so there is at least some risk to having limited partners assume unlimited control.

V.3.3.   Fiduciary and Similar Obligations

Given the rules governing a limited partner's presumed role in the limited partnership, it is not surprising that the statutes also include the rule that "[a] limited partner does not have any

---

[71]   Ark. Code Ann. § 4-43-303(b) (repealed).

fiduciary duty to the limited partnership or to any other partner solely by reason of being a limited partner." § 4-47-305(a). To the extent that the statute and/or any partnership agreement imposes duties or responsibilities on a limited partner, however, the statute does provide that they are to be exercised "consistently with the obligation of good faith and fair dealing." § 4-47-305(b). Under the statute, the fact that the limited partner's conduct might further his or her own interest is not sufficient to show a breach of obligation owed under the statute or partnership agreement. § 4-47-305(c). This rule, however, should be subject to the contrary agreement of the parties. The agreement may not "eliminate" this obligation of good faith and fair dealing, but it may "prescribe the standards by which the performance of the obligation is to be measured, if the standards are not manifestly unreasonable." § 4-47-110(b)(7).

V.3.4. Rights of Limited Partners

Traditionally, the passivity of limited partners has been reflected not only in the limited management role and authority given to them under the statutes, but also in terms of the statutory rights accorded to them. Limited partners have certain voting rights, but only on very limited matters. For instance, the statute provides that in order for a limited partnership to be bound by the "act of a general partner which is not apparently for carrying on in the ordinary course the limited partnership's activities or activities of the kind carried on by the limited partnership binds the limited partnership," that act must be actually authorized by all other partners, presumably including any limited partners. § 4-47-402(b). Similarly, the consent of "each" partner is required to:

(1)   amend the partnership agreement;
(2)   amend the certificate of limited partnership to add or . . . delete a statement that the limited partnership is a limited liability limited partnership;

207

and

(3)   sell, lease, exchange, or otherwise dispose of all, or substantially all, of the limited partnership's property, with or without the good will, other than in the usual and regular course of the limited partnership's activities.

§ 4-47-406(b).

Similarly, it takes the approval of all partners to waive the obligation of another partner to make a contribution or return funds that were improperly paid or distributed to such partner. § 4-47-502(c). Conversion of the limited partnership, at least under default rules, also takes unanimous approval of all partners. § 4-47-1103. Finally, voluntary dissolution must be approved by not only all general partners but also a majority in interest of the limited partners. § 4-47-801(2).

While not a voting right per se, limited partners also have the right to petition a court for judicial dissolution if equitable grounds for such an order exist. § 4-47-802. They can also involve the courts by bringing a legal action against their limited partnership, either direct (§ 4-47-1001), or derivative (§ 4-47-1002).

In addition to voting rights, the statute gives limited partners certain rights to receive or obtain information about the partnership. § 4-47-304. Information that is required to be kept at the limited partnership's designated office, which includes things like a list of partners and copies of basic partnership documentation,[72] may be inspected and copied on 10 days' notice, with no particular purpose for seeking the information being required. § 4-47-304(a). Other information "regarding the state of

---

[72]   See Ark. Code Ann. § 4-47-111 for a complete list of such information.

the activities and financial condition of the limited partnership and other information regarding the activities of the limited partnership" may be obtained if it is "just and reasonable" that the information be released, the limited partner's purpose in asking is "reasonably related to the partner's interest as a limited partner," the request to release the information describes "with reasonable particularity the information sought and the purpose for seeking the information," and "the information sought is directly connected to the limited partner's purpose." § 4-47-304(b).

Finally limited partners may, under appropriate circumstances bring direct or derivative actions against the limited partnership or other partners, for legal or equitable relief, "to enforce the rights and otherwise protect the interests of the partner." § 4-47-1001(a). They must plead and prove "an actual or threatened injury that is not solely the result of an injury suffered or threatened to be suffered by the limited partnership." § 4-47-1001(b). Before bringing a derivative action, the partner must "first make [ ] a demand on the general partners, requesting that they cause the limited partnership to bring an action to enforce the right" and either the general partners must fail to bring the action in a reasonable time or the demand must be futile. § 4-47-1002. A derivative complaint must also "state with particularity: (1) the date and content of plaintiff's demand and the general partners' response . . . or (2) why demand should be excused as futile." § 4-47-1004. The person bringing the suit must have been a partner at the time the action is commenced as well as at the time the conduct giving rise to the claim occurred, or the plaintiff's status as partner must have "devolved upon the person by operation of law or pursuant to the terms of the partnership agreement from a person that was a partner at the time of the conduct." § 4-47-1003.

In addition to the foregoing rights, which are rather limited, the statute gives limited partners the power to transfer their economic interest to other persons. §§ 4-47-701 to- 702. They also have, at least under the default rules, the power to dissociate from the limited partnership, but this power can be taken away by agreement. § 4-47-601(b). And, of course, they can be given additional rights and responsibilities in the partnership agreement or thereafter, as the general partners deem appropriate.

V.3.5. Limited Liability

In addition to limited management rights and responsibilities, limited partners are also, by statute, given limited personal liability for debts of the business. In fact, the default rule is that they are not to be personally liable for such debts solely by virtue of their role as limited partners, regardless of whether the debt arises in contract, tort, or otherwise. § 4-47-303. Limited partners can still be liable for their own misconduct, of course; if they agree to be liable for one or more debts of the partnership (for example by signing a guarantee); or if the veil of limited liability is pierced.[73]

V.4. Erroneous Belief in Status as a Limited Partner

Obviously, the limited liability of limited partners is typically a matter of some importance, and there are special rules for what happens if a person erroneously believes him or herself to be a limited partner. § 4-47-306. If a person erroneously but in good faith believes that he or she is a limited partner, and he or she causes a corrected certificate to be filed or withdraws from future equity participation in the business, that will end future liability.

---

[73] For a more complete discussion of "veil piercing," see Chapter 8 of this book.

§ 4-47-306(a). In addition, the person who incorrectly believed him or herself to be a limited partner is liable to pre-existing creditors as a general partner only if the third person believed in good faith that the person was a general partner at the time the debt was incurred. § 4-47-306(b). A person acting diligently and in good faith may withdraw under this provision even if it would otherwise breach an agreement about withdrawing. § 4-47-306(c).

There is no specific requirement that the withdrawal be made within any certain time frame, but the person seeking relief under this provision must have held the belief that he or she was a limited partner in "good faith," and the corrective action is taken upon "ascertaining the mistake." At some point, there may be problems with the good faith requirement. In addition, if the withdrawal would violate a provision in the agreement limiting a partner's right to withdraw, there is a requirement that the corrective action be made diligently and in good faith.

V.5.   Sharing of Profits and Losses; Distributions

V.5.1.   General Rules

In many respects, a limited partnership resembles a general partnership with the addition of a class of limited partners. It would be a serious mistake, however, to assume that all of the important default rules governing partnership operations are the same. One of the most important differences involves the default rules governing how profits and losses, as well as distributions, are to be shared.

With regard to general partnerships, in the absence of an agreement between the partners, the default rule is that "[e]ach partner is entitled to an equal share of the partnership profits and is chargeable with a share of the partnership losses in proportion to the partner's share of the profits." § 4-46-401(b). In a limited partnership the default rule is a little harder to figure out and very different in operation. There is no express provision governing allocation of profits and losses; instead the ULPA (2001) speaks only in terms of distributions. The language of the statute, which appears on its face to be mandatory, is in fact subject to the contrary agreement of the partners, but the default rule is that "[a] distribution by a limited partnership must be shared among the partners on the basis of the value, as stated in the required records when the limited partnership decides to make the distribution, of the contributions the limited partnership has received from each partner." § 4-47-503.

This section emphasizes the importance of partnership records that set out the agreed-upon value of each partner's contribution if any partner has contributed property other than cash in exchange for his or her partnership interest. It also implies that the records of the partnership with respect to agreed-upon value can change over time, as it is the time when the distribution is decided upon that governs the determination of value. It would be theoretically possible to have a presumption of distributions based on agreed-upon value of the contributions, while profits and losses were to be "allocated" in a different manner with an accounting upon the termination of the partnership, but fortunately this is not the way the statute works. The only distributions that are set out as a matter of course in the statute are those that would occur upon dissolution of the partnership, and those final liquidating payouts are simply treated as distributions, subject to the same presumptions. § 4-47-812(b).

This rule is likely to have more appeal than an automatic assumption that all partners share equally in all profits and losses, as is the case with general partners. However, it is probably worth pointing out to clients that this may not be an ideal arrangement to set out in the partnership agreement. Perhaps the best way to explain the potential issue is to use the example of the corporation.

People make an equity investment in a corporation by purchasing stock. Their share of profits (and losses if the corporation is organized as a Subchapter S corporation so that losses can pass through to the owners) is based on how many shares of stock they buy. While it is common for all shareholders who buy stock at the same time to pay the same price, the value of the stock is almost certain to change over time. If the corporation is doing well, and has good prospects, the price will go up, and a given amount of cash will buy fewer shares and hence a smaller share of profits. If the corporation is failing, and an investment is very risky, the price of stock will have fallen, and the same amount of cash will buy both more shares and a greater share of any future profits.

This same result can be accomplished in a limited partnership, but only by drafting around the default rules. One relatively common way to accomplish this objective is to provide that profits and losses are to be shared based on the number of "units" or "interests" owned, and to give the general partners (or those with management authority) power to set the price of such units or interests over time. Rather than listing the ownership of units in the partnership agreement, they can be set out in an exhibit or attachment to the partnership agreement, making future amendments much simpler and easy to keep up with.

Note that these rules only govern the manner in which profits are shared. Losses are handled differently, but only because limited partners do not have personal liability any losses of the partnership. The rule as between the general partners is that each "general partner when the obligation was incurred . . . [who has not been previously released from liability for that obligation] shall contribute to the limited partnership for the purpose of enabling the limited partnership to satisfy the obligation. The contribution due from each of those persons is in proportion to the right to receive distributions in the capacity of general partner in effect for each of those persons when the obligation was incurred." § 4-47-812(c)(1). Limited partners will not bear a proportionate share of these liabilities, and presumably would not even if the default rules on sharing of profits are modified.

Whether or not to retain the default rule governing sharing of distributions, or to choose an alternative such as those described here, is of course a matter for the client to decide.

V.5.2.   Timing of and Limits on Distributions

The statutes do contain a number of other rules that relate to distributions. First, the statutes have, as a default rule, a provision that there is no "right" to interim distributions and that interim distributions will be made only if the limited partnership decides to make them. § 4-47-504. This is subject to the contrary agreement of the partners, and it is common to see language providing for regular distributions, or distributions that are to be made when certain conditions (such as minimum reserves are met), or minimum distributions that would be sufficient to pay the taxes which might be incurred by the partners as a result of allocations of profits.

As discussed in Chapter 3, dealing with partnership taxation, partners are taxed on the amount of profits allocated to them, even if those sums are not actually paid out to them.[74] To avoid the problems of owing tax on money that is not actually available to pay the tax, it is very common to provide for

---

[74]   See section III.2, Chapter 3.

distributions sufficient to pay income taxes. While relatively simple to state in principle, the actual drafting of this kind of language can be quite complicated.

The same language suggested for a general partnership agreement with regard to interim distributions to pay taxes would work as well for a limited partnership. Possible language, which also appears in chapter 4, might read as follows:

> For each fiscal year, to the extent that the partnership has operating income sufficient to make such payments and to retain in its net reserves an amount equal to at least $_____, each partner shall be entitled to receive within 90 days after the end of such fiscal year a tax distribution equal to the product of (a) the net profits for that fiscal year, if any, allocated to that partner and (b) the sum of (i) the highest marginal rate of federal income tax applicable to ordinary income for individuals for that fiscal year plus (ii) the highest marginal rate of state income tax applicable to ordinary income for individuals residing in Arkansas for that fiscal year, in each case determined without regard to phase-outs, alternative taxes and the like, and without regard to any other tax attribute of the individual partner. Such tax distribution is an advance to help partners to pay their taxes resulting from partnership operations and is not intended to indemnify partners against their taxes on partnership income.

As was mentioned in the preceding chapter, this is not "the ideal" tax distribution provision, and it does not purport to cover every conceivable circumstance. Your clients may have different preferences or needs, and may need other issues to be addressed. The possible questions mentioned in chapter 4 as being left open by this language apply to limited partnerships as much as to general partnerships.[75]

In addition to the general rule that there is no entitlement to interim distributions, ULPA (2001) also provides that partners will not receive a distribution merely because they dissociate from the partnership. § 4-47-505. Partners will receive a liquidating distribution if their dissociation triggers winding up of the partnership (§ 4-47-812(b)), but the withdrawal of partners from a limited partnership does not automatically mean a dissolution of the partnership. For example, withdrawal of a limited partner is not listed as an event of dissolution unless there are no remaining limited partners and no new limited partner is added within 90 days (§ 4-47-602(a)(3)); and a general partner's withdrawal results in dissolution only if (1) a majority in interest of partners vote to dissolve within 90 days of the partner's withdrawal or (2) there is no remaining general partner and no new general partner is added within 90 days. § 4-47-801(3). These rules are all also subject to the contrary agreement of the parties, except that a limited partnership by definition must have at least one general partner and one limited partner.

The default rules also incorporate a number of limitations on distributions from the limited partnership, particularly on the amount of such distributions. § 4-47-508. A limited partnership may not make a distribution in violation of the partnership agreement (§ 4-47-508(a)), although the partnership agreement can be amended to change the permissible distributions. More importantly, the statue provides that no distribution is permitted if:

(1)   the limited partnership would not be able to pay its debts as they become due in the ordinary course of the limited partnership's activities; or

(2)   the limited partnership's total assets would be less

---

[75]   See section IV.5.3, Chapter 4.

than the sum of its total liabilities plus the amount that would be needed, if the limited partnership were to be dissolved, wound up, and terminated at the time of the distribution, to satisfy the preferential rights upon dissolution, winding up, and termination of partners whose preferential rights are superior to those of persons receiving the distribution.

§ 4-47-508(b).

This limitation may not be avoided by agreement of the parties, because it affects the rights of creditors who are neither partners nor transferees. § 4-47-110(13). There is no such limitation on distributions in the general partnership statute (because general partners would all be personally liable for any debts that the partnership cannot repay anyway, unlike limited partners), but the uniform fraudulent conveyances statute would require the same result, if the general partnership elected LLP status.[76]

The limited partnership statute also includes rules for determining how the persons authorizing the distribution should determine propriety of the distribution, and the time at which that determination is to be made. The determination of whether a distribution is prohibited may be made on the basis of "financial statements prepared on the basis of accounting practices and principles that are reasonable in the circumstances or on a fair valuation or other method that is reasonable in the circumstances." § 4-47-508(c). In determining whether the distribution is permissible, it is important to known when to measure the economic effect of the distribution. Is it to be measured when approved? When the payments are made? What if the distribution takes the form of indebtedness or is deferred for a substantial period of time?

---

[76]   The Arkansas Fraudulent Transfer Act is codified at Ark. Code Ann. §§ 4-59-201 to- 209.

The statute begins by suggesting that if the distribution is in the form of indebtedness, the important time to gauge the economic effect is the date of each payment of interest or principal. § 4-47-508(g). Subject to this rule, the statute also says that "in the case of distribution by purchase, redemption, or other acquisition of a transferable interest in the limited partnership, [the effect of the distribution should be measured] as of the date money or other property is transferred or debt incurred by the limited partnership." § 4-47-508(d)(1). Presumably, in the case of a distribution in the form of indebtedness, it is still the date of payment that governs. The statute then says that in other cases, the effect of the distribution is to be measured as of the date: (A) the distribution is authorized, if the payment occurs within 120 days after that date; or (B) the payment is made, if payment occurs more than 120 days after the distribution is authorized." § 4-47-508(d)(2). This is also made subject to the rule that of distributions in indebtedness, it is the date of payment that determines the legality of the distribution.

Because there is an apparent lack of consistency between these provisions, it is probably advisable not to make distributions from a limited partnership in the form of indebtedness from the limited partnership. This suggestion is likely to be particularly important for general partners, who are made personally liable to the limited partnership for improper distributions to which they consent (§ 4-47-509(a)), but this liability is limited to circumstances where the general partner was "grossly negligent or reckless," or engaged in intentional or knowing misconduct (§ 4-47-509(a), cross-referencing § 4-47-408, which in turn limits a general partner's duty of care to these standards). Partners who knowingly receive an improper distribution may also be liable to the partnership to the extent that the distribution which they received exceeded permissible amounts. § 4-47-509(b). There is a two year statute of limitations on these actions (§ 4-47-509(d)), and a general partner who is sued may implead other general partners who also consented to the payments and any person who knowingly received improper distributions in order to compel such persons to contribute in the event that liability is imposed (§ 4-47-509(c)).

V.5.3.   Right to Distributions

In addition to the foregoing limitations on the timing and amount of distributions, the statutory default rules have other provisions relating to the payment of distributions that limit a partner's rights to obtaining such payouts. The first of these is a provision that specifies there is no right to demand or receive distributions in kind. § 4-47-506. The partnership may distribute an asset in kind, but under the default rules only "to the extent each partner receives a percentage of the asset equal to the partner's share of distributions." § 4-47-506.

Finally, the statute establishes the extent of partners' and transferees' right to receive distributions that have been approved. In the words of the statute "[w]hen a partner or transferee becomes entitled to receive a distribution, the partner or transferee has the status of, and is entitled to all remedies available to, a creditor of the limited partnership with respect to the distribution." § 4-47-507. The statute does allow the partnership to reduce its obligation by offsetting amounts due to the partnership from "the partner or dissociated partner on whose account the distribution is made." § 4-47-507.

There is no specific provision prohibiting modifications to these default rules, but to the extent that the rights of third persons might be impaired, partners are not permitted to change these rules.

V.6.   Partnership Interests

Changing topics, the partners may want the partnership agreement to describe the partnership interests that are acquired by the partners, and the rights associated with those interests. The default rules may be acceptable, but there are number of issues that should at least be raised with clients thinking about forming a limited partnership.

V.6.1.   Nature of Partnership Interests

Absent agreement to the contrary, when a partner buys into a limited partnership, he or she acquires a certain bundle of rights and responsibilities. Those differ depending on whether the purchaser of that interest become a general or limited partner. However, under the default rules, in either case the only portion of the partnership interest that is readily transferable is the right to receive, in accordance with the terms of the transfer, "distributions to which the transferor would otherwise be entitled" and, upon dissolution and winding up, "the net amount otherwise distributable to the transferor." § 4-47-702(b). The transferring partner "retains the rights of a partner other than the interest in distributions transferred and retains all duties and obligations of a partner." § 4-47-702(d).

This "transferable interest" is deemed by statute to be personal property (§ 4-47-701), which is important for things like knowing how the statute of frauds applies to transfers of that interest, or how creditors might go about obtaining a security interest in the event of a pledge by the partner to a creditor.

As mentioned earlier, in order to facilitate investments at different times (when the reasonable value of a certain percent of partnership profits might differ from what was paid at earlier times) it is not at all uncommon to see partnership agreements refer to partnership interests as units, interests, or even shares. Units (or interests, or shares) may be designated as units of limited partners' interest and general partners' interest, and the simplest way of permitting amendments when ownership changes, is to have the name and mailing address of the partner, the type and number of units (or interests, or shares), and the consideration paid along with its agreed value, listed on an exhibit (or attachment, or addendum) to the agreement. In this way, only that supplemental document would need to be amended when changes occur.

Some partnership agreements list percentage ownership instead of breaking down ownership into units, interests, or shares, and there is certainly nothing wrong with this. However, if this drafting alternative is chosen, every time an interest changes, that will also affect the percentage ownership of every other partner, making it slightly more difficult to keep the partnership agreement accurate and up to date.

V.6.2.   Issuance of New Interests (Becoming a Partner)

The limited partnership statute distinguishes between the admission of general and limited partners. Limited partners are added: (1) as provided in the partnership agreement; (2) as a result of conversion that provides for this; or (3) upon the unanimous consent of all partners. § 4-47-301. General partners are admitted under any of those three procedures, or if the last general partner dissociates from the partnership, upon the consent of a majority in interest[77] of the limited partners within 90 days of that dissociation.

---

[77]   The term "majority in interest" as used in these materials generally refers to action by partners (which may in a particular case be either general, limited, or all partners) owning a majority of the rights to receive distributions out of the rights held by all such partners. The rights of transferees are not included in this determination. For

§ 4-47-401. The initial certificate of limited partnership must name the original general partners (and list their street and mailing addresses) (§ 4-47-201(a)(3)), and the certificate must be amended every time new general partners are added. § 4-47-202(b)(1).

These default rules require unanimous consent of the partners (including limited partners) before new partners are allowed to join. This may make it difficult to raise additional capital through the sale of partnership interests, and it is very common to see partnership agreements that delegate authority to the general partners to decide upon the conditions for admission of new limited partners. If the partners do not want unfettered discretion to rest in the hands of the general partners, the partnership agreement can be set up to authorize the admission of up to a specified number of additional limited partners, or can impose conditions on who can join or what consideration must be received, or can authorize the sale of a certain number of units or interests. In order to go beyond the authorization in the partnership agreement, the agreement would need to be amended (either pursuant to its terms, or through unanimous vote of all the partners under the default rules). § 4-47-406(b)(1).

It is also possible, although less common, to change the rules requiring unanimous consent for the admission of new or additional general partners. In many cases limited partners will not want a new general partner to be added without unanimous consent, but it is also possible that obtaining unanimous consent might be difficult and, if this is a concern, the partnership agreement can easily provide that a new general partner can be added upon the vote of a certain specified number or percentage of the partners.

---

a fuller discussion of the concept of "majority in interest," see section V.9.1 of this Chapter.

V.6.3.   Transfers of Interests by Existing Partners

It is possible for persons to become partners when they purchase an interest from an existing partner rather than directly from the partnership. In general terms, the default rules specify that partners (whether general or limited) may transfer only the right to receive distributions when they sell their partnership interests (or units), and not the right to become a partner (either general or limited). A transferring partner in fact retains status as partner, unless or until being removed by the other partners or pursuant to the partnership agreement, and the transferee becomes a partner only in accordance with the rules announced above.

The specific statutory provisions governing transfers of interests owned by partners start with the rule that the only portion of the partner's interest which can be conveyed is the "partner's transferable interest." § 4-47-701. "Transfer" is defined to include "an assignment, conveyance, deed, bill of sale, lease, mortgage, security interest, encumbrance, gift, and transfer by operating of law." § 4-47-102(21). Regardless of which form of transfer takes, and irrespective of whether it is a transfer in whole or part, the transfer neither causes the transferring partner to dissociate nor triggers dissolution and winding up of the partnership. § 4-47-702(a)(2). The transferee does not, by virtue of the transfer alone, become entitled "to participate in the management or conduct of the limited partnership's activities, to require access to information concerning the limited partnership's transactions [unless it is dissolving, and then only from the date of dissolution] . . . or to inspect or copy the required information or the limited partnership's other records." § 4-47-702(a)(3). Absent agreement to the contrary (which in many cases may be done in advance, in the partnership agreement), a transferee obtains only the "right to receive, in accordance with the transfer: (1) distributions to which the transferor would otherwise be entitled; and (2) upon the dissolution and winding up of the limited partnership's activities the net amount otherwise distributable to the transferor." § 4-47-702(b).

The non-financial interests and rights of the transferee are strictly limited under the default rules. A transferee may obtain an accounting of a dissolution and winding up, for instance, only of partnership transactions from the date of dissolution. § 4-47-702(c). Moreover, all of the management and other rights that are usually associated with being a partner remain with the transferring partner rather than passing to the transferee. § 4-47-702(d).

Even these rights may be limited, but only if the transferee is given notice of the limitation of transfer. Normally an agreement of the parties may not restrict the rights of third parties (§ 4-47-110(b)(13)), but ULPA (2001) explicitly states that the "transfer of a partner's transferable interest in the limited partnership in violation of a restriction on transfer contained in the partnership agreement is ineffective as to a person having notice of the restriction at the time of transfer." § 4-47-702(f). This makes it clear that if the transferee does have notice of the restriction, it should be binding.

The partnership agreement may certainly loosen the default rules and permit transfer of additional rights to transferees. One possible adjustment is to allow transferees to become partners automatically, and the statute specifies that if they do, they become liable for the transferor's obligations to make any promised contributions or return illegal distributions, unless those obligations were unknown to the transferee at the time he or she became a partner. § 4-47-702(g), cross referencing §§ 4-47-502, -509. The partnership agreement may also give transferees specified informational or voting rights, to help preserve the value of a partner's investment, if this is desired by the parties. Because limited partners' rights are usually so limited anyway, it is often specified that a limited partner's units or interests are freely transferable (including the right to become a substitute limited partner), or at least transferable without the need to have unanimous approval of the other partners before the transferee is admitted as a limited partner. General partner's interests are generally not made freely transferable in this manner, although it is possible to permit a transferee of a general partner's interest to automatically become a limited partner with respect to the interest transferred.

There is one other special category of transfers that needs to be considered. When a partner dies, this obviously means that the interest must go somewhere. The default rule is that the legal representative of the deceased partner steps into the role of transferee, and for the limited purpose of settling the estate may also act as a limited partner for the purpose of obtaining information. § 4-47-704, cross referencing § 4-47-304. Absent agreement to the contrary, neither the personal representative nor any heir would have any status in the partnership beyond that of mere transferee. If the partners wish a different rule, for example to allow heirs to have the same rights as other limited partners, this will need to be spelled out in the partnership agreement.

V.6.4.   Creditors and Charging Orders

The partnership statute also addresses specific rights of creditors with regard to partnership interests. In general, in order for a creditor to proceed against a partner's partnership interest, the claim must first be reduced to judgment. Then, the creditor may apply for a charging order which, if granted, will entitle the creditor to receive distributions that would otherwise have gone to the partner who owed the debt. The charging order does not entitle the creditor to order or accelerate the timing of any distributions, nor does it give the creditor any management authority. The charging order may be foreclosed, which will cause a permanent transfer of the transferable interest so foreclosed, but this also does nothing more than result in the creditor becoming a transferee.

The statutory language starts with giving the judgment creditors of a partner the power to apply to "a court of competent jurisdiction" to have that court "charge the transferable interest of the judgment debtor with payment of the unsatisfied amount of the judgment with interest. To the extent so charged, the judgment creditor has only the rights of a transferee." § 4-47-703(a). The court then also has the authority under the statute to "appoint a receiver" for any distributions from the partnership, and that receiver may also be empowered to "make all other orders, directions, accounts, and inquiries the judgment debtor might have made or which the circumstances of the case may require to give effect to the charging order". § 4-47-703(a).

Once obtained, a charging order acts as a lien on the judgment debtor's transferable interest, and the statute specifically provides for foreclosure of that charging order "at any time." § 4-47-703(b). The purchaser of such a foreclosed interest gains only "the rights of a transferee." § 4-47-703(b). Prior to foreclosure, the interest that has been charged may be redeemed by: (1) the debtor; (2) by any other partner (so long as this is not done with partnership property); or (3) the limited partnership, with partnership property, but only upon unanimous consent of all partners. § 4-47-703(c).

These provisions are designed to give "the exclusive remedy by which a judgment creditor of a partner or transferee may satisfy a judgment out of the judgment debtor's transferable interest." § 4-47-703(e). In addition, the statute specifies that the chapter is not intended to and will not "deprive any partner or transferee of the benefit of any exemption laws applicable to the partner's or transferee's transferable interest." § 4-47-703(d).

V.7.   Leaving the Partnership (Dissociation)

V.7.1.   Limited Partners

As a starting point for looking at the rules governing dissociation of limited partners from a limited partnership, it is worth emphasizing that the statutory language relating to dissociation as a limited partner does not necessarily mean that the person dissociates entirely from the limited partnership. Because it is possible for the same person to own both limited and general partnership interests, the statute is very careful to speak in terms of dissociating as a limited partner, and the rules discussed in this section specifically apply only to dissociation from that particular role.

Arkansas' limited partnership statute sets out rules for dissociation of limited partners that mirror in many respects the rules applicable to general partners in general partnerships. In fact, much of the statutory language is identical, except for certain provisions that the drafters deemed to be inappropriate for limited partners. One such difference was the omission of bankruptcy or insolvency as events of dissociation for limited partners, since their financial status should have no substantial impact on the operation of the limited partnership or the other partners. Although the language mirrors Arkansas' current general partnership statute, it has changed substantially from the earlier rules governing limited partners and limited partnerships.

Under prior Arkansas law, a limited partner could withdraw from the limited partnership upon six months' written notice, and at that time would become entitled to receive the fair value of the limited partnership interest. This was subject to modification if the partnership agreement provided different exit rights or included a definite duration for the limited partnership. §§ 4-43-603 to- 604 (repealed). Under our current statute, a limited partner is given the power to dissociate, even if the dissociation is wrongful under the terms of the partnership agreement, but at that time becomes a transferee of its own transferable interest rather than being entitled to the value of the interest. Somewhat confusingly, even though the statute provides for wrongful withdrawal, it also does not prohibit the partners from changing a limited partner's "power" as well as their "right" to withdraw. To make this point a little clearer, it is probably necessary to look at the actual statutory language.

The starting point for the current Arkansas statutes applicable to the dissociation of a person as limited partner is the default rule that "[a] person does not have a right to dissociate as a limited partner before the termination of the limited partnership." § 4-47-601(a). Instead, dissociation "as a limited partner" occurs: (1) when the limited partnership has notice of the "person's express will to withdraw as a limited partner or on a later date specified by the person;" (2) upon the happening of an event specified in the partnership agreement; (3) when the person is expelled as a limited partner (with the statute providing a number of ways in which such expulsion might occur); (4) upon the person's death or termination (if the limited partner is not a natural person); or (5) upon conversion or merger of the limited partnership under terms pursuant to which the limited partnership itself no longer survives or the person ceases to be a limited partner. § 4-47-601(b).

The first of these options is the voluntary withdrawal of the limited partner, simply by giving notice to the limited partnership.

§ 4-47-601(b)(1). This should mean that a provision in the partnership agreement saying that withdrawal before a certain date or event is wrongful would not actually prevent dissociation of a person as limited partner. The comments to the official version of ULPA (2001) make it clear that this was in fact the original intent of the language. However, consider the section of the statute dealing with "non-waivable" provisions. That section prohibits the partners from eliminating the power of a person "to dissociate as a general partner" but contains no comparable restriction on the ability to remove a person's "power" to withdraw as a limited partner. § 4-47-110(b)(8). Therefore, a clearly worded provision specifying that attempted withdrawal in violation of a particular partnership provision is not merely wrongful but ineffective should be binding on limited partners.

The next subsection of the statute simply specifies that the partners may, by agreement, set out events upon which a person may be dissociated as a limited partner. Things like the sale or other transfer of all of the person's limited partnership interest, for example, are common events of dissociation that are not spelled out as default rules in the statute, but are found in many partnership agreements. § 4-47-601(b)(2).

The next few subsections of the statute all deal with expulsion of a limited partner. First, the partnership agreement itself may contain rules governing when a limited partner may be expelled. § 4-47-601(b)(3). In addition, even if the partnership agreement itself is silent, the default provisions allow a person to be expelled as a limited partner "by unanimous consent of the other partners" in these situations: (1) it becomes unlawful to continue the partnership activities with such person as a limited partner; (2) all of that person's transferable interest in the partners has been transferred (other than for security purposes) or there has been a charging order on such interest, which has not been foreclosed; (3) the limited partner is a corporation that has filed articles of dissolution or the equivalent, and it has been given 90 days' notice that expulsion will happen unless the dissolution is revoked or the corporate charter reinstated; or (4) the limited partner is a partnership or LLC that has been dissolved and is being wound up. § 4-47-601(b)(4).

It is also possible to have a person expelled as limited partner if the limited partnership applies to court and shows that the person: (1) was "engaged in wrongful conduct that adversely and materially affected the limited partnership's activities"; (2) "willfully or persistently committed a material breach of the partnership agreement or of the obligation of good faith and fair dealing"; or (3) "engaged in conduct relating to the limited partnership's activities which makes it not reasonably practicable to carry on the activities with the person as limited partner." § 4-47-601(5). Note that these rules may be modified or even eliminated as grounds for judicial dissolution if the partnership agreement so provides.

Not surprisingly, death of an individual partner is an event of dissociation (§ 4-47-601(6)), and there are comparable triggers for dissociation of non-individual limited partners. If a limited partner is a trust or estate, the distribution of that trust's or estate's entire transferable interest in the partnership (albeit not to a successor trustee or successor personal representative) is an event of dissociation. § 4-47-601(7) - (8). "Termination" of a limited partner that "is not an individual, partnership, limited liability company, corporation, trust, or estate" is an event of dissociation. § 4-4-601(9).

Finally, if the limited partnership participates in a conversion or merger, and is not the surviving entity, or if pursuant to the terms of the reorganization, the person is dissociated, this

will also end the person's status as a limited partner. §
4-47-601(10).

It is worth emphasizing that dissociation as a limited
partner does not automatically mean, as it did under prior law, that
the person is entitled to be bought out for the fair value of the
interest. While dissociation terminates that person's rights as a
limited partner, and prevents new obligations of good faith and fair
dealing from arising, the person continues to have an association
with the limited partnership, albeit as a mere transferee. §
4-47-602. The only continuing rights as a limited partner are if the
person again becomes a limited partner (as any assignee could).
§ 4-47-704. The only obligations of good faith and fair dealing
that remain must arise out of matters and events that occurred prior
to the dissociation. § 4-47-602(a)(2). Finally, any obligations
owed to the limited partnership or other partners are not discharged
merely because of the dissociation. § 4-47-602(b).

V.7.2.   General Partners

The current limited partnership statute in Arkansas uses
essentially identical language covering withdrawal of general
partners from a limited partnership to that found in our current
general partnership statute. Speaking generally, a general partner
always retains the legal ability to withdraw, even if that withdrawal
violates the terms of an agreement. This may be referred to as the
distinction between the "power" and the "right" to withdraw. Note
that a withdrawal in violation of an agreement may give rise to
various causes of action against the wrongfully dissociating
general partner, but such person may not be compelled to remain
in the capacity.

The statutory language that makes it clear that a general
partner always has the power to dissociate is unambiguous: "[a]

person has the power to dissociate as a general partner at any time, rightfully or wrongfully, by express will." § 4-47-604(a). Moreover, that general section lists the limited circumstances under which the withdrawal may be considered "wrongful." Dissociation as a general partner is "wrongful only if": (1) it violates an express provision in the partnership agreement; or (2) it occurs before the termination of the limited partnership, and the person withdraws by express will, is expelled by judicial determination, is dissociated as a result of bankruptcy, or (for non-individuals) dissolves or terminates. § 4-47-604(b). The official comment to the uniform version of ULPA suggests that the language about withdrawal being wrongful if it was prior to termination of the limited partnership was intended to reflect the expectation that each general partner is expected to stay in that role through the winding up process, absent agreement to the contrary. In the event of a dissociation that is wrongful, the general partner who wrongfully dissociates as a general partner becomes liable to the limited partners and potentially the other partners for any damages caused by the dissociation. § 4-47-604(c). This liability "is in addition to any other obligation" owed by the wrongfully dissociating general partner.

Dissociation need not, however, be wrongful. The statutes set out a number of circumstances under which a person will dissociate as a general partner, only some of which fit the above definitions. The listed events of dissociation are as follows: (1) the person gives the limited partnership notice of express will to withdraw as general partner (§ 4-47-603(1)); (2) the occurrence of any event agreed to in the partnership agreement as causing such dissociation (§ 4-47-603(2)); (3) the person's expulsion as a general partner under specified circumstances (§ 4-47-603(3) - (5)); (4) the person becomes bankrupt or insolvent as defined in the statute (§ 4-47-603(6)); (5) if the person is an individual, he or she dies or is determined to be incompetent (§ 4-47-603(7)); (6) if the person is a trust or estate, distribution of its entire transferable interest in the partnership as explained in the statute (§ 4-47-603(8) - (9)); (7) termination of a general partner that is not an individual, partnership, LLC, corporation, trust, or estate (§ 4-47-603(10)); or (8) the limited partnership participates in a conversion or merger in which it is not the surviving entity or as a result of which the person ceases to be a general partner (§ 4-47-603(11)).

The ability to withdraw by express will is one of the non-modifiable provisions of the limited partnership statute. § 4-47-110(b)(8). As discussed earlier, however, unless the partnership agreement provides otherwise, voluntary withdrawal as a general partner prior to termination of the limited partnership is presumed to be wrongful, and may also be given additional consequences by express agreement of the parties. § 4-47-604.

The parties are also free to add other events of dissociation, which will depend on the specific needs of the partners and the business. This could include triggers like leaving employment, net assets falling below a specified amount, or anything else that might suit the needs of the partners. The partnership agreement can add optional events of dissociation, or mandatory ones, or ones that give a specified number of partners owning a specified percentage of the outstanding partnership interests, the right to trigger dissociation.

The third category of events of dissociation parallels that found in both the Arkansas general partnership statute and the limited partnership statutory provisions applicable to limited partners. These are the statutory provisions relating to expulsion of a general partner. The first possibility is that a person may be expelled as a general partner pursuant to something agreed to in the partnership agreement. § 4-47-603(3). Even if the agreement itself is silent, however, the default rules give the other partners, upon unanimous consent, the right to expel a general partner if: (1) it becomes unlawful to carry on the partnership business with such person as a general partner; (2) the person has transferred all or substantially all of his or her transferable interest in the partnership (other than for security), or has a charging order on such interest, which has not been foreclosed; (3) the person is a corporation that has filed articles of dissolution or the equivalent, and it has been given 90 days' notice that expulsion will happen unless the dissolution is revoked or the corporate charter reinstated; or (4) the general partner is a partnership or LLC that has been dissolved and is being wound up. § 4-47-603(4).

Finally, it is also possible to have a general partner expelled by judicial order if the limited partnership shows that the person: (1) "engaged in wrongful conduct that adversely and materially affected the limited partnership activities"; (2) "willfully or persistently committed a material breach of the partnership agreement or of a duty owed to the partnership or the other partners"; or (3) "engaged in conduct relating to the limited partnership's activities which makes it not reasonably practicable to carry on the activities of the limited partnership with the person as a general partner." § 4-47-603(5). The official comment to the uniform version of the statute makes it clear that these provisions are intended to be subject to the contrary agreement of the parties, which was not the case under prior law.

While not listed as default events of dissociation as a limited partner, person will be dissociated as a general partner upon becoming "a debtor in bankruptcy"; executing "an assignment for the benefit of creditors"; seeking or agreeing to the appointment of a trustee, receiver or liquidator of all or substantially all of such persons's property; or failing to have the appointment of any such trustee, receiver, or liquidator vacated within 90 days of appointment. § 4-47-603(6).

Death or incapacity also acts as an event of dissociation for a general partner. § 4-47-603(7). Incapacity occurs upon the appointment of a guardian or general conservator for the person, or upon "a judicial determination that the person has otherwise become incapable of performing the person's duties as a general partner under the partnership agreement." Trusts and estates that are general partners are dissociated once their entire transferable interest in the partnership is transferred (other than to a success trustee or personal representative). § 4-47-603(8) - (9). Termination of other entities will cause the person to be dissociated as a general partner. § 4-47-603(10). Finally, as is the case for limited partners, a person is dissociated as a general partner if the limited partnership participates in a conversion or merger and it either does not survive, or the terms of the conversion or merger provide that such person ceases to be a general partner. § 4-47-603(11).

Once a person is dissociated as a general partner, even if he or she continues to be a limited partner, that person's rights and responsibilities as a general partner end. This means that hr or she no longer has the right to participate in management as a general partner, is free to compete with the limited partnership, and his or her other duties of care and loyalty continue "only with regard to matters arising and events occurring before the person's dissociation as a general partner." § 4-47-605(a)(1)-(3).   In addition, upon dissociation, a former general partner gains the right to sign and deliver to the Secretary of State "a statement of dissociation," and at the request of the limited partnership is to sign an amendment to the certificate of limited partnership reflecting the dissociation. § 4-47-605(a)(4). Finally, upon dissociation, the former general partner becomes a mere transferee of any transferable interest owned as general partner (§

4-47-605(a)(5)), except in the case of the limited special rights of a personal representative of a deceased partner (§ 4-47-704) or special rights that may apply if the person is dissociated as a general partner by virtue of a conversion or merger of the limited partnership (§ 4-47-605(a)(5) which cross references subchapter 11 of ULPA (2001)).

In addition to noting the things that do change upon dissociation as a general partner, the statute also specifies that "dissociation as a general partner does not of itself discharge the person from any obligation to the limited partnership or the other partners which the person incurred while a general partner." § 4-47-605 (b). The partners may by agreement change the impact of dissociation as a general partner on obligations that are owed to them, but may not change obligations to the limited partnership if that would affect the rights of persons other than partners (such as creditors).

V.8. Continuation of the Limited Partnership following Dissociation of a Partner

As described in the preceding section of these materials, dissociation of partners does not necessarily mean that the partnership is dissolved and its affairs wound up. In fact, the presumption is that a dissociated partner continues to hold his or her interest as transferee. (§ 4-47-602(a)(3) (as to dissociation as a limited partner) and § 4-47-605(a)(5) (as to dissociation as a general partner)). In addition, the dissociated partner has no right to be paid the fair value of the partnership interest as a result of dissociation. § 4-47-505.

There are some exceptions to the rule that dissociation does not trigger dissolution. One such exception occurs upon dissociation of the last remaining limited or general partner, if no replacement can be found in a timely fashion, because a limited partnership is specifically defined as an entity having one or more general and one or more limited partners. § 4-47-102(11). Dissociation of the last limited partner results in dissolution if 90 days pass without admission of at least one new limited partner by the limited partnership. § 4-47-801(4). Dissociation of the last general partner results in dissolution unless, prior to the passage of 90 days following such dissociation, a majority in interest of the limited partners consent to continue the business and a new general partner is added in accordance with that consent. § 4-47-801(3)(B). Another exception occurs if any general partner dissociates and majority in interest of all partners (general and limited) consent to dissolution. § 4-47-801(3)(A). Unanimous consent of the remaining partners would also result in dissolution. § 4-47-801(2). And, of course, the partnership agreement itself could provide for dissolution upon dissociation of one or more partners. § 4-47-801(1). Absent these circumstances, however, a limited partnership should continue notwithstanding dissociation of a partner. This possibility raises the issue of a dissociated partner's lingering power to affect or bind the partnership.

The statute addresses the lingering authority of dissociated general partners, but not of dissociated limited partners. The reason for this is that limited partners do not, simply by virtue of their status as limited partners, have power to bind the partnership or affect its legal relations. If the partnership agreement gives such power, presumably normal rules of agency law should apply. This would mean that as an agent of the limited partnership, actual authority would be terminated upon termination of the agency relationship (which would normally be when the agent has notice that his or her authority has ended), while apparent authority would continue so long as it was reasonable for a third person to believe based on the partnership's manifestations that the former limited partner had such power.[78] The rules applicable to lingering authority of dissociated general partners under ULPA (2001) are similar, but a little more specific.

Under the Arkansas limited partnership statute, a dissociated general partner can bind the partnership by an act that would have bound the partnership prior to such partner's dissociation. § 4-47-606(a)(1). This means that the act must have been "apparently carrying on in the ordinary course the limited partnership's activities or activities of the kind carried on by the limited partnership" and the third party must not have had notice that the partner was not, in fact, authorized to act in such a way. § 4-47-402(a). In addition, this lingering power lasts only two years following dissociation, and at the time of the transaction, the third party must not have had notice of the dissociation and must have reasonably believed that the person was a general partner. § 4-47-606(a)(2). If the partnership is bound in such a manner, the dissociated general partner is made liable to the partnership and any other general partner for any damages arising out of obligations caused by the dissociated partner. § 4-47-606(b).

As to a dissociated general partner's liability to others, the statute provides generally that dissociation by itself does not discharge a person's liability as general partner "for an obligation of the limited partnership incurred before dissociation," but there is no liability "for a limited partnership's obligation incurred after

---

[78]   § 3.11 of the Restatement (Third) of Agency deals with the topic of "Termination Of Apparent Authority." It provides that "(1) The termination of actual authority does not by itself end any apparent authority held by an agent"; and "(2) Apparent authority ends when it is no longer reasonable for the third party with whom an agent deals to believe that the agent continues to act with actual authority."

dissociation." § 4-47-607(a). However, if the dissociation does not result in dissolution and winding up of the partnership, and assuming that the partnership in question has not registered as an LLLP,[79] a dissociated general partner will be liable for post-dissociation transactions if it is the type of obligation for which general partners would be liable, less than two years have passed since the dissociation, and "the other party does not have notice of the dissociation and reasonably believes that the person is a general partner." § 4-47-607(c).

In the event that a dissociated partner would be liable under any of these provisions, the statute also addresses how such liability may end. First, the dissociated partner may enter into an agreement with the limited partnership's creditor, pursuant to which the dissociated partner is released from liability. § 4-47-607(d). Alternatively "[a] person dissociated as a general partner is released from liability for an obligation of the limited partnership if the limited partnership's creditor, with notice of the person's dissociation as a general partner but without the person's consent, agrees to a material alteration in the nature or time of payment of the obligation." § 4-47-607(e).

V.9.   Winding up a Limited Partnership

V.9.1.   The Normal Process

Aside from the possibility of judicial dissolution, the statute lists the "only" circumstances under which a limited partnership is to be dissolved and wound up. § 4-47-801. The first possibility does, however, make it clear that the partners are in control in establishing when their business will end. A limited

---

[79]   See section V.10. of this Chapter for a fuller discussion of the rules applicable to limited liability limited partnerships (LLLPs).

partnership will be dissolved and its business wound up as provided in the partnership agreement if either the Secretary of State signs and files a declaration of dissolution, upon the withdrawal of the last general or limited partner unless a replacement is agreed to within 90 days in accordance with the statute or the partnership agreement, or upon the consent (which under the default rules need not follow any particular formalities or be in writing) of: (1) all general partners and a majority in interest of limited partners; or (2) a majority in interest of all partners if the consent is obtained within 90 days following the dissociation of a general partner when at least one general partner remains.

The first of these options is for the partners to specify in their partnership agreement events upon which the limited partnership is to be dissolved. § 4-47-801(1). This could either be the occurrence of a specified event, accomplishment of a particular goal, the passage of a certain amount of time, or anything else necessary to accomplish the partners' goals. The statute does not limit the rights of the partners to set out events of dissolution in their agreement. The statute does not impose any requirement that the partnership agreement provisions relating to dissolution be in writing or in any other form of record, although the partnership agreement itself could impose that requirement. On the other hand, if the provisions relating to dissolution and winding up are not "contained in a partnership agreement made in a record," one of the items of required information that must be kept at the partnership's offices is a record which states "any events upon the happening of which the limited partnership is to be dissolved and its activities wound up." § 4-47-111(9)(D).

Putting aside for a moment the possibility of administrative dissolution, which will be covered in a subsequent section of this chapter, the next second possibility listed in the statute is consent of all general partners and "of limited partners owning a majority of the rights to receive distributions as limited partners at the time the consent is to be effective." § 4-47-801(2). These materials often use the short hand phrase "a majority in interest" of the partners to describe this, but the statute makes it quite clear that: (1) only partners (and not transferees) are counted for purposes of the determining the required consent; and (2) it is the consent of partners owning the right to a majority of any distributions, out of all interests in distributions held by such partners, that matters. In addition, where (as here) the statute talks in terms of a majority in interest of "limited partners," if the same person holds interests both as general and limited partner, it is only the interest in distributions attributable to the interest held as limited partner that would be counted. See official comment to ULPA (2001) § 801.

The next possibility set out in the statute is that a limited partnership is to dissolve and its affairs be wound up if any general partner dissociates, and one of two things happens. First, the partnership is to dissolve if there is at least one remaining general partner, but partners owning "a majority of the rights to receive distributions as partners at the time the consent is to be effective" consent to dissolve within 90 days of that partner's dissociation. § 4-47-801(3)(A). Note that for this provision, while it is still true that only the distribution rights of partners count, and not those of transferees, it does not matter if the interests are owned as general or limited partners. If a majority in interest (as of the date the consent would be effective) agree to dissolve, that constitutes a trigger under the default rules. This is, however, subject to a contrary agreement by the partners. Alternatively, dissolution is triggered is if a general partner dissociates and there is as a result no remaining general partner. In this case, the partnership dissolves after 90 days, unless within that time a majority in interest of the limited partners consent to continue the business of the limited partnership, agree to admit a new general partner and at least one new general partner is added in accordance with the terms of that consent. § 4-47-801(3)(B).

The next listed event that would trigger dissolution is the passage of 90 days after the dissociation of the limited partnership's last limited partner, unless at least one limited partner is added by the partnership during that time period. § 4-47-801(4). This provision does not specify the vote required to continue the business under these circumstances, and does not in fact require an explicit consent to continue the business. Instead, if a limited partner is added within 90 days of the dissociation of the last limited partner, continuation of the limited partnership is automatic. If no limited partner is added, the partnership must be dissolved and wound up. To some extent, this can be modified by agreement. The partners could, for example, require a vote to continue even if a new limited partner is added. They would not, however, be free to have the business continue as a limited partnership with no limited partners.

Finally, the last option is "the signing and filing of a declaration of dissolution by the Secretary of State" under the administrative dissolution provisions, which will be examined in more detail in section V.9.3. of this Chapter. § 4-47-801(5).

V.9.2.   Judicial Dissolution

The statutory provision authorizing a court to order dissolution of a limited partnership is considerably shorter but potentially quite broad. "On application by a partner the circuit court may order dissolution of a limited partnership if it is not reasonably practicable to carry on the activities of the limited partnership in conformity with the partnership agreement." § 4-47-802. This provision may not be varied by the partners. § 4-47-110(b)(9).

There are no cases in Arkansas interpreting this provision, nor (as of the date these materials were prepared) are there reported decisions quoting this language from any other state. On the other hand, the earlier partnership statute (RULPA) permitted judicial dissolution when it was "not reasonably practicable to carry on the business in conformity with the partnership agreement." RULPA § 802. Commentators have described a number of instances in which courts have awarded dissolution under this provision, and a similar interpretation is certainly likely under ULPA: "Courts have found a dissolution decree appropriate if a general partner engages in misconduct, a breach of fiduciary duty making it impracticable to carry on the business, a breach of the limited partnership agreement causing permanent damage to the limited partnership, and a willful refusal to furnish the limited partners with financial information concerning partnership business operations. Also, a limited partnership can be dissolved when there is continued dissension among the partners and the likelihood of insolvency. Finally, a court may order dissolution when it is no longer practicable to carry on the limited partnership's business." It is also clear that the standard in the statute is not that it is impossible to carry on the business or activities, but that it is not reasonably likely.

V.9.3.   Administrative Dissolution

In addition to voluntary and judicial dissolution, the statute also contains relatively detailed provisions governing administrative dissolution. These provisions relate to the right of the Secretary of State to intervene when a limited partnership fails to make required reports or payments under Arkansas law. Current rules allow the Secretary of State to administratively dissolve a limited partnership if, within 60 days after the due date, a limited partnership fails to either: "(1) pay any fee, tax, or penalty due to the Secretary of State under this chapter or other law; or (2) deliver its annual report to the Secretary of State." § 4-47-809(a).

The steps to be taken by the Secretary of State to actually dissolve the limited partnership are also set out in the statute. First, there must be a determination by the Secretary of State that there are grounds under the statute for dissolution. Then, it must file a record of determination, which must be served on the limited partnership. § 4-47-809(b).[80] The limited partnership has 60 days after service of the copy of that determination in which to correct the grounds for dissolution or to prove to the reasonable satisfaction of the Secretary of State that the grounds do not exist. § 4-47-809(c). If this does not happen, the Secretary of State "shall administratively dissolve the limited partnership by preparing, signing and filing a declaration of dissolution that states the grounds for dissolution," and serve the limited partnership with a copy of this declaration. § 4-47-809(c).

Although administrative dissolution of a limited partnership does not instantaneously terminate the partnership's existence, following such an act by the Secretary of State, the partnership retains only authority to carry on "activities necessary to wind up its activities and liquidate its assets" and to "notify claimants." § 4-47-809(d). The administrative dissolution does

---

[80]   Service of process is governed by the Model Registered Agents Act in Arkansas, which provides that service may normally be had on the registered agent of the entity, and if there is none or the entity's registered agent cannot, with" reasonable diligence" be served, then any of the "governors" of the entity may be served at the entity's principal office as shown in the most recently filed annual report, or if none, the original document filed to create the entity. § 4-20-113(b). If these options do not work, service can be made "by handing a copy to the manger, clerk, or other person in charge of any regular place of business or activity of the entity if the person served is not a plaintiff in the action." § 4-20-113(c). In the case of a limited partnership, this would mean service should first be attempted on the registered agent (if any is serving), then on any of the general partners (who have the managing authority sufficient to qualify them as the governors under the Model Registered Agents Act), and then on a manager or other agent at a regular place of business.

not act to terminate the authority of the agent for service of process. § 4-47-809(e).

Administrative dissolution need not be final. A limited partnership has a two year period following the date of dissolution during which it may apply for reinstatement. In order to do this, the partnership must file an application with the Secretary of State which states: (1) "the name of the limited partnership and the effective date of its administrative dissolution; (2) that the grounds for dissolution either did not exist or have been eliminated; and (3) that the limited partnership's name [complies with the requirements of the statute]. . . ." § 4-47-810(a). If the Secretary of State determines that such an application complies with these requirements, and contains information which is factually accurate, a declaration of reinstatement stating this finding shall be prepared, signed and filed by the Secretary of State, with a copy to be served on the limited partnership. § 4-47-810(b). An effective reinstatement " relates back to and takes effect as of the effective date of the administrative dissolution and the limited partnership may resume its activities as if the administrative dissolution had never occurred." § 4-47-810(c).

If an application for reinstatement is denied by the Secretary of State, the partnership must be served with a copy of a notice of reasons which must be prepared, signed, and filed by the Secretary of State. § 4-47-811(a). After being served with this notice of denial, the limited partnership has 30 days in which to petition the circuit court appealing the denial; the petition must ask the court to set aside the dissolution; must contain a copy of the declaration of dissolution; the application for reinstatement and the notice of denial; and must be served on the Secretary of State. § 4-47-811(b). The statute gives the court authority to take summary action ordering reinstatement, or any "other action the court considers appropriate." § 4-47-811(c).

If the two year window in which an application for reinstatement may be filed has passed, there is no other statutory recourse. They parties are, of course, free to form another limited partnership, but it will date only from the time the new documents are filed, and will not relate back to the date of administrative dissolution.

V.9.4.   Winding up Process

Assuming that a limited partnership has been dissolved and is proceeding with the liquidation of the business, the question becomes how this is to happen. The statutes actually have fairly detailed guidance about the winding up process. The starting point is the rule that once a limited partnership is dissolved, it continues in existence only for purposes of winding up. § 4-47-803(a). A general partner who, knowing of the dissolution, binds the partnership to acts not appropriate to the winding up of the business, will be liable to the partnership, other partners or third parties for any damages caused by such actions. § 4-47-805(a).

The limited partnership act includes a list of activities that are permissible but may not be necessary during the winding up of a limited partnership. These activities include: amending the certificate of limited partnership to specify that the partnership is dissolved, preserving the limited partnership business or property as a going concern for a reasonable time, prosecuting and defending actions and proceedings, transferring partnership property, settling disputes by mediation or arbitration, filing a statement of termination once the winding up has been finished, and taking other "necessary" acts. § 4-47-803(b)(1). Presumably, "necessary" in this context means an act that is reasonably necessary to conduct the termination of the partnership's activities and liquidation of its assets as well as appropriate distributions to creditors and partners. In addition to these acts, the statute also provides that the limited partnership "<u>shall</u> discharge the limited partnership's liabilities, settle and close the limited partnership's activities, and marshal and distribute the assets of the partnership." § 4-47-803(b)(2) (emphasis added). These last steps are apparently mandatory.

The statutes also cover the issue of who is to be in charge of this process. Presumably, in most cases, the winding up process will be supervised by the general partners. "A limited partnership is bound by a general partner's act after dissolution which . . . is appropriate for winding up the limited partnership's activities." § 4-47-804(a)(1). A dissociated general partner may also bind the limited partnership by taking acts that are appropriate to wind up the partnership, but the partnership is only bound if the third person does not have notice of that partner's dissociation and reasonably believes that he or she is still a general partner. § 4-47-804(b)(1)(B). A dissociated general partner who causes the partnership to incur an obligation under this provision is liable to the partnership for any damages, or to any other person for damages caused as a result of such obligation. § 4-47-805(b).

If there is no general partner, a person may be appointed to conduct the winding up "by the consent of limited partners owning a majority of the rights to receive distributions as limited partners at the time the consent is to be effective." § 4-47-803(c). (Note that only limited partners get to vote, not transferees, and only the distributional rights of limited partners count for determining when consent of a majority in interest has been obtained.) If someone is appointed in this manner, that person acquires the same powers to manage the limited partnership during the winding up process that a general partner would have, and is required to amend the certificate of limited partnership to state that there is no general partner, and to provide the name and address (both street and mailing) of the person appointed to wind up the partnership. §

4-47-803(c)(1)-(2).   The person appointed in this manner does not, however, become a general partner, and therefore would not be subject to a general partner's usual fiduciary obligations. If the parties wish to impose a particular standard of care upon a person appointed to wind up the business of the limited partnership, that would need to be agreed to as part of the appointment.

Alternatively, if this process does not work, any partner may apply to circuit court for judicial supervision of the winding up if there is no general partner and within a reasonable time the limited partners have not appointed someone to supervise the winding up in accordance with the prior rules. § 4-47-803(d). Any partner also has the right to seek judicial supervision of the winding up under this provision for any other good cause.

V.9.5.   Creditors, Claims, Liabilities, and Contribution

Because a limited partnership has a class of owners who have no personal liability for debts of the business, the rights of creditors are of particular concern in the dissolution and winding up process. The statutes contain a number of provisions relating to creditors, how their claims are to be handled, when they may be extinguished, who might be liable for debts incurred and how those are to be collected, and general obligations of partners to contribute to pay off unpaid debts.

The rules and procedures for handling creditors' claims in the limited partnership statute are modeled on the rules applicable to corporations. There are specific procedures for handling known claims (and a relatively abbreviated time frame in which creditors in this category must act to preserve their claims) and other claims (with a lengthier period of time in which such claims may be made). The processes specified are optional in the sense that the statute says that a limited partnership "may" handle known and unknown claims as suggested, but there is a strong incentive to follow the suggested process because doing so will cut off the rights of potential creditors, often more quickly than would otherwise be the case. This allows the business affairs of the partnership to be completely settled expeditiously.

With regard to claims that are known by the limited partnership, the statutes specify that a dissolved limited partnership "may" notify known claimants of the dissolution by providing a record that includes all of the following information: (1) it must set out the information required to be included in a claim; (2) it needs to include a mailing address to which the claim is to be sent; (3) it must state the deadline for receipt of the claim, which may not be less than 120 days after the date the notice is received by the claimant; (4) it must notify the recipient that the claim will be barred if not received by the deadline; and (5) it must notify the claimant that barring of claims against the limited partnership will also bar any corresponding claims against any general partner or dissociated general partner. § 4-47-806(b). The final section may be omitted if the limited partnership was, for its entire existence, an LLLP (as described in the final section of this chapter). If this notice is sent out, any claims that are not received by the specified deadline are barred. § 4-47-806(c)(1). Even if a claim is timely received, if the dissolved limited partnership rejects the claim and so notifies the claimant, the claim will be barred unless an action is commenced within 90 days following receipt of the notice of rejection. § 4-47-806(c)(2). These rules do not apply to claims based on events that occur subsequent to the effective date of the dissolution or if the liability was contingent on that date. § 4-47-806(d).

In order to bar other claims, a dissolved limited partnership is to publish notice of the dissolution and set out the process by which such claims are to be presented. § 4-47-807(a). The notice must be "published at least once in a newspaper of general circulation in the county in which the dissolved limited partnership's designated office is located or, if it has none in this State, in the county in which the limited partnership's designated office is or was last located." § 4-47-807(b)(1). It must include the following information: (1) a description of all information required to be included with a claim; (2) the mailing address to which the claim must be sent; (3) a statement to the effect that any claim against the limited partnership will be barred unless an action to enforce the claim is brought within five years of the date on which the notice is published; and (4) a notification that barring of claims against the limited partnership will also bar any corresponding claims against any general partner or dissociated general partner. § 4-47-807(b)(2)-(4). The final provision may be omitted if the limited partnership was, for its entire existence, an LLLP (as described in the final section of this chapter). Failure to commence an action to enforce a claim within five years of such a publication bars claims by: (1) persons who did not receive notice as a known claimant; (2) persons who did receive notice as a known claimant but whose claims were not acted on in a timely fashion by the limited partnership; and (3) claimants whose claims were contingent or based on events that occurred following the effective date of the partnership's dissolution. § 4-47-807(c).

If a claim is made within the five year period, the issue is often how it is to be enforced. The limited partnership is not required to hold its assets for this period, pending the resolution of contingent or unknown claims. Instead, the statute provides that claims that have not been barred may be enforced "against the dissolved limited partnership, to the extent of its undistributed assets," but more importantly, also against partners or transferees to the extent of each such person's proportionate share of the claim or the partnership assets distributed to such person in liquidation, whichever is less, provided also that the total liability for all claims under this provision can not exceed the total amount of assets distributed to such person as part of the winding up process. § 4-47-807(d). If the limited partnership has general partners and is not a registered LLLP, the general partners may also be sued if they are personally liable for the debt. § 4-47-807(d)(3), cross referencing § 4-47-404.

If a claim against the limited partnership is barred either because the process for known claims was followed, or five years has passed since publication notice for other claims, then the corresponding claims against general partners or dissociated general partners will also be barred. § 4-47-808.

The last major section of the statute that deals with the winding up process covers both the proper disposition of partnership assets and the topic of when additional contributions are required. The order in which partnership assets are to be paid out is both logical and not subject to contrary agreement of the parties, at least insofar as a purported agreement would affect the rights of third parties. § 4-47-110(b)(13). As between the partners themselves, the order, timing, and manner of distributions may be modified by agreement. Keep in mind that some changes from the default rule of treating all liquidating payments in the same manner that other distributions are handled could have substantial tax consequences, or might even be disregarded for tax purposes. Therefore, special arrangements as to distributions (whether liquidating or otherwise) should be review with the clients' tax advisor(s).

The first order of priority when it comes to paying out partnership assets is to creditors. "In winding up . . . the assets of the limited partnership, including the contributions required . . . must be applied to satisfy the limited partnership's obligations to creditors, including, to the extent permitted by law, partners that are creditors." § 4-47-812(a). Because this section obviously relates to the rights of persons other than partners, it is not subject to modification by the partners. As for the reference to the fact that sometimes payments to partners who are creditors may not be given the same priority as payments to other creditors, this merely reflects the law embodied in the common law doctrine of equitable subordination, and statutory provisions in both the Bankruptcy Code,[81] and the Arkansas Fraudulent Transfer Act.[82]

Equitable subordination may be ordered by a court in a number of different situations, but one of them is "when a fiduciary of the debtor misuses his position to the disadvantage of other creditors."[83] Because general partners are fiduciaries, they are subject to a rule that does not apply to outsiders in the same way, and this means that they may not always be permitted to stand on the same footing as other creditors. The Bankruptcy Code codifies this rule.[84] The Arkansas Fraudulent Transfer Act works in a similar way, providing that the insider status is one of the characteristics that might make it easier to treat a debt as having

---

[81]   11 U.S.C. § 510.

[82]   This act is codified at §§ 4-59-201 to- 212.

[83]   Matter of Cajun Electric Power Co-Operative, Inc. v. Cajun Power Cooperative, 119 F.3d 349, 357 (5th Cir. 1997) (also noting that the other two commonly cited possibilities are when a third party controls the debtor to its advantage, or when a third party actually defrauds other creditors). See also In re Graycarr, Inc., 330 B.R. 741, 749 (Bkrtcy.W.D.Ark. 2005) (citing In re Bellanca Aircraft Corp., 850 F.2d 1275, 1282 (8th Cir. 1988)). Courts within the Eighth Circuit Court of Appeals commonly cite to decisions of the Fifth Circuit Court of Appeals on equitable subordination. For example, Bellanca cites to Wilson v. Huffman (In re Missionary Baptist Found.), 712 F.2d 206, 212 (5th Cir. 1983).

[84]   Section 510 of the Bankruptcy Code has been described as "an extension of the common law doctrine of equitable subordination." In re Raney, 132 B.R. 63, 67 (Bkrtcy.D.Wyo. 1991)

been fraudulently incurred, so that it might be subordinated to the claims of other creditors.[85]

After creditors have been paid off, the surplus is to be paid, in cash, as a distribution. § 4-47-812(b). Aside from the default rule that payments are to be made in the form of cash, this section does not describe how distributions are to be shared, but the main section on distributions specifies that "[a] distribution by a limited partnership must be shared among the partners on the basis of the value, as stated in the required records when the limited partnership decides to make the distribution, of the contributions the limited partnership has received from each partner." § 4-47-503. Although seemingly mandatory, this provision is subject to the contrary agreement of the parties. Normally, however, liquidating distributions would be presumed to be shared and paid in the same way as interim distributions. Other arrangements are, of course, quite possible, but a tax advisor should definitely be consulted before unusual allocation and distribution provisions are included in a partnership agreement.

The first two subsections of this statutory provision therefore deal with how assets of the limited partnership are to be shared, and in what order. The next subsections cover the situation in which there are insufficient partnership assets to cover the claims of creditors. (Partners receive liquidating distributions only out of the amounts left over after creditors are paid, so if the partnership has nothing left over, they will not be entitled to any distribution.)

In the event that the limited partnership is unable to satisfy all of its obligations to creditors, all persons who were general partners when the obligation was incurred and who have not been

---

[85]   § 4-49-204(b)(1).

released from liability must contribute to the limited partnership to enable it to meet its obligation. § 4-47-812(c)(1). Each such person is liable "in proportion to the right to receive distributions in the capacity of general partner in effect for each of those persons when the obligation was incurred." *Id*. If someone does not contribute their required share, those partners who are contributing must cover the deficiency, in proportion to their right to share distributions in the capacity of general partner in effect of each of the persons still contributing as of the date the obligation was incurred. § 4-47-812(c)(2). Further additional contributions may be required in the same manner until creditors are paid in full. § 4-47-812(d). Anyone who makes an additional contribution under this provision may recover the extra amounts paid from the person who failed to make a required contribution. *Id*. Estates of deceased individuals are liable for obligations under these provisions. § 4-47-812(e). Obligations to contribute may also be enforced by either an assignee for the benefit of creditors of the limited partnership or a court appointed representative for creditors. § 4-47-812(f).

The only way to change these rules would be to have the limited partnership register as a limited liability limited partnership (LLLP) as described in the final section of this chapter.

V.10   Electing to become an LLLP

V.10.1   What is an LLLP

In the most simple terms, an LLLP (a "limited liability limited partnership") is a limited partnership that has elected to be a limited liability limited partnership under state law, in order to insulate the general partners in the business from the unlimited personal liability that was traditionally associated with the limited partnership form of business. Note that the new status does not turn the general partners into limited partners, and does not impact the existing limited partners. The form of business still needs to have at least one general partner (with presumptive management rights, apparent authority as a general partner, fiduciary obligations, and the absolute power to withdraw as a general partner) and at least one limited partner (who, absent agreement to the contrary will have virtually no management rights or power, no fiduciary obligations, and no right to withdraw from participation in the venture).

In Arkansas, a limited partnership can choose to be a limited liability limited partnership ("LLLP"), by the simple expedient of electing such status in the certificate of limited partnership. § 4-47-201(a)(4). The LLLP must have a name that indicates the business's status as an LLLP (§ 4-47-108(c)), but there is no other substantive difference in the document required to organize the business than that which is required for any limited partnership. The effect of this election is to eliminate personal liability of the LLLP's general partners (§ 4-47-404(c)). In essence, this is the only substantive difference between LLLPs and limited partnerships.

The limitation on personal liability for general partners is not absolute in an LLLP; general partners in this form of business still stand to lose any contribution, are still personally liable for personal fault, may be responsible if they execute a guarantee of a business debt, and can lose personal assets if the veil of limited liability is pierced. This option does, however, place general partners on a par with limited partners, and with owners in a business set up as either an LLP, an LLC or corporation.

The one particular potential disadvantage to the LLLP is that there are still a number of states that do not expressly recognize the LLLP as a valid form of business. While this may change over time as the newer ULPA is adopted more widely, it is still a matter of concern for businesses that may enter the stream of commerce in other jurisdictions. The issue of whether Arkansas law providing for limited liability of the general partners in an LLLP would be respected in the event of litigation arising out of injuries caused in a jurisdiction that simply does not recognize the LLLP has not been resolved. The risk that limited liability might not work creates a noteworthy limitation on this option for businesses that anticipate doing business across state lines.

V.10.2   How to Elect

A business that wishes to become an LLLP may do so either at the time the business is initially formed or any time thereafter by including the election in the certificate or amended certificate that operates as the organic organizational document of the business.

For a business that simply wishes to organize as an LLP from the outset, the certificate of limited partnership should specify that it is to be a limited liability limited partnership (as required by § 4-47-201(a)(4)) and should have a name that includes the phrase "limited liability partnership" or the abbreviation "LLLP" or "L.L.L.P." and must not include the abbreviation "L.P." or "LP". § 4-47-108(c), which is cross referenced in § 4-47-201(a)(1). All of the other requirements for filing a certificate of limited partnership (duplicate copies, appropriate execution, other information, filing fees, etc.) remain the same.[86] As of the date these materials were written, the fee to register as an LLLP was $50. § 4-47-1302(9).

---

[86]   See section V.1.2. of this Chapter for a fuller description of the requirements associated with filing a certificate of limited partnership.

If an existing limited partnership wishes to become an LLLP, it will have to do so by filing an amendment to its existing certificate. The amendment must be approved by a consent of all partners, presumably including limited partners. § 4-47-406(b)(2).[87] In order to effectuate the amendment, the amended or amended and restated certificate must be delivered to the Secretary of State. This document must have the name of the limited partnership ,the date its initial certificate was filed, the changes being made (which in this case would be an election to become an LLLP and a change in the name of the business). § 4-47-202. This particular kind of amendment must be signed by all of the general partners listed in the certificate. § 4-47-204(a)(2). The appropriate fee ($25 as of the date these materials were prepared) must also be sent. § 4-47-1302(a)(2).

One other provision of the statute relating to an amendment to become an LLLP is worth mentioning here. An existing limited partnership that elects to become an LLLP (or an existing LLLP that wishes to become a regular limited partnership) remains the same entity for purpose of holding title to or conveying interests in property and for all other purposes. § 4-47-1208. This means that the words or abbreviations "limited partnership," "limited liability limited partnership," "LP," "LLP," "L.P." or "L.L.P.," are interchangeable in a chain of title.

V.10.3   Termination of Election

An LLLP can elect to terminate an election in essentially the same way as an election is made. All partners must consent (§ 4-47-406(b)(2)), and then an amended or amended and restated

---

[87]   I use the word "presumably" because this section is supposed to deal with the management rights of "general partners," but subsection (a) talks about when consent of a majority of general partners is needed. Thus, subsection b seems to be talking about both general and limited partners rather than just general partners.

certificate must be filed (§ 4-47-202). This amendment would require a change in name to reflect that the limited partnership is no longer an LLLP, and must include an express statement to that effect. This amendment also needs to be signed by all general partners named in the certificate as amended or restated. § 4-47-204(a)(2). A filing fee ($25 as of the date these materials were written) is also required. § 4-47-1302(a)(2).

CHAPTER VI.   THE LIMITED LIABILITY COMPANY

VI.1. Background and Overview

Limited Liability Companies (LLCs) were originally created in order to take advantage of then-current tax regulations that allowed businesses to possess the corporate characteristic of limited liability for owners, but still obtain partnership tax status. The earliest state LLC statutes were modeled on partnership law except that members were offered the presumption of limited liability for business debts. Because partnership rules were not always ideal for operating businesses, and because the tax regulations then in effect allowed for businesses to look somewhat like a corporation and still be taxed as partnerships, statutory innovations allowed organizers a great deal of flexibility in moving along the spectrum toward possessing other corporate characteristics, such as centralized management, continuity of life, and free transferability of interests.   Eventually, those tax regulations (which had been known as the corporate resemblance test) became too time-consuming to administer, and the IRS abandoned that approach in favor of a simplified presumption that domestic, unincorporated entities would not wish to be taxed as corporations. Under the current rules, as explained in more detail in Chapter 3, multiple owner LLCs are presumed to be taxed as partnerships, and the LLC may have as many traditional corporate characteristics as it deems desirable without jeopardizing that presumption.   However, because the original statutes were modeled on partnership law (with the exception of limited liability), most default rules under the LLC Act continue to resemble the rules that traditionally applied to general partnerships.

Arkansas' LLC statute is codified at §§ 4-32-101 et seq., and is officially called the "Arkansas Small Business Entity Tax Pass Through Act." § 4-32-101. Virtually no one uses this nomenclature however, except in formal documents, and the statute is simply commonly referred to as the Arkansas LLC Act.

VI.2. Formation and the Operating Agreement

VI.2.1.   Formation and the Articles of Organization

An Arkansas LLC is formed by filing "articles of organization" with the Secretary of State. § 4-32-202. The articles of organization perform a similar function and contain similar information to articles of incorporation for a corporation or a certificate of limited partnership for a limited partnership. Like its corporate and limited partnership counterparts, the articles of organization will contain relatively little information. In fact, in most cases, the document will be a single page. The on-line form available from the Secretary of State is only one page long.[88]

The heart of the LLC is the "operating agreement," which, according to the Arkansas Act, "means the written agreement which shall be entered into among all of the members as to the conduct of the business and affairs of a Limited Liability Company." § 4-32-102(11) (emphasis added). Note that there are some interesting issues raised by this statutory language since, despite the apparently mandatory language about having a written operating agreement, the statutes do not expressly require than anything be in that written agreement. The interrelationship of the operating agreement and the provisions of the LLC Act is probably most akin to that between a limited partnership agreement and the

---

statutory provisions of ULPA (2001). The statutes provide rather complete models for the LLC and the limited partnership, but are, in a variety of places, expressly made subject to a contrary agreement by the parties.

In the case of the LLC, the LLC Act provides statutory "default" provisions with respect to most key issues. For many issues, therefore, the operating agreement may simply incorporate, either expressly or impliedly, the default provisions of the LLC Act. However, significant flexibility is usually allowed the parties to vary the statutory default approach by agreement.

As indicated above, an Arkansas LLC is formed when one or more persons sign and file "articles of organization" with the Office of the Secretary of State. § 4-32-201. That office has developed a standard form which can be used for this purpose. Be aware that the form was updated in 2011, so older printouts of the document may be somewhat out of date.

The basic requirements for filing articles of organization are as follows:

(1)   The articles of organization must be signed by one or more persons who need not be members of the LLC. § 4-32-201. The term "persons" for this purpose is liberally defined to include individuals, partnerships, other LLCs, trusts, estates, associations, corporations, other legal entities, and custodians and nominees. § 4-32-102(12). The person signing may do so as an attorney-in-fact. The name of the person signing and the capacity in which he or she signs should appear below the signature. § 4-32-204.

(2)   An original signed copy of the articles and a duplicate copy that may be a signed, photocopied, or conformed copy

must be filed with the Secretary of State. § 4-32-205. The Secretary's office will retain the original and return the copy, marked "filed." On-line filing is permissible, but not required.

(3)   The articles must comply with the requirements of the applicable statute. § 4-32-202.

(4)   If mailed in, the articles of organization must be accompanied by a filing fee of $50. § 4-32-1301(a)(1). For an electronic filing on line, there is a $40 filing fee and a $5 processing fee, for a total discounted rate of $45. § 4-32-1301(d)(1).

(5)   Unless the on-line services are used, the articles and filing fee should be mailed to:
>   Secretary of State
>   Attn: Corporations Division
>   State Capitol
>   Little Rock, AR 72201

Note that under the terms of § 4-32-206(a), "[u]nless a delayed effective date is recited in the articles of organization, a limited liability company is formed when the articles of organization are delivered to the Secretary of State for filing, even if the Secretary of State is unable at the time of delivery to make the determination required for filing by §4-32-1308." The Secretary of State is not required to, and historically has not kept, official records of when it receives articles that are mailed in–they are stamped filed when the Secretary of State agrees to accept them. If it is important to know exactly when the articles are delivered, either the on line filing system should be used, or articles should be mailed in with a return receipt requested. If the parties do wish to specify a delayed effective date, they need to do so in the articles, although the delayed date may not be more than

90 days after the date of filing. § 4-32-1308(f)(4).

The Arkansas LLC Act requires relatively little be included in the articles of organization, and is similar in this respect to the ULPA (2001) and the Arkansas Business Corporation Act, which also do not require that a great deal of information be included in the certificate of limited partnership and the articles of incorporation.

The articles must include the name of the LLC. § 4-32-202(1), cross referencing § 4-32-103. The name of a nonprofessional LLC may generally not be the same as or deceptively similar to the name of any other LLC, limited partnership, or corporation organized in or transacting business in Arkansas, or to a name that has previously been reserved by someone else. The name of a nonprofessional LLC must contain the words "Limited Liability Company" or "Limited Company" or the abbreviations "L.L.C.," "L.C.," "LLC," or "LC." "Limited" may be abbreviated as "Ltd." and the word "company" may be abbreviated as "Co." A name can be reserved in advance for a $25 fee. § 4-32-104. (Note that it is only necessary or desirable to pay this extra amount if your clients know in advance the name they want to use and do not want anyone else to take that name between the time they decide on it and the time the documents are ready for filing.)

The articles must also include the name of an agent for service of process and the address of the registered office of the LLC. § 4-32-202(2). This section cross references a provision in the Model Registered Agents Act, requiring that the organic document for an LLC include the name of an agent for service of process and, unless the agent is a commercial registered agent, an address for service of process. § 4-20-105(a).

Up until the 2001 legislative session, the Arkansas LLC Act required that the articles set forth the latest date on which the LLC was to dissolve. The requirement that this be included in the articles (which was apparently the result of a misunderstanding of the tax requirements in effect at the time the original LLC legislation was promulgated) was removed in 2001 although some older forms may still show that as being included. The current on line form no longer includes a space for even an optional maximum term for a domestic LLC, although the statute itself does make mention of the possibility that the articles could include a maximum term for the LLC. § 4-32-901(1).

The last provision in the articles of organization is only required if the management of the LLC is to be vested in one or more managers. If this is the case, the articles are required to include a statement to that effect. § 4-32-202(3).

The on-line form does not include room for any optional provisions, and the general section dealing with the articles of organization does not specifically mention optional provisions. On the other hand, there are a few references in the statute to terms that could be included in the articles, but are not required. One section mentions the possibility that the articles could set out a maximum term for the LLC (§ 4-32-901(1)); another suggests that the articles can give members the right to withdraw (§ 4-32-802(c)); a third suggests that the articles should be able to provide that the LLC will not continue for the default 90 day period if it ceases to have any members (§ 4-32-901(3)). Presumably these provisions could be included in the articles, although they are not mandatory.

Once filed, the articles of organization are subject to amendment or restatement. § 4-32-203. This assumes, of course, that the members can agree to the amendment in accordance with whatever terms the operating agreement may set for such action.

VI.2.2. The Operating Agreement

Buried amidst the harmless and generally helpful definitions section of the Arkansas LLC Act is the following language describing the LLC's "operating agreement": "'Operating agreement' means the written agreement which shall be entered into among all of the members as to the conduct of the business and affairs of a limited liability company." § 4-32-102(11). The problems with this provision are the inclusion of the word "written," and the apparent requirement that "all members" must enter into the agreement if it is one that governs "conduct of the business and affairs" of the LLC. While a careful review of the entire statute does not reveal anything that has to be in an operating agreement, these rules do specify that an LLC has to have one, and it apparently has to be in writing. § 4-47-102(11).

One fear is that failure to comply with the minimal statutory formalities associated with an LLC (including the statutory requirement of a written operating agreement) might increase the risk that the veil of limited liability will be pierced. As of the date these materials were written, however, only one reported case appears to involve a piercing attempt where an LLC failed to have a written operating agreement. In K.C. Properties of N.W. Arkansas, Inc. v. Lowell Inv. Partners, LLC, 373 Ark. 14, 280 S.W.3d 1 (2008), the court declined to pierce the veil of limited liability even though the owners of the LLC had apparently admitted in discovery that a number of formalities had been ignored, including failure to have an operating agreement, or to properly admit members, receive contributions, keep books and records, or maintain assets to pay for its own debts. 373 Ark. at

33, 280 S.W.3d at 16.[6]

In any event, in order to take a conservative approach to the issue, it would be quite advisable to prepare a written operating agreement. The obvious question would be what to include in such a document.

While the Arkansas LLC Act does not list anything that must appear in the operating agreement, there are a few written records that an LLC is supposed to keep at its principal place of business, and it makes sense to incorporate those into the operating agreement. Included in the list of information that is generally required to be kept (in addition to things like the operating agreement and various filings made in recent years) is the following: (1) alphabetical lists of current and a past members and managers, including full names, and the last known mailing address of each; (2) a listing of the amount of cash and a statement of the agreed value of other property or services contributed by each member and the conditions under which any additional contributions are to be made by each; and (3) a list of the events upon which the LLC is to be dissolved and its affairs wound up. § 4-32-405. Although these are supposed to be maintained, it is worth emphasizing that the statute specifies that failure of the LLC to keep or maintain these records shall "not be grounds for imposing liability on any member or manager for the debts and obligations of the limited liability company." § 4-32-405(d). In addition, while it seems desirable to include this kind of information in a single document such as the operating agreement, these are not the only provisions that could or should appear in an LLC's operational document.

---

[6]   A more recent Arkansas case awarded piercing, but the opinion includes no facts from which one could determine whether failure to follow formalities was important. Marx Real Estate Investments, LLC v. Coloso, 2011 Ark. App. 426 __ S.W3d __, 2011 WL 2368343 (2011).

As is the case with partnerships, it is possible to simply adopt the default rules, and have an extremely brief agreement explaining how the business is to run. However, even if you (as an attorney) have ready access to the statutes and are familiar with the default rules, clients are unlikely to have the same access or familiarity. It therefore makes sense to set out in one place a relatively complete understanding and agreement about how the business is to run. This also has the benefit of forcing clients to focus on the various rules that they might not otherwise consider or understand.

Before listing the provisions that might be included in an operating agreement, it should be pointed out that there are a number of provisions in the Arkansas LLC Act that are expressly made subject to contrary provisions in the operating agreement. Oddly enough, some of these sections make no mention of any requirement that this kind of provision be in writing, while others specify that the default rule may only be changed "in writing" in an operating agreement.

For example, the management of the affairs of the limited liability company are to be managed by a majority of the members, "unless otherwise provided in an operating agreement." § 4-32-401. The duties of members and managers are set out in the statute, again "[u]nless otherwise provided in an operating agreement." § 4-32-402. An operating agreement can change the obligation of members to make promised contributions. § 4-32-502(b), (d). Removal of members may be as provided in the operating agreement. § 4-32-802(a)(3)(A). The operating agreement may also allow a member to withdraw, although the default rules would not allow that prior to dissolution and winding up of the LLC. § 4-32-802(c). Dissolution may also occur as provided in an operating agreement. § 4-32-901.

On the other hand, most of the default rules that are made subject to the operating agreement specifically require that the contrary provision be in writing. For example, the statute sets out default voting requirements to authorize certain actions, but with regard to the vote required to amend an existing operating agreement or to authorize an act that would otherwise violate an existing operating agreement, the statute says that any change in the vote required must appear "in writing in an operating agreement." § 4-32-403(b). Similarly "[a]n operating agreement which is in writing" may change the liability of members and managers for monetary damages for breach of duty, or provide for indemnification. § 4-32-404. The list of records and information that is required to be maintained by the LLC is itself subject to contrary provisions "in writing in an operating agreement." § 4-32-405(a). It also takes a written provision in the operating agreement to change the default rules regarding sharing of profits. § 4-32-503. Assignment of membership interests may be governed by written provisions in an operating agreement. § 4-32-704. The rights of assignees to become a member are also subject only to written provisions. § 4-32-706. Admission of members generally is governed by a written operating agreement. § 4-32-801. Unless an operating agreement provides otherwise in writing, a member can be removed by a majority vote of members if he or she has assigned all of his or her membership interest. § 4-32-802(a)(3)(B). (This mention of the "writing" requirement is especially odd since the preceding subsection says merely that members may be removed as provided in the operating agreement, with no mention of a writing requirement. § 4-32-802(a)(3)(B).) There are a number of other default rules governing dissociation of members, most of which are subject to "written" provisions in the operating agreement. § 4-32-802. The procedure for winding up a dissolving LLC may be changed from the default rules "in writing in an operating agreement." 4-32-903. Virtually the entire topic of distributions is subject to the operating agreement, with some of the statutory provisions saying that a contrary agreement has to be in writing and some of them being silent about any such requirement. §§ 4-32-601 to- 603.

The primary concern about this drafting inconsistency is that it gives the impression that an oral modification to an operating agreement might be acceptable as to some kinds of provisions. However, because the definitions section of the LLC Act says that an operating agreement must be in writing, this result is not at all certain. By far the best advice, until Arkansas' statute is updated, would be to have the operating agreement and all amendments made in writing.

So what should an operating agreement include? An LLC's operating agreement is much like a partnership's partnership agreement, and can cover a long list of topics. If you are responsible for drafting one, you might want to consider the following substantive subjects (in addition to normal drafting considerations like an appropriate document name, table of contents, definitions section, date, signatures, etc.):

*Name of LLC
> Keep in mind the requirements under Arkansas law for naming an LLC, and remember that merely forming a business under Arkansas law does not register that name as a tradename or prevent its use in other jurisdictions.

*Names and Addresses of Members
> Under Arkansas law, an LLC should have a list of current and past members, organized alphabetically, along with the last known mailing address of each member. To avoid or minimize the necessity of amending the entire document every time the list of members changes, it might be desirable to keep these lists as attachments or exhibits to

the main agreement.

*LLC's Purpose

Many operating agreements list a purpose for the LLC, which may be either informational or limiting, depending on the nature of the LLC. Particularly in the case of a manager-managed LLC, if the members want to restrict the power of managers to conduct business other than that related to a particular purpose, this may be an important provision. It may also be appropriate to include in this section any limitations on members' rights to engage in activities that might be seen as competing with the LLC.

*Addresses and Agent for Service of Process

Arkansas requires that every LLC have a designated office and an agent upon whom service of process may be had, together with an address for such person, unless it is a commercial registered agent in this state. This need not be in the agreement itself, and because it is also subject to change, it might be desirable to include this in an exhibit, attachment, or other addendum, to make amendments simple to do. One reason for including this in the agreement is to help remind non-lawyer members that when the information relative to service of process changes, it is a good idea to not only amend the agreement but also to update the required filings as well.

* Initial Contribution of Members

Arkansas law also requires that the LLC maintain a list of the contributions and agreed-upon value of all non-cash contributions at the principle office for the LLC, although failure to keep this information is not supposed to be grounds for imposing liability on members or managers. Because members may be added or may leave, this is also the kind of information that it might be advisable to include on exhibits or attachments. Ideally, for each member, the agreement should include the date of the contribution, a legal description of the contribution, its agreed-upon value, and the effect of failure to comply with any terms of the agreement to contribute (this is particularly important if a contribution takes the form of a promise to pay or perform services over time).

*Any Agreement about Additional Contributions

The default rule in Arkansas is that members are not required to make additional contributions beyond the amounts originally agreed to, so if the members want to provide for additional contributions, the procedure for making or requiring additional contributions should be spelled out, along with effect of failure to make a required additional contribution.

*Allocation of Profits and Losses

In an Arkansas LLC, the presumption is that profits and losses are shared equally by all members, as is the case with general partnership. This is a rule which may surprise some clients and may frequently be different from what they want. Most investors will want and expect their return to be based on the value and timing of their contributions, and if this is the case, the operating agreement should spell out how profits (and losses, for tax purposes at least) are to be shared. Setting up an LLC so that members receive units or interests in exchange for their contributions, and then share in profits and losses based on the number of units or interests purchased, may be more likely to coincide with clients' interests or expectations. If the LLC is going to have special allocations, which happens when the allocation of a particular kind of gain or loss differs from the usual way in which allocations are made between the members, that should be spelled out as well, after consultation with a tax advisor because there are very complicated rules applicable to special allocations.

*Distributions

The operating agreement can spell out when distributions will be made, when they are required, who decides on timing and amount, if there are any limitations of distributions, and also any rules applicable to advances draws or loans made in anticipation of distributions. In the absence of any specific provisions, the members (or managers in a manager-managed LLC) would presumably have authority to decide on distributions as part of their general management authority.

*Salaries

Members who are also employees may want to have their salary arrangements approved in the operating agreement or at least have the agreement mention that members who act as employees shall be entitled to receive salaries. The distinction between salary and return on investment can have tax consequences, and should definitely be reviewed with the clients' tax advisors.

*Management and Control of Business

The default rule for LLCs is that all members share management authority equally, and that every member has a single vote on management decisions regardless of the relative value of contributions or the share that each might have in profits. The default rules also give all members apparent authority to make decisions on behalf of the LLC, which might result in the company being bound by acts that were not actually authorized but look to outsiders like they were in the ordinary course of the LLC's business. The LLC Act does give Arkansas LLCs the option of electing manager-management, by including a provision to that effect in the articles of organization. If this option is chosen, the operating agreement should specify who the managers will be, how long they will serve, how they are removed, replaced ,or supplemented, their voting powers, and any limits on their actual authority. In addition, the agreement should establish any required formalities for decision-making by either the members or managers (as the case may be) because the statutes do not set out much in the way of procedural requirements, and clients will generally appreciate having such guidance. Notice, meeting, quorum, and voting requirements should be considered. The agreement should also specify what kinds of records of decisions should be made and kept. If there is an expectation that certain members or classes of member must spend a certain amount of time managing the business, this should also be in the agreement. This might also be an appropriate place to include authorization for or prohibition against outside or competing activities, depending on client needs and preferences.

*Duties of Members and Managers

Under current Arkansas law, default rules provide that members in a member-managed LLC and managers in a manager-managed LLC are liable to the LLC and other members only for "gross negligence or willful misconduct." They are also bound to account for profits and benefits derived from transactions connected with the conduct and winding up of the LLC and use of the LLC's confidential or proprietary information. If the parties wish to change these default rules, the operating agreement should specify the level of care expected. For example, although common law might already provide this result, it might be desirable to specify that all contractual obligations will be fulfilled in a manner consistent with the obligations of good faith and fair dealing. This would be consistent with the level of care expected of those with management responsibilities in most other forms of business. This might also be an appropriate place to add any language about indemnification or the extent to which persons with management power will be liable for monetary damages to the LLC or other members.

*Adding Members

At some place, the agreement should address how new members can be added to the LLC. The agreement should specify who must agree to the new member and should set out any minimum qualifications before a new member can be accepted. The impact of new members should also be addressed, which means, for example, explaining how the addition of a new member affects distribution or allocation of profits and losses, and voting rights among all members. Note that this kind of information needs to address both members who contribute directly to the LLC as well as those who are transferees of membership interests seeking to be accepted as members. If there are limits on the addition of new members in either of these situations (for example, a requirement that before the LLC issues units or interests to new members, existing members must first be given the right to buy the units and thereby maintain or increase their share of the LLC's economic or managerial rights) or on the right of existing members to sell interests (such as an obligation to first offer their interest to other existing members) this would need to be in the agreement. Limitations and conditions on when members can be admitted, terms upon which payment can be accepted by the LLC, and the impact of new members on LLC rights and obligations should all be spelled out.

*Rights of Transferees

Following or accompanying the discussion of new members, the LLC agreement should include language discussing the rights of transferees who do not become members. It would probably be convenient to explain their rights to distributions and allocations, their informational rights, and any other rights that they might have, in the LLC agreement. If there are differences in the rights of different classes of transferees, such as transferees as a matter of law (for example, as part of a divorce settlement or foreclosure of a charging order entered on a debt owed by a member) or transferees who have in some way been agreed to by the other members, that would also need to be explained. Note that restrictions on the rights of transferees may not be binding on third parties without notice of such restrictions, and may not be effective as against transferees by operation of law such as judgment creditors of members.

*Withdrawal of Members

The agreement should address both voluntary and involuntary withdrawal of members. The consequences of death or incapacity and its effect on the LLC should also be mentioned. Rights of heirs should be covered as well, both in terms of rights to the economic interest and conditions under which they may be named as substitute members. Voluntary transfers, such as sale or gift of a membership interest, should also be covered. If the other members are to have a right of first refusal or an option to buy such membership interests, this should be specified. If not included in another section, limits on the right of purchasers to become members could be spelled out, even if the clients simply want to adopt default statutory rules. It is probably also important to consider involuntary transfers, such as those that might be ordered by a court in the event of divorce or bankruptcy. The rights of other members or the LLC to buy out membership interests in such a case could be set out.

*Termination of LLC

The agreement should spell out the circumstances under which the LLC will end. In fact, the Arkansas statute requires LLCs to keep a record of the events requiring dissolution at the LLC's principle office, so it makes sense to include that in the operating agreement. Events of dissolution and the process of winding up (including who has the authority to arrange to dissolution and any rules as to how it should proceed) should also be addressed. The agreement might also explain how participants are to be compensated for arranging the winding up of the LLC business.

*Amendment of the Agreement

This would include the process by which the agreement can be amended, the vote required, and whether amendments must be in a signed writing or may be proven by conduct or testimony about oral arrangements.

*Provisions Often Regarded as Boilerplate

This could include a wide variety of topics. For example, it is now common to include an arbitration clause in operating agreements, although this is, of course, completely optional with the client. Many operating agreements address relatively routine things like who will be the tax matters member, whether the books will be kept on the cash or accrual method, the fiscal year of the LLC, and where the LLC will bank. There may also be language stating that section headings are merely for convenience, that the plural includes the singular and vice versa unless the context clearly requires otherwise, and similar statements relevant to the interpretation of the document.

While not a comprehensive list of topics that might be covered in a LLC agreement, the preceding list at least gives an idea of what might be appropriately documented in a written agreement among the members.

VI.2.3.   Mandatory Rules

When advising clients, it might also be appropriate to emphasize to them the things that cannot be changed by agreement. Fortunately, as is the case with partnerships, there are relatively few rules that are not subject to contrary agreement of the parties. In fact, of all the available business options in Arkansas, the LLC is the most flexible. Because our current statute is not modeled on any uniform or model act, however, the non-waivable rules are not collected in one place, and each individual provision must be considered to determine whether the statutory rule is in fact subject to the contrary agreement of the parties.

Obviously, many of the requirements associated with executing and filing documents are mandatory and may not be changed by the members or managers of an LLC. The following items appear to fit in this category and do not appear to be subject to contrary agreement: name requirements for the business (§ 4-32-103); requirement of a registered agent and office (§ 4-32-202(2), cross referencing § 4-20-105(a)); requirements about who may sign documents to be filed (§ 4-32-204), although the statute does change the rules depending on whether the parties have elected member or manager management; fees (§ 4-32-1301); and general filing requirements (§ 4-32-1308).

There are also a handful of provisions relating to the operation of the LLC, or rights of members, that do not appear to be subject to change by the members. For example, there is no provision in the LLC Act allowing members to agree to an oral operating agreement or to dispense with one completely. § 4-32-102(11) (defining operating agreement as the "written agreement which <u>shall</u> be entered into among all the members," emphasis added). The operating agreement may not take away the rights of members to inspect and copy LLC records (§ 4-32-405(b)), although the operating agreement can change what records are required to be kept at the LLC's principal place of business. It does not appear that the operating agreement can remove the right of members to petition for dissolution. § 4-32-902. The right of the LLC to sue in its own name is not made subject to the operating agreement (§ 4-32-1101), and the members do not appear to be free to change the governing law applicable to a domestic LLC. § 4-32-1314

Not surprisingly, many of the topics that address rights of third parties may not be modified. For example, members may not change the apparent authority of those with management power to bind the business by acts that appear to be carrying on the ordinary business of the LLC (§ 4-32-301), although they may change who has the apparent authority by choosing between the member-management and manager-management models. Liability of the LLC to third parties may not be changed. § 4-32-309. Nothing in the statute allows an operating agreement to limit the rights of a member's judgment creditor to obtain a charging order on that person's membership interest. § 4-32-705. Priority of creditors to payment upon winding up of the business is another provision that does not appear to be subject to contrary agreement by the members. § 4-32-905.

For the most part, however, the remaining subjects addressed in the Arkansas LLC Act, including management, sharing of profits and losses, sale of membership interests, addition of new or substitute members, dissociation of members, events triggering dissolution and winding up, and even the process of winding up, may be changed by agreement of the parties. The following materials focus on the default rules, but it should certainly be kept in mind that these are generally subject to contrary agreement in order to meet the needs and preferences of clients desiring to form an Arkansas LLC.

VI.3. Management, Authority, and Fiduciary Duties

Most forms of business come with a pre-set management model. Partnerships are managed by the general partners, and it is not possible to eliminate the power of those partners to bind the partnership by acts that appear to be carrying on the business of the partnership (although actual authority may be taken away from one or more of the partners and may be delegated to others). This rule is true for traditional general partnerships, LLPs, limited partnerships, and LLLPs. The corporation is even more rigid, generally requiring that all management authority be exercised by or under the authority of a board of directors (§ 4-27-801(b)), although there is at least the possibility of changing this in the articles of incorporation for corporations having fewer than 50 shareholders (§ 4-27-801(c)). The LLC statutes, however, build in two distinct management models that the members or organizers are free to choose between, the member-management model and the manager-management model. In addition, it is possible to have a hybrid model where the articles of organization set out one choice, but the operating agreement varies from the default rules. Each of these options will be discussed separately.

VI.3.1.   The Member-Managed LLC

While the Arkansas LLC Act provides a great deal of flexibility in terms of choices among different management models, if nothing is said in any of the parties' documents or agreement, the members will retain management authority, just as general partners do in a general partnership. In other words, if the parties do not agree otherwise, an LLC will be member-managed, with all members having equal rights to participate in management. § 4-32-401(b), cross referencing § 4-32-301. All members also have apparent authority to manage the business under this model. § 4-32-301(a).

If you are called upon to create an LLC for clients, it is important to keep in mind that under the default model "every member is an agent of the limited liability company," and every member has the power to bind the entity to any act "apparently carrying on in the usual way the business or affairs of the limited liability company." § 4-32-301(a). This means that a member who lacks actual authority from the other members can nevertheless, by individual action, bind the LLC, which may or may not be a risk that the members of an LLC are willing to take. This should be a major business consideration in choosing a management model for an Arkansas LLC. Note that while the LLC may have a cause of action against a member who acts contrary to the limits of such member's authority, this may be of small consolation if the member does not have the financial resources to pay for any damages incurred by the LLC. In addition, such cause of action is only likely to arise if the member was grossly negligent or engaged in wilful misconduct. (On the other hand, if manager-management is chosen, all managers will have this apparent

280

authority, but at least the parties can specify who will act as managers.)

The default rules governing voting of members in a member-managed Arkansas LLC provide that, as to most matters, "the affirmative vote, approval or consent of more than one-half (1/2) by number of the members . . . shall be required to decide any matter connected with the business of the limited liability company." § 4-32-403(a). The requirement of collective action does not necessarily apply with respect to actions which are "for apparently carrying on in the usual way the business or affairs of the limited liability company," because in this case a single member (in a member-managed LLC) has the ability to bind the company. § 4-32-301(a). An act by a single member outside the usual course of business would not bind the LLC unless the act was taken with actual authority, and such authorization would generally require collective action by the members.

While the usual rule is that such collective action may be taken by a majority in number of the members, the default rules also provide that a number of actions will require consent of all members. Unanimous approval of the members is required, under the default voting rules, to amend a written operating agreement (§ 4-32-403(b)(1)) or authorize any act on behalf of the LLC that contravenes a written operating agreement including any written provision which expressly limits the purpose, business, or affairs of the LLC (§ 4-32-403(b)(2)). In addition, a careful reading of the rest of the LLC Act reveals that under the default rules (i.e., unless the operating agreement provides otherwise), it also takes unanimous agreement of the members to do any of the following:
> (1) Compromise an enforceable obligation of a member to make a contribution to the LLC (§ 4-32-502(d));
> (2) Admit as a new member a person who acquires an LLC interest directly from the entity (§ 4-32-801(a)(1));

(3) Admit an assignee of an LLC interest from another member to membership in the LLC (§ 4-32-706(a));

(4) Retain a member as a member despite the occurrence of a number of specified "events of dissociation" which would otherwise terminate the member's membership in the LLC (§ 4-32-802(a)(4) -(10), covering events like bankruptcy, reorganization, death, incapacity, dissolution, or termination)); or

(5) Voluntarily dissolve an LLC (§ 4-32-901(2)).

The operating agreement may provide a lesser approval standard for any or all of these decisions, or may delegate authority to make any of these decisions to managers or others.

The language of the LLC Act is that virtually all of these actions may be authorized by the "affirmative vote, approval or consent" of the applicable members. § 4-32-403(a). The comment to the corresponding section of the Draft Prototype LLC Act,[7] from which this language was apparently derived, indicates that members may be deemed to have authorized an act by a course of dealing or even failure to dissent within a reasonable time, or in other words that "the members" . . . right to vote on an ordinary

---

[7]   Because there were no uniform or model LLC acts at the time Arkansas adopted its LLC statute, the original proponents of LLC legislation for Arkansas chose to model their bill on a preliminary draft of a statute that had been produced by the Working Group on the Prototype Limited Liability Company Act Subcommittee on Limited Liability Companies, of the Committee on Partnerships and Unincorporated Business Organizations in the Section of Business Law of the American Bar Association (report of November 19, 1992). (You can find the text of the draft prototype act in 2 L. RIBSTEIN & R. KEATINGE, LIMITED LIABILITY COMPANIES, (1992).) This subcommittee produced drafts of a Prototype Limited Liability Company Act, which include significant commentary (although none of that commentary has been cited by any Arkansas court in interpreting our statute). The last draft from the working committee was dated Mar. 4, 1992, but the Prototype LLC Act was never promulgated in final form, since the ABA Working Group agreed to stop work on the project at the request of the National Conference of Commissioners on Uniform State Laws (NCCUSL).

transaction may arise only if they manifest a difference of opinion regarding a proposed transaction." If members want to be guaranteed the right to vote on particular matters, ideally those matters should be spelled out in the operating agreement. If they are not, a dispute may well arise as to whether the members in fact "consented" to a particular act even without any formal approval. The one provision that does include a specific requirement of additional formality is that in order to admit a new member under the default rules, "written consent of all members is required". § 4-32-801(a)(1).

While LLC statutes in most states provide that members' voting power will vary with their relative contributions, this is not the default rule which has been adopted in Arkansas (and this is one reason why it is risky to use sample LLC forms from other jurisdictions). Arkansas, apparently agreeing with the rationale of the drafters of the Draft Prototype LLC Act, employs a per capita voting approach which is certainly easier to apply, but does not take into consideration the relative investment of members in apportioning voting rights. Under this approach, for most matters, approval of "more than one-half by number of the members" is required, and (as mentioned earlier) for certain acts, such as amendments to a written operating agreement or to authorize any act in contravention of a written operating agreement, "consent of all members shall be required."

By way of example, if A, B, and C form the ABC Limited Company, an Arkansas LLC, and do not include any provision on voting rights in their operating agreement, A, B, and C will have equal voting power, regardless of the amounts of their capital contribution. A, B, and C each get one vote on all LLC business matters, even if A contributed $10,000, while B and C each contributed no more than $1. This means that B and C could outvote A on any ordinary business decision, although A would have veto power over amendment to any written operating agreement or other matters requiring unanimity.

This apportionment of voting rights is, of course, subject to contrary agreement in a written operating agreement. One common way of altering the apportioning of voting rights would be to bring it into line with the members' investments. The major drafting concern if this alternative is chosen is in choosing a mechanism whereby the relative value of capital contributions can be determined readily and accurately. If an LLC is going to be operated informally, with different forms of consideration being accepted as capital contributions, this may be difficult to accomplish in a manner that is satisfactory to all concerned. On the other hand, the LLC Act requires a writing reflecting the assigned values of various forms of contributions, and voting rights could be apportioned on the basis of the relative values assigned to the contributions of the members. Even this approach would impose some accounting requirements, however, if the parties intend to adjust the relative values to reflect, for example, distributions to members that are not pro rata. In addition, this may not be a satisfactory allocation of voting power, since the level of risk associated with investment in the LLC may change over time. Another very common way in which voting rights might be allocated is to have members buy units or interests in the LLC, the price of which might vary over time, and to have votes based on the number of units or interests owned. It would even be possible to have different classes of units or interests, with different voting rights associated with each class. The possibilities are virtually endless, and the preferences and needs of clients should drive the eventual drafting of this kind of provision.

In addition to changing the default rules with regard to the apportionment of voting rights, the Arkansas LLC Act allows the members of an LLC to change the minimum votes or consent required in order to accomplish various actions. For example, there may be a business reason for requiring a super-majority vote or consent before certain decisions can be approved. There might be decisions that the parties want to have approved by a vote of at least 2/3 or 3/4, or a specified percentage of members (or of the outstanding units or interests). Alternatively, the members may wish to be able to amend the operating agreement or add new members with less than unanimous agreement. In this case, the operating agreement would be reducing the vote required under the default rules. Such changes are permitted, so long as they are included in a written operating agreement.

It may also make sense to look at what happens when the members act in ways that are contrary to the best interests of the LLC, or contrary to their actual authority. Generally speaking, management actions, under the default rules, fall into one of two categories: (1) actions which are apparently in the usual course of business, and (2) those which are not. As to the first category, members in member-managed Arkansas LLCs, who lack actual authority, can bind the LLC as to third parties without knowledge of the lack of authority. While the LLC <u>may</u> have a cause of action against a member for such an action, this is unlikely to be entirely satisfactory. First, such cause of action is only likely to arise if the member was grossly negligent or engaged in willful misconduct. Second, this option is only viable if the LLC does not have a provision eliminating monetary damages due from members or requiring indemnification of the member. Finally, the cause of action is worthless if the member does not have the financial ability to pay for any damages caused by the misconduct. In any event, the Arkansas LLC Act does not appear to permit an LLC to restrict this authority to bind the LLC by acts apparently in the usual course, except that the organizers can choose whether to give the power to members or managers.

VI.3.2.   The Manager-Managed LLC

The primary alternative management model for an Arkansas LLC is similar to the centralized management model of a corporate board of directors. Under this model, designated managers, who need not be members, are given exclusive power to manage the LLC. § 4-32-301(b). In this case, the managers, but not the members, have the apparent authority to manage the business. This option must be elected in the articles of organization.

The default rules governing voting of managers in a manager-managed LLC work in the same way as for members in a member-managed LLC, and provide that, as to most matters, "the affirmative vote, approval or consent of more than one-half (1/2) by number of the . . . managers . . . shall be required to decide any matter connected with the business of the limited liability company." § 4-32-403. There are no rules governing notice requirements, quorum, proxy voting, actual meeting requirements, or records that must be kept. If any of these formalities are expected or preferred by the parties, they should be incorporated into the LLC's operating agreement.

Note also, that as is the case with regard to members in a member-managed LLC, the typical requirement of collective action by a majority of the managers does not necessarily apply with respect to actions which are " for apparently carrying on in the usual way the business or affairs of the limited liability company," because in this case a single manager has the ability to bind the company. § 4-32-301(b)(2). An act by a single manager outside the usual course of business would not bind the LLC unless the act was taken with actual authority, and such authorization would generally require collective action by the managers (or members for certain kinds of actions).

Although managers have the power to make most decisions under the manager-management model, this is not true for all decisions. Under the default rules, members in a manager-management LLC still retain authority to make a number of decisions, and typically those require unanimous consent unless the operating agreement provides otherwise. Unanimous approval of the members is required under the default voting rules applicable to manager-managed LLCs, to do any of the following:

(1)   Amend a written operating agreement (§ 4-32-403(b)(1));

(2)   Authorize any act on behalf of the LLC that contravenes a written operating agreement including any written provision thereof which expressly limits the purpose, business or affairs of the LLC or the conduct thereof (§ 4-32-403(b)(2));

(3)   Compromise an enforceable obligation of a member to make a contribution to the LLC (§ 4-32-502(d));

(4)   Admit as a new member a person who acquires an LLC interest directly from the entity (§ 4-32-801(a)(1));

(5)   Admit an assignee of an LLC interest from another member to membership in the LLC (§ 4-32-706(a));

(6)   Retain a member as a member despite the occurrence of a number of specified "events of dissociation" which would otherwise terminate the member's membership in the LLC (§ 4-32-802(a)(4)-(10), covering events like bankruptcy, reorganization, death, incapacity, dissolution or termination); or

(7)   Voluntarily dissolve an LLC (§ 4-32-901(2)).

The operating agreement may provide a lesser approval standard for any or all of these decisions, or may delegate authority to make any of these decisions to managers. In addition, members retain the default authority to select and replace managers, although this takes a simple majority consent (by number) of the members rather than unanimity. § 4-32-401(c)(1).

While the statute offers very little guidance about the way in which managers are to operate, it does offer default rules governing the selection and removal of the managers. Normally, managers may be "designated, appointed, elected, removed, or replaced by a vote, approval, or consent of more than one-half (½) by number of the members." § 4-32-401(c)(1). The managers need not be members of the LLC, nor do they need to be natural persons. § 4-32-401(c)(2). In addition, unlike corporate directors whose terms are limited by statute, an LLC's managers "hold office until their successors shall have been elected and qualified," unless they resign or are removed before that time. § 4-32-401(c)(3). Because this default rule may be different from what is expected, particularly by clients who are familiar with the model of the corporate board of directors, these rules should be clearly explained, and alternative arrangements (such as limited or staggered terms for managers) discussed. Keep in mind that if the clients want even more certainty with regard to who will be managing the LLC, the right of members to remove managers without cause may also be modified, or a supermajority vote required for such removal.

VI.3.3.   Hybrid Management

Somewhat oddly, the LLC Act specifically contemplates an arrangement where the articles of organization and the operating agreement are not consistent with regard to who has management power over the company. Where there are inconsistencies (either the articles do not authorize managers but the operating agreement provides for them or the articles specify manager-management but the operating agreement gives actual authority to the members), the statute provides that as to persons other than members, the articles will control (§ 4-32-401(a)), but as to members the operating agreement will control (§ 4-32-401(b)). Because there will be different rules as to insiders and outsiders, and because these two possibilities bifurcate actual and apparent authority to at least some extent, these are generally referred to as "hybrid management" arrangements.

Recall that the default rule is a member-managed LLC where all members have apparent authority to bind the company by acts that appear to be carrying on the usual business of the LLC. If the articles do not specifically elect manager-management, the LLC's members will all have this apparent authority, and the operating agreement will not control as to persons other than members. However, as to allocations of actual authority between the members, the operating agreement can set up any management structure that the parties desire. Managers or officers or committees with specific roles are all possibilities that should be discussed with clients who are concerned about leaving all management decisions to a majority of the members. Particularly if there are a large number of members or they are widely dispersed, it may make day to day operations very difficult if actual authority is not delegated to representatives.

Alternatively, if the articles do specify manager-management, the managers will have apparent authority to bind the company by acts that appear to be carrying on the LLC's usual business. This is so regardless of how the operating agreement allocates actual authority or purports to limit the actual authority of certain managers to take certain actions.

Clients are generally free to set up any management structure they like, with the important caveat that the LLC's members will have apparent authority (if the articles say nothing about management), or the managers will have such power (if the articles provide for managers). There is no effective way to remove this apparent authority although clients can choose between giving the power to members or managers.

If the operating agreement is silent, the managers will be able to act if one-half by number of them give their vote, approval or consent to a particular course of action. § 4-32-403. There are no default rules for meetings, notice, quorum, formal voting, proxies, or records of action taken. If any of these issues are important to your clients, they should be covered in the operating agreement. It is particularly likely that unrelated investors will want to have some assurance that there will be actual and perhaps even regular meetings, and that records of actions taken might be kept and therefore available for inspection. Clients should, however, be counseled that informality is one of the advantages of the LLC form of business, and this benefit dissipates the more detailed the requirements for meetings and records are.

VI.3.4.   Duties   Owed   by   Those   with Management Authority

The Arkansas LLC Act provides that, absent agreement to the contrary in the operating agreement, neither members nor managers are to "be liable, responsible, or accountable in damages or otherwise to the limited liability company or to the members of the limited liability company for any action taken or failure to act on behalf of the limited liability company unless the act or omission constitutes gross negligence or willful misconduct." § 4-32-402(1). There is a separate provision (also subject to the contrary agreement of the parties) obligating members and managers to account to the LLC "and hold as trustee for it any profit or benefit derived by that person without the consent of more than one-half (1/2) by number of the disinterested managers or members, or other persons participating in the management of the business or affairs of the limited liability company, from any transaction connected with the conduct or winding up of the limited liability company or any use by the member or manager of its property." § 4-32-402(2). This duty to account specifically includes, without limitation, the use of "confidential or proprietary information" of the LLC and other matters entrusted to the member or manager. *Id.*

Although members with management authority and managers generally owe the same level of care to the LLC, if the LLC in question is manager-managed, a member who is not a manager "shall have no duties" to the LLC or other members "solely by reason of acting in the capacity of a member." § 4-32-402(3). Obviously, if the member in question acts as a manager or assumes responsibility beyond that of a member as such, this limitation would not apply.

Arkansas' current partnership statutes (for both general and limited partnerships) apply a similar level of care on partners, but both UPA (1996) and ULPA (2001) limit the power of participants to reduce the statutory duties of care and loyalty (although there are no statutory limitations on how much the standards might be heightened). There are no such limits in the Arkansas LLC Act. Thus, if the parties want to remove the duty of care or duty to account completely, there does not appear to be any statutory prohibition on this choice. While there is no statutory limitation on the power of parties to remove the duties imposed as a default rule under the statute, this does not necessarily mean that the courts would respect an agreement that purports to allow members to act in bad faith or in a manner inconsistent with the common law of fair dealing. These obligations are not necessarily imposed as a matter of statute, but as a result of the common law of contracts. Parties to contracts (an operating agreement or agreement between members or managers and an LLC are contracts) have generally been required to exercise their contractual obligations in good faith. A recent article makes a compelling argument for the retention of a "mandatory core of minimum decencies" under the LLC Act. Frances S. Fendler, *A License to Lie, Cheat, and Steal? Restriction or Elimination of Fiduciary Duties in Arkansas Limited Liability Companies*, 60 Ark. L. Rev. 643, 676 (2007). Not only would interpreting the LLC Act to require at least minimal standards help reconcile the law applicable to different unincorporated businesses in the state, but it seems a desirable result from public policy perspectives. *Id.* at 676-86. Of course, if the parties want to impose a stricter level of care, such as the obligation to act as an ordinarily prudent person under similar circumstances, they should be free to do this as well.

In addition to reducing the level of care required, the parties in an LLC are also free to relieve members or managers from liability for monetary damages to the LLC or other members. By including a provision in a written operating agreement, members of an LLC may "[e]liminate or limit the personal liability of a member or manager for monetary damages for breach of any duty provided for in § 4-32-402." § 4-32-404(1). If this does not go far enough, the statute also allows a written operating agreement to "[p]rovide for indemnification of a member or manager for judgments, settlements, penalties, fines, or expenses incurred in a proceeding to which a person is a party because the person is or was a member or manager." § 4-32-404(2).

VI.4. Liability of and Contributions by Participants in an LLC

An Arkansas LLC is a limited liability enterprise, which

means that its members and managers will not be personally liable for debts of the business simply because they act as such. The statute is actually broader than that, specifying that, with the exception of acts and omissions of those providing certain professional services, no "member, manager, agent or employee" of an LLC is "liable for a debt, obligation, or liability of . . . [the company], whether arising in contract, tort, or otherwise or for the acts or omissions of any other member, manager, agent, or employee." § 4-32-304. Instead, the LLC itself is "liable to third parties for its valid obligations." § 4-32-309.

Obviously, as is the case with other limited liability enterprises, this does not mean that a member or manager will never be personally liable even if the LLC is also liable. As will be discussed shortly, business owners may also be liable for their promised contributions (provided that the promise to make the contribution is otherwise enforceable). Similarly, owners can be liable if they guarantee a debt of the business. In addition, even if the members are not providing professional services, members may be held liable for their own conduct, and in this case their status as owner in a limited liability business will not shield their personal assets.[8] For example, if they act as agents of the business and in the course of acting, they commit a tort, they will be personally liable for any damage they inflict. The LLC may also be liable, for example, for negligent hiring or supervision, or under the doctrine of respondeat superior,[9] but the fact that the individual

---

[8]   See Scott v. Central Arkansas Nursing Centers, Inc., 101 Ark. App. 424, 434, 278 S.W.3d 587, 595-96 (2008), noting that while shareholders are "not ordinarily liable for the acts of their corporation or LLC," they "may be liable for their own acts or conduct."

[9]   The current Restatement of Agency specifies that "[a]n employer is subject to liability for torts committed by employees while acting within the scope of their employment." Rest (3rd) Agency § 2.04. "Employer" and "employee" are terms of art, designed to replace the old fashioned language of "master and servant" that was

actors are LLC members will not insulate them from responsibility for their own misconduct. Alternatively, if they act as agents for the business and fail to fully disclose the existence and identity of the principle, they can be liable as agents for an unidentified principle under traditional agency law rules.[10] Finally, if the veil of limited liability is pierced, the owners may also find themselves being held personally liable.[11]

Of the preceding possibilities, the only one that will be covered in more detail here is the obligation of members to make contributions. The reason for this is that the LLC Act has some specific rules governing contributions that may be important to explain to clients. The first is a specific authorization for the LLC to issue its members interests "in exchange for property, services rendered, or a promissory note or other obligation to contribute cash or property or to perform services." § 4-32-501. The remaining provisions all cover when such a promise may be enforced, how, and by whom.

---

found in earlier restatements of the law.

[10]   See, e.g., Oliver v. Eureka Springs Sales Co., 222 Ark. 94, 95, 257 S.W.2d 367, 368 (1953), applying the doctrine but using the phrase "partially identified principal," which was the language of the earlier restatements rather than the current Restatement (3rd) of Agency. In Beech v. Crawford, Not Reported in S.W.3d, 1999 WL 1031310 (Ark. App. 1999), the Arkansas Court of Appeals applied these principles without referring to the restatement or its terminology. The court stated: "It is the agent's duty to disclose his capacity as agent of a corporation if he is to escape personal liability for contracts made by him, and the agent bears the burden of proving that he was acting in his corporate, rather than individual, capacity." Id, citing 19 C.J.S. Corporations § 540 (1990). Liability was imposed because there was no evidence showing that the agent told the third party "that he was contracting on behalf of the corporation."

[11]   This issue is discussed in more detail in Chapter 8 of these materials.

The first of these requirements is that in order to be enforceable, a promise to make a contribution to an LLC must be in a writing signed by the member. § 4-32-502(a). Absent agreement to the contrary in the operating agreement, a member's death, disability, or other incapacity does not excuse failure to make a required contribution. § 4-32-502(b). Under the statutory default rules, a member who fails to make an enforceable contribution may be compelled, at the option of the LLC, "to contribute cash equal to that portion of value of the stated contribution that has not been made." § 4-32-502(c). In addition, although this is also subject to a contrary agreement, it takes unanimous consent of the members to compromise an enforceable obligation of a member to make a contribution. § 4-32-502(d). On the other hand, while the obligation may be enforced by the LLC, the only creditors who can enforce the obligation to contribute are those who have extended credit in reliance on the obligation or have otherwise relied on it after the written agreement to contribute has been signed. § 4-32-502(e).[12]

VI.5. Sharing of Profits and Losses; Distributions

VI.5.1. Profits and Losses Generally

From an individual member's standpoint, the economic claims of the member against the LLC may have paramount importance among all the issues with which the member will be concerned. Therefore, you will likely want to insure that these economic claims, above all other matters, are clearly defined and understood by clients seeking your assistance in organizing an LLC.

---

[12] Subsection (e) includes a misleading cross reference to an obligation to contribute pursuant to subsection (d). The actual obligation to contribute appears in subsection (a). § 4-32-502.

At the outset, it is probably worth focusing on the terminology utilized in connection with profits and losses. This is important in order to understand the statutes, advice you might get from a client's tax advisor, and in order to be able to communicate these issues back to your clients. A member's interest in profits or losses is generally referred to as the member's share, distributive share, or allocative share. All of these labels mean the same thing–this is the amount to which the member would have a claim if the LLC were to be liquidated and everything paid out. It is an important concept for both tax and economic purposes, as it will determine tax liabilities and will provide an approximation of the economic value of the membership interest. Actual payouts are referred to distributions–a cash distribution is paid (obviously) in cash and an in-kind distribution is where the LLC pays out some of its assets to members without first converting those assets to cash. Finally, remember that although an LLC is a distinct entity under state law, it will either be taxed as a tax partnership or as an association taxable as a corporation (usually the former). So for tax purposes, the LLC is typically a tax partnership, even though the "partnership" label means something different for state business law purposes.

A number of specific issues will have to be addressed, as a practical matter, at both the entity and member levels in order to fully assess the economic status of the LLC and any economic claims the members may have against it. At the entity level, determinations will have to be made as to the profits or losses of the entity for tax purposes, since these will have to be reported on federal and state income tax returns. If the LLC is classified as a partnership for federal income tax purposes, IRC § 703 requires the determination of an entity level "taxable income," and IRC § 6031(a) requires the filing of an entity federal income tax return. Under Arkansas law, an LLC will have the same tax status as they have for federal tax purposes (§ 4-32-1313), which is a change from prior law requiring LLCs with two or more members to be taxed as partnerships under state law.

The profits and losses of the entity in an economic sense, which may be different from the tax profits or losses, will have to be determined in order to present a complete picture of the financial resources to which creditors and members may lay claim. For example, the proceeds received by an LLC from a life insurance policy may not be included in computing profits for income tax purposes (IRC § 101(a)(1)) but these proceeds may constitute a significant addition to the assets of the entity. The operating cash flow of the entity will also have to be determined in order to assess what may be available for interim distribution to members at any particular time.

These same three general determinations will also have to be made from the perspective of individual members. Thus: (1) individual members will need to know what their reportable shares of profits or losses are for tax purposes, since they must take these into account in computing their separate income tax liabilities; (2) determinations will have to be made in some fashion as to the allocable share to each member of the economic profits and losses of the entity, since, for example, each member will want such member's share of both taxable and tax exempt income of the LLC; and (3) a determination will have to made as to the right each member has to share in particular distributions being made by the LLC to its members.

The operating agreement need not address any of this. Default rules are provided in the LLC Act as to distribution rights of members, and the Internal Revenue Code sets out similar presumptions as to the right to share in profits and losses for tax purposes. Other determinations can be made as a matter of sound accounting principles which need not be specifically addressed in the operating agreement. On the other hand, because of the paramount importance of these issues to most members, only the operating agreements of the most informal LLCs will likely remain completely silent as to these matters.

If the operating agreement is silent, the statutory default rules will come into play. This means that "each member shall be repaid that member's contribution to capital and share equally in the profits and assets remaining after all liabilities, including those to members, are satisfied." § 4-32-503. Because members have no personal liability for debts of the enterprise under normal circumstances (§ 4-32-304) there is no default rule for making members contribute to offset any excess losses. For tax purposes, however, losses would normally be allocated to the members in the same manner as profits.

All of this is, of course, subject to contrary agreement by the members of the LLC. Remember, however, that if there is a "special" allocation of either income or loss, the allocation might be disregarded if it does not have substantial economic effect. This matter is discussed in somewhat greater detail in the chapter on tax considerations,[13] but because this is a very complicated area of the tax code, and because individual tax situations will vary from client to client, it is always advisable to have clients consult with their individual tax advisors as to the consequences of any special arrangements with regard to allocations of profits and losses.

VI.5.2.   Distributions

Let us turn now from allocations to distributions, keeping in mind, of course, that the two are by necessity related. The

---

[13]   See Chapter 3 of these materials.

economic claims that a particular member, as a member, will have against the LLC will generally be discharged in one or both of two ways: (1) through sharing by the member in interim (non-liquidating) distributions made by the LLC to its members as such; and (2) through sharing in liquidating distributions. Liquidating distributions would occur either on the termination of a particular member's membership interest in an LLC that does not thereby dissolve, or as part of the general liquidation of a dissolved LLC. If you are called upon to draft an operating agreement for an Arkansas LLC, you should direct your clients to consider a number of basic issues. These would include: (1) the mechanism for determining how much in the aggregate is available for distribution on an interim basis; (2) the mechanism for determining how much of what is available for distribution in any given year may or must be distributed; (3) the mechanism for determining the manner in which the available amounts will be allocated among the members entitled to share in the distributions; and (4) the mechanism for determining when these distributions will be made.

Assuming the LLC is classified as a partnership for tax purposes, the tax rules governing partnerships and partners should apply to the LLC and its members. The discussion which follows makes this assumption unless otherwise indicated. The general rule which should serve as the starting point for an analysis of the taxation of LLCs is that a multi-member LLC will generally compute its taxable income or loss in the same manner as an individual, subject to specified exceptions. (Under current tax regulations a single member LLC is disregarded for tax purposes, so it would presumably compute its taxable income exactly like the owner, and if the owner happens to be an individual, the result would be akin to taxation in the case of a sole proprietorship.)[14]

If the parties fail to specify any of these things in their operating agreement, interim distributions of cash or other assets are to be shared equally among all members. § 4-32-601. Unless the operating agreement specifies otherwise, it takes a majority by number of members or managers, as the case may be, to determine the amount and timing of such a distribution. *Id.*, cross referencing § 4-32-403. A member who dissociates is normally entitled to receive, "within a reasonable time after dissociation the fair value of the member's interest" in the company as of the date of dissociation, based on the member's right to share in distributions. § 4-32-602. Finally, if the LLC itself is dissolving and the members have not agreed otherwise, members are to receive a distribution consisting first of the value of their contributions and second a portion of any assets remaining, in proportion to their respective rights to share in distributions. § 4-32-905(3).

Any or all of these default distribution rights can be modified by appropriate provisions in the operating agreement. These modifications can take a number of different forms: (1) distributions can be decided by a select group of members or managers; (2) distributions can be made mandatory in at least certain circumstances; (3) those with the power to order distributions may be directed to at least consider whether distributions are appropriate on a regular basis; (4) overall distribution rights may be determined in some manner other than on a per capita (equal) basis; (5) provision may be made for preferred distributions to some members; or (6) provision may be made for the sharing of particular items (e.g., the profit on the sale

---

[14] If you are unclear about what this means, Chapter 3 of these materials provides a general overview of partnership taxation.

of a particular property) in a manner that is different from the general distributions rights. The parties are generally free to divide up the economic pie of the LLC in whatever manner they choose, and the flexibility afforded here (a characteristic carried over from the partnership) is one of the most attractive features of the LLC. However, any variation from the default rules should be clearly expressed in the operating agreement.

Distributions are generally based on cash flow rather than "profits" in either an economic or tax sense. Some operating agreements may contain an express formula for determining the amount of cash flow available for distribution. Other agreements will not contain specific formula provisions, assuming instead, as a general matter, that the LLC will not distribute what it does not have, and that those charged with managing the LLC should generally have discretion to declare distributions as they deem advisable.

Equally important to the determination of the amount available for distribution is when the distributions are to be made. The LLC Act says this will be as provided in the operating agreement or as the members in a member-managed or managers in a manager-managed LLC may decide. In other words, there are no specific "default" provisions concerning the timing of interim distributions. The most informal way of handling the timing issue is to say nothing about it in the operating agreement. In that event, those in charge of management of the LLC, either members or managers, will decide when distributions will be made. On the other hand, the operating agreement may mandate that distributions be made when available cash flow will permit it. The availability of the cash flow could be assessed on whatever schedule the operating agreement provides, such as monthly, quarterly, etc.

The choice of whether to specify in the operating agreement when distributions are to be made may depend on whether the LLC is member-managed or manager-managed. If the LLC is being managed by representatives of the members rather than the members themselves, the members may be more likely to prefer that the operating agreement provide greater assurances that distributions will in fact be made with some regularity.

In the case of liquidating distributions by an LLC, the LLC Act protects the rights of creditors by giving them a higher claim to the LLC assets than members have and by generally providing that their claims will not be discharged before they are notified (actually or constructively) and given an opportunity to present their claims to the LLC. No express limitations are placed, however, on interim (nonliquidating) distributions made by the LLC to its members. For example, there are no provisions similar to those in the Arkansas Business Corporation Act which prohibit distributions by a corporation to its shareholders that would render the entity unable to pay its debts "as they become due in the usual course of business" or would render it insolvent in a balance sheet sense.

It is not logical to assume, however, that the LLC could circumvent creditors' claims by simply distributing assets to its members in interim distributions which would leave the LLC unable to pay those creditors' claims on dissolution. The Arkansas Fraudulent Transfer Act would operate to prevent any such strategy from being effective. This act gives creditors a variety of remedies, ranging from the right to avoid any transfers in violation of the act, to injunctions against future transfers and the appointment of a receiver. By its terms, the act makes a transfer fraudulent whenever the transfer is made with "actual intent to hinder, delay, or defraud any creditor" or where the transfer is made "[w]ithout receiving a reasonably equivalent value in exchange" and the debtor's assets were unreasonably small. § 4-59-204(a)(1)-(2). Even absent express guidance in the LLC Act, these standards do provide a limitation on interim distributions which should protect creditors' interests.

Assuming the LLC is taxed as a partnership, entity income, determined as of the end of the year, passes through for tax purposes to the members, who must report it, regardless of whether the tax profits have actually been distributed to the members. On the other hand, actual distributions which do not exceed a member's share of previously taxed profits should not produce additional taxable income to the member as a result of the distribution. This single tax approach is accomplished by providing that a member's basis in the entity is increased, at the end of the entity's taxable year, by the member's share of entity income, and decreased by actual distributions. On the other hand, an actual distribution to a member does not result in additional gain to the member, generally, except to the extent a cash distribution to the member exceeds that member's basis in the entity before the cash distribution is taken into account.

Although this was covered in the prior chapter on partnership taxation, it is worth repeating that the timing and nature of distributions can cause tax problems. Take this simple example. A/B LLC has $100,000 in tax profits at the end of 2010. If A and B are the sole members and they share profits equally, A and B will each report $50,000 of the LLC's profits, and will each increase their basis in their LLC interests by $50,000. If, for example, the LLC then actually distributes $50,000 cash to each in January 2011, the distribution would not exceed the previously taxed share of each, as represented by the increased basis of each in their interests in the LLC. No additional gain would be recognized on the distribution, and the basis of each in their respective entity interests would be reduced by $50,000. Assume this distribution brings the basis of each back to zero. Assume further than the LLC has enough available cash flow to make a further cash distribution to each on July 1, 2011, in the amount of $10,000 each. If this is an unconditional distribution to each, they would both recognize an immediate taxable gain of $10,000, since the cash distributed will exceed the zero basis of each in the company. On the other hand, if this July distribution is delayed until after the end of 2011, the members will be able to increase their basis in the LLC interests for their share of the 2011 profits before any recognition event, and assuming those shares were at least $10,000 each, no gain will be recognized with respect to the actual distribution.

Thus, generally, if an interim distribution during the year simply represents the undistributed share of previously taxed profits, no additional gain should be recognized on the distribution. On the other hand, if all previously taxed profits have already been distributed, and the interim distribution is from the current year's earnings, gain may be recognized if the interim distribution is unconditional. This problem is solved where the distribution against current earnings is clearly characterized as such as an "advance," or "loan," or "draw" against those current earnings. In this event, the interim distribution is tantamount to a loan which will be paid back out of earnings determined at the end of the year, and subject to repayment by the member to the extent those earnings are not sufficient to fully offset the earlier draw. The tax regulations provide that no distribution occurs with respect to a loan, draw, or advance, until such is canceled against earnings, which would take place after the members' earnings for the year have been determined, and after their bases in their entity interests have been increased to reflect such earnings. If the advance to a member does not exceed the member's profit share for the entire year, therefore, no additional gain should occur with respect to the actual distribution.

Thus, for example, if the $10,000 distributed to each A and B on July 1, 2011, is treated as an advance or draw against 2011 profits only, A and B would not be taxed on receipt of the advance on July 1. If the LLC has $20,000 of profits for all of 2011, A and B would report their $10,000 share each, as determined at the end of the year. The basis of each would increase by that $10,000. Then, when the $10,000 advance to each is canceled against the $10,000 share of 2011 profits allocated to each, the cancellation will be treated as a deemed distribution. No additional gain will be recognized on the deemed distribution since A and B will each have $10,000 of new basis in their LLC interests to offset the deemed distributions.

If you are called upon to include language in your clients' operating agreement that allows such preliminary, conditional payments, language like the following might work:

> A drawing account shall be established and maintained for each member. On the first business day of each month, the account shall be credited with 1/13th of that member's share of the prior year's net profits. On the first business day of each month, each member shall have the right to withdraw up to 100% of the amount in such member's drawing account. At the end of the LLC's fiscal year, each member's drawing account shall be credited with the additional amount, if any, equal to such member's share of profits for that year reduced by the sum of the amounts previously credited to his or her drawing account. If, however, such member's share of profits for that year is less than the amounts credited during the year, the account shall immediately be reduced by the amount by which amounts previously credited exceed such member's share of profits. At the end of each fiscal year, each member shall receive the amount, if any, equal to the share of profits for that year reduced by the sum of the amounts

withdrawn from such member's drawing account during the year. If, however, any member's share of profits for that year is less than the amounts withdrawn during the year, such member shall promptly repay the difference to the LLC. A credit balance in a member's drawing account shall be considered a debt of the LLC to that member, payable upon demand, and a deficit balance therein shall be a debt of that member to the LLC, payable upon demand. Except with the prior unanimous written consent of the other members, no member shall make withdrawals from his drawing account that will result in a deficit balance.

Obviously, this language will not work in every situation, for every client, but it provides a starting point for considering how such a provision might be included if the clients desire to provide for such payments.

There is a second tax-related issue regarding distributions from an LLC that is taxed as a partnership. Recall that members in such an LLC would be taxed when income is allocated to them; not when distributions are made (so long as the member has sufficient basis in his or her capital account to offset the amount that is distributed). This means that members may find themselves facing the obligation to pay taxes on income that they have not received and have no "right" to receive. This may be quite unpalatable to many clients or potential investors. To alleviate the burden of having to pay taxes in the absence of a distribution sufficient to offset such obligation, it is not uncommon for operating agreements to have a mandatory distribution provision sufficient to offset taxes. Such a provision might read something like this:

For each fiscal year, to the extent that the LLC has operating income sufficient to make such payments and to retain in its net reserves an amount equal to at least $_____ , each member shall be entitled to receive within 90 days after the end of such fiscal year a distribution equal to the product of (a) the net profits for that fiscal year, if any, allocated to that member and (b) the sum of (i) the highest marginal rate of federal income tax applicable to ordinary income for individuals for that fiscal year plus (ii) the highest marginal rate of state income tax applicable to ordinary income for individuals residing in Arkansas for that fiscal year, in each case determined without regard to phase-outs, alternative taxes and the like, and without regard to any other tax attribute of the individual member. Such tax distribution is an advance to help members pay their taxes resulting from LLC operations and is not intended to indemnify members against their taxes on income from the LLC.

This is <u>not</u> a perfect tax distribution provision and does not cover every conceivable circumstance. It is to be expected that your clients will have special needs, and you should consider a variety of factors in tailoring the operating agreement language to meet their needs.   You may wish to pay special attention to such issues as how mandatory these distributions should be, whether the distribution should be sufficient to pay minimum or maximum tax liability, whether and to what extent it should include potential liability for state taxes and if so which state, whether local taxes should be considered, whether prior losses allocated to a member should be considered in setting minimum distributions, whether interest needs to be paid on the distributions and if so when and at what rates, the timing of the mandatory distribution, whether it would be better to calculate the distribution based on net taxable income allocated rather than net profits (which might be especially important if there is built-in gain associated with property contributed to the partnership by one or more members), whether there should be quarterly advances to cover estimated tax payments, the effect of tax credits allocated by the LLC, whether the provision should continue in effect if the LLC has gone into liquidation, the impact of subsequent tax audits, etc. Each deal is different, and how you choose to address mandatory distributions to offset taxes should be rethought for every operating agreement you draft.

VI.6. Membership Interests

VI.6.1. Nature of Membership Interests

The LLC Act provides simply that a membership interest is "personal property." § 4-32-703. This does not appear to be subject to contrary agreement of the parties, presumably because it could impact the rights of third parties. Among other things, this provision means that transfers or assignments of membership interests need not comply with any statute of frauds requirement applicable to transfers of interests in real property, even if the only assets of the LLC are real estate. It also means that the way to perfect a pledge of a membership interest as security for a debt would be to treat the membership interest as personal property, even if the only underlying assets of the LLC are real property.

VI.6.2. Issuance of New Interests (Becoming a Member)

An LLC membership interest may be issued by the LLC in exchange for "property, services rendered, or a promissory note or other obligation to contribute cash or property or to perform services." § 4-32-501. In order to be enforceable, this obligation must be in writing, signed by the member. § 4-32-502(a). A person making a contribution may become a member at the time the LLC is formed, or thereafter, as provided in the operating agreement or under the statutory default rules if the operating agreement is silent.

The LLC Act specifies that an LLC can admit members directly either in compliance with the written provisions of the operating agreement or upon the written consent of all members. § 4-32-801(a)(1). Note that this is one of the very few places in the LLC Act where any specific formalities for action by the members are included; agreement to admit a new member under the default rules must be in a "written consent of all members." The effective date of admission as a member is the later of the date the LLC is formed, the time specified in the operating agreement, or (if the operating agreement does not provide) when the person's admission as member is shown in the LLC's records. § 4-32-801(b).

VI.6.3. Sales and Voluntary Transfers of Interests by Existing Members

The provisions governing how persons may join an LLC by purchasing a membership interest from an existing member are somewhat more complicated. While the members are generally free to modify the default provisions concerning how and what may be transferred, the default rules essentially bifurcate a membership interest into a transferable interest (which includes only the right to distributions) and the management and other rights associated with being a member. Somewhat confusingly, the statute says that (unless otherwise provided in a written operating agreement) an LLC "interest is assignable in whole or in part." § 4-32-704(a)(1). This is misleading, however, because even an assignment "in whole" merely "entitles the assignee to receive, to the extent assigned, only the distributions to which the assignor would be entitled." § 4-32-704(a)(2). It does not dissolve the LLC, cause the transferring member to dissociate as a member, or give the assignee any rights to participate in the management of the company. § 4-32-704(a)(3)-(4). The transferring member only ceases to be a member if the assignee is admitted as member (§ 4-32-704(4)) or if the transferring member is removed   in accordance with the operating agreement or statutory default rules (§ 4-32-802(a)(3)(B)). Assignment neither makes the assignee liable as member nor releases the transferor from any such liability. § 4-32-704(a)(5)-(6).

If the parties for some reason desire to have certificated ownership interests, the statute gives them the power to require that membership interests be evidenced by a certificate issued by the LLC. § 4-32-704(b). If such a provision is included in the operating agreement, it may also provide for the assignment or transfer of such interests. *Id.*

The default rule concerning how an assignee would become a member is that it takes unanimous consent of all members to admit an assignee as member. § 4-32-706(a). In addition, while a written operating agreement may change this rule, in the absence of a provision specifying how the consent is to be documented, the LLC Act requies that each member consent to the admission of the assignee in a signed writing. *Id.*

It is highly advisable to have clients consider modifying or explaining the effect of admission of assignees as members in their operating agreement, particularly if the LLC has adopted the default rules concerning sharing of profits and management rights. Remember that the default rule allows assignment "in part," which is fine so long as the assignee obtains only a partial interest in the profits that were originally allocated to the assigning member. If, however, the assignee is ever added as a member, he or she would automatically be presumed to share equally in profits of the business, and have an equal vote in the management under the default rules. This could cause some drastic and unanticipated changes in economic rights and voting power if the members were not fully aware of the impact of admitting the assignee of part of a member's interest to the LLC as member.

If an assignee is admitted as a member, he or she automatically gains the "the rights and powers and is subject to the restrictions and liabilities of a member under the articles of organization, any operating agreement" and the statutes. § 4-32-706(b). The new member also becomes obligated to make any required contributions that the transferring member would have had to make, but this obligation will not apply if the new member did not know of these obligations at the time of becoming a member and if the LLC's written records did not reflect the obligation. *Id.*, cross referencing the records required to be kept under § 4-32-405. Even if the assignee becomes a member, this does not release the transferring member from an otherwise enforceable obligation to make additional contributions. § 4-32-706(c), cross referencing § 4-32-502, dealing with required contributions.

VI.6.4.   Creditors and Charging Orders

Creditors of individual members of an LLC typically have little access to assets of the LLC. One possibility for them to recover against the LLC's assets is in the relatively unusual case of reverse piercing, which is addressed in somewhat more detail in chapter 8 of these materials. Absent facts sufficient to justify reverse piercing however, the LLC Act itself gives creditors only the right to obtain a charging order against the LLC.

The first step under the LLC Act is for the creditor to reduce his, her, or its claim against the member to a judgment, because only judgment creditors may proceed against the membership interest in this manner. The statute gives such judgment creditors the right to obtain a charging order against the debtor's membership interest. § 4-32-705. "To the extent so charged, the judgment creditor has only the rights of an assignee of the member's limited liability company interest." *Id*. In the simplest terms, a charging order works like a garnishment, with the LLC being required to pay to the creditor amounts that would otherwise have been distributed to the member, up to the amount of the judgment covered by the charging order together with any accrued interest. The charging order does not entitle the creditor to order distributions, to cause the sale of assets, or in any way to participate in the management of the LLC. The debtor, in fact, retains all of his or her management power and rights, unless the operating agreement provides otherwise. Under the statutory default rules, becoming a judgment debtor whose membership interest is subject to a charging order does not automatically entitle the other members to remove the debtor as a member.

In many ways, the provision for a charging order mirrors what can happen to partners who become judgment debtors. The judgment creditors may obtain a charging order under UPA (1996) for general partnerships and LLPs (§ 4-46-504) and ULPA (2001) for limited partnerships and LLLPs (§ 4-47-703). Both of these statutes, however, provide significantly more detail about the charging order than is present in our LLC Act. Under both UPA (1996) and ULPA (2001), the charging order works like a lien, may be bought out at any time prior to foreclosure by other partners or the partnership, and may be foreclosed upon. § 4-46-504(b)-(c) (for general partnerships and LLPs) and § 4-47-703(b)-(c) (for limited partnerships and LLLPs). The LLC Act has none of this detail. The LLC Act also does not specify that charging orders are the exclusive remedy, as do both of the Arkansas partnership statutes.

The issue of whether charging orders are an exclusive remedy under our LLC statute is not one that has been addressed by the Arkansas courts in any reported decision to date. Charging orders were created as a creditors' remedy under the original uniform general and limited partnership acts, in order to protect such partnerships from potential disruption by creditors of individual partners. UPA (1914) § 28; ULPA (1916) § 22. "The charging order became the judgment creditor's 'exclusive' (and, emphatically, indirect) access to those assets. That is, a judgment creditor of a partner had no rights whatsoever in the assets of the firm but was exclusively remitted to collecting whatever income stream those assets might produce for the judgment debtor."[15]

It is not, however, accurate to assume that the holder of charging order has traditionally had to sit around indefinitely waiting for distributions that are never ordered. At least under partnership law, the creditor could elect to foreclose on the charged interest. UPA (1914) § 28(2), permitting redemption "at any time before foreclosure." The foreclosed interest holder becomes entitled to all the rights of an assignee, but also becomes potentially subject to adverse tax consequences. One who forecloses on a partnership interest, although a mere assignee and not a partner under state law, is considered a partner for federal tax purposes. Rev. Rul. 77-137, 1977-1 C.B. 178. This means the purchaser at the foreclosure sale becomes liable for income that is allocated to that interest, even if it is not actually distributed. Although there is no direct authority from the IRS on point, the general assumption seems to be that the mere holder of a charging order is not a partner for tax purposes, and thus is only liable for tax on income actually received.

---

[15]   Daniel S. Kleinberger, Carter G. Bishop, Thomas Earl Geu, *Charging Orders and the New Uniform Limited Partnership Act Dispelling Rumors of Disaster*, 18 Prob. & Prop. 30, 31 (2004).

Presumably, even though the Arkansas LLC Act does not specify, a charging order on a member's interest could be foreclosed. If this is not a possibility, creditors' rights could be limited quite dramatically, as there would then be no mechanism by which the holder of a charging order could oppose the decision of an LLC not to order distributions. It should be emphasized, however, that the availability of foreclosure for a charging order under current Arkansas law is not certain. In addition, because of the risk of adverse tax consequences, it is not entirely clear that it would be desirable in every case. Without it, however, the rights of creditors as expressly outlined in the statute are extremely limited. What, then, about other potential creditor's remedies?

In Olmstead v. Federal Trade Commission,[16] a recent, highly publicized and much-criticized opinion, the Florida Supreme Court found that a charging order was not the exclusive creditor's remedy under the Florida LLC statute. The statute in question reads much like the equivalent provision under Arkansas law, providing for a charging order but not specifically indicating whether the remedy was to be exclusive.[17]   The creditor in Olmstead, the FTC, was not satisfied that a charging order would adequately protect its interest and asked the court for a more vigorous remedy. The Florida Supreme Court ultimately agreed that a charging order would not fairly protect the creditors and therefore ordered the members (the Olmsteads) to sign over to the FTC all their "right, title, and interest" in each of their single

---

[16]   44 So.3d 76 (Fla. 2010).

[17]   Fla. Stat. Ann. § 608.433(4) (West 2007) states: "On application to a court of competent jurisdiction by any judgment creditor of a member, the court may charge the limited liability company membership interest of the member with payment of the unsatisfied amount of the judgment with interest ...."

member LLCs.[18] The actual holding of the case, as stated by the court, was that "the [Florida LLC act's] statutory charging order provision does not preclude application of the creditor's remedy of execution on an interest in a single-member LLC." [19]

There are important parallels between the statutory law that was under consideration by the Olmstead court and that in Arkansas. As is the case in Arkansas, the Florida partnership statutes contain a provision making the charging order the exclusive remedy, while the Florida LLC statute does not. The Florida LLC act allows for single member LLCs, and because the sole member can give "unanimous" approval to the admission or substitution of any other member, it is not inaccurate to think of such LLCs as having freely transferable membership interests. This is also the rule in Arkansas. In deciding that the charging order was not the exclusive remedy for the sole member's creditor, the Florida Supreme Court specifically commented on the differences in statutory language between the partnership and LLC statutes (which also exists in Arkansas), and also addressed the potential unfairness that could arise if a charging order were the only remedy for creditors of the member of a single member LLC.

The opinion does not address whether charging orders are the exclusive remedy for LLCs that are not owned by a single member. It does not discuss the possibility that membership interests may be made freely transferable in other kinds of LLCs, or what happens if there are technically multiple members but they are bound by familial or contractual ties. It does, however, clearly raise the possibility that the statutory charging order will not be the exclusive remedy for creditors of LLC members in Florida,

---

[18]   Olmstead, 44 So. 3d at 83.

[19]   Olmstead, 44 So. 3d at 78.

because the LLC statute does not make it exclusive. To the extent that Olmstead may be considered persuasive authority in Arkansas, this is therefore an issue that may be very important to discuss with clients.

It should also be noted that there is a strongly worded dissent criticizing the result in Olmstead. In addition, academic commentary about the opinion has generally been quite critical of the result. It is also unclear if Arkansas courts will agree with the reasoning of the Florida court and extend creditor's remedies beyond the charging order that is expressly mentioned in the LLC Act. However, there is at least the possibility that additional remedies will be available, which does potentially limited the asset protection function that the LLC had previously been thought to offer.

VI.7.   Leaving the LLC (Dissociation)

VI.7.1.   Effect on the LLC

Under traditional partnership law, dissociation of a partner triggered at least technical dissolution of the partnership. The remaining partners often had the right to continue the business, but the "association" of the original partners itself would no longer be in existence. There was therefore an uncomfortable divergence between the very technical meaning of "dissolution" under the UPA (1914) (it was defined as the change in association caused when any member dissociated, and did not indicate whether the business itself was to continue) and the meaning of that word in other contexts.

More recently, the partnership statutes have moved away from treating the partnership as a mere association of persons and now recognizes that the business itself, for most purposes at least, has a separate identity and existence. Fortunately, the LLC Act, although generally modeled after general partnership law, does not conflate dissociation and dissolution in the same way as partnership law traditionally did.

In the context of the LLC, the LLC Act sets out events of dissociation (which are the events upon which a member will cease to be associated with the LLC as a member). § 4-32-802. These may or may not trigger dissolution of the LLC under the separate section on that topic, which lists the events upon which an LLC "is dissolved and its affairs ... wound up." § 4-32-901.

The remaining subsections of this topic focus on the events that trigger dissociation of members. The triggers for dissolution and winding up, and the actual process of winding up, as described in the LLC Act, are set out in the last section of this chapter.

VI.7.2.   Events that Cause Dissociation

A member in an Arkansas LLC, under the statutory default rules, ceases to be a member (or in other words dissociates) upon any of the following events: (1) the member withdraws in accordance with the articles or operating agreement; (2) the member sells his or her entire interest, and the assignee is accepted as a member as to the entire interest; (3) the member is removed as a member in accordance with the operating agreement; (4) there is an affirmative vote of a majority of the members removing a member for transferring all of his or her interest in the LLC (regardless of whether the assignee becomes a member); (6) the member becomes bankrupt or insolvent, as such terms are defined in the statute; (5) 120 days expire after the member seeks reorganization, liquidation, has a receiver appointed or equivalent proceedings are initiated; (67 the member dies or is adjudicated incompetent; or (8) a non-individual member dissolves and winds

317

up, terminates, or (for estates) distributes all of its assets, except for a corporation which has its charter revoked (in which case the corporation has 90 days to reinstate the charter before it is automatically dissociated from the LLC). § 4-32-802. The LLC statute specifically provides, however, that the operating agreement can provide additional events of dissociation, and in all of the preceding cases, the operating agreement can also eliminate the event of dissociation from the list or provide circumstances under which the other members can vote to excuse what would otherwise result in dissociation of the member. In some cases, the statute itself sets out a vote by which the remaining members, or some of them, may vote to avoid the dissociation of the member.

Some of the language of the Arkansas statute seems questionable. For example, the statute currently says that death is an event of dissociation "[u]nless otherwise provided in writing in an operating agreement or by the written consent of all members at the time. . . ." § 4-32-802(6). Frankly, it is difficult to understand how death can be waived as an event of dissociation. This provision also seemingly conflicts with another section of the LLC Act which says that upon a member's death, the member's executor or other legal representative "shall have all of the rights of an assignee of the member's interest." § 4-32-707. This section is not made subject to the contrary agreement of the members.

There are, however, some of the default rules concerning dissociation that clients seeking to form an LLC may wish to reconsider. For example, the members may wish to be able to waive an event of default with something less than the written consent of all members. They may wish to make sale or transfer of all of a member's economic (transferable) interest an automatic event of dissociation so that a vote of a majority of the remaining members is not required. They may not feel the need to make bankruptcy or insolvency an automatic event of dissociation. They may not wish to wait 90 days after a corporate member's charter has been revoked to have that member dissociate. And finally, they may wish to give members the right to dissociate (i.e., convert to assignee status upon the giving of notice to the LLC).

This last possibility raises the issue of voluntary withdrawal, an issue that has caused considerable confusion and a number of amendments to the LLC Act. As originally enacted, the LLC Act simply allowed members to dissociate by giving notice to the LLC. Amendments in 1997 proved to be unsatisfactory, and the statue was amended again in 1999 so that the statute now provides that "[a] member may withdraw from a limited liability company only at the time or upon the happening of an event specified in the articles of organization or an operating agreement. Unless the articles of organization or an operating agreement provides otherwise, a member may not withdraw from a limited liability company prior to the dissolution and winding up of the limited liability company." § 4-32-802(c). Under the default rules, even the sale of all of the member's economic interest does not amount to an effective withdrawal as member, which might prove problematic for a member so concerned about the way in which the company is being operated that he or she is worried about potential liability if the veil of limited liability is pierced. In addition, in a member managed LLC, the inability to withdraw may result in continued application of fiduciary duties to the member who no longer has an economic stake in the business and does not wish to be associated with it. These are the kinds of considerations that may make a right to withdraw a good rule for clients to consider when setting up an operating agreement for their LLC.

Arkansas is not alone in struggling with withdrawal rights of members in LLCs now that the IRS has abandoned the corporate resemblance test which provided a significant rationale for permitting voluntary withdrawal as the default rule for such enterprises. Several other states have also chosen to eliminate or modify the rights of members to withdraw voluntarily and be bought out at the time they withdraw as the default rule.[20]

VI.8.   Winding up an LLC

VI.8.1.   Events that Cause Winding Up of the LLC

As noted earlier, dissociation of one or more members is not automatically tied to dissolution of the LLC, as has traditionally been the case for the general partnership. Rather, dissolution of an LLC is triggered, at least under the current default rules, under the following circumstances: (1) at the time or upon the occurrence of events specified in writing in the articles of organization or an operating agreement; (2) upon the written consent of all members; (3) whenever there are no members unless the personal representative of the last remaining member agrees within 90 days after dissociation of the last member to become and is added as a member; or (4) upon the entry of a decree of judicial dissolution. § 4-32-901. Judicial dissolution is to be awarded to any member if the court finds that "it is not reasonably practicable to carry on the business of the limited liability company in

---

[20]   *See, e.g.,* OKLA. LEGIS. 145 § 6 (1997) (codified at OKLA. ST. tit. 18 § 2036); OR. ST. § 63.205 (both eliminating power to withdraw unless provided in operating agreement). Other states have enacted legislation providing that in the event of withdrawal, there is no "right" to be paid off, but instead the withdrawing member continues as an assignee of the interest. *See, e.g.,* COLO. REV. STAT. § 7-80-603; MO. STAT. § 347.103; 1997 NEB. LAWS L.B. 631 (codified at NEB. STAT. § 21-2619(3)); GEN. STAT. N.C. § 57C-3-02. Finally, some states have chosen to discourage voluntary withdrawal by eliminating a withdrawing member's right to distributions at the time of withdrawal. *See* CAL. CORP. CODE § 17252(b); 31 ME REV. STAT. § 672. *See also* MICH. STAT. § 450.4509 (eliminating the right to a distribution if the withdrawal is wrongful).

conformity with the operating agreement." § 4-32-902.

If the operating agreement does not provide a way in which the LLC is to be terminated, its normal existence is deemed to be perpetual, and the default rule is that in order to dissolve and wind up the business, the written consent of all members must be obtained. § 4-32-901(b). The operating agreement cannot take away the power of all members to dissolve the LLC by written agreement.

The language explaining the default rules that are to apply whenever an LLC has no remaining members is convoluted. This portion of the statute says that an LLC is to be dissolved and its affairs wound up:

> At any time there are no members, provided that, unless otherwise provided in the articles of organization or an operating agreement, the limited liability company is not dissolved and is not required to be wound up if within ninety (90) days or such other period as is provided for in the articles of organization or an operating agreement after the occurrence of the event that terminated the continued membership of the last remaining member, the personal representative of the last remaining member agrees in writing to continue the limited liability company and to the admission of the personal representative of the member or its nominee or designee to the limited liability company as a member, effective as of the occurrence of the event that terminated the continued membership of the last remaining member . . . . § 4-32-901(3).

The first reference to a contrary provision in an operating agreement is itself ambiguous. Can an operating agreement say that an LLC will continue indefinitely even with no members? Because it is difficult to see how an LLC can continue with no members, assume that the answer to this question is "no." Then there is a second reference to the power of the articles or operating agreement to change the presumptive 90 day default period in which a new member could be added by the personal representative of the last member. Can this period be increased? For how long a period of time can a memberless LLC continue? What if the last remaining member has no personal representative?

Ideally, an operating agreement should explain what the parties prefer to happen if the last member dissociates. Although the statute is not clear, it is unlikely that the courts would recognize a memberless LLC for an extended period, so it would probably be unwise to attempt to extend the period in which a substitute member could be found beyond 90 days. Nonetheless, the statutory language here is ambiguous, and will remain so unless and until it is amended or interpreted by the Arkansas courts.

VI.8.2.   The Winding Up Process

The process of winding up as described in the LLC Act is borrowed primarily from corporate law. The members (or managers for a manager-managed LLC) who are left at the time dissolution begins retain actual authority to wind up the business and apparent authority to continue conducting business as usual as to third parties without notice of the dissolution. § 4-32-903(1),-904(a). Their actual authority specifically extends to prosecuting and defending suits, settling and closing out the business of the company, disposing of the company's assets, discharging its liabilities, and making liquidating distributions to the members out of what is left. § 4-32-903(2). The extent of their statutory authority is limited, however, to acts "appropriate for winding up the limited liability company's affairs or completing transactions unfinished at dissolution," (§ 4-32-904(a)(1)), and lingering apparent authority is limited to entering into "transaction[s] that would have bound the . . . company if had not been dissolved" (§ 4-32-904(a)(2)). If the LLC files articles of dissolution, this will act as notice sufficient to terminate a third party's ability to rely on lingering apparent authority. § 4-32-904(b). An LLC may choose to authorize additional acts, which would then be binding on the LLC. § 4-32-904(c). In addition, if the LLC restricts a member or manager's actual authority, this restriction is binding on any third party who knows of the restriction. § 4-32-904(d).

Essentially, the members or managers with authority to conduct the winding up are supposed to liquidate everything and pay out the proceeds in the following order of priority: (1) first to creditors, including members and former members, for everything other than liability for distributions; (2) to members and former members for amounts owed as previously declared distributions; (3) to members as a return of their contributions; and (4) to members in accordance with their interest in profits. § 4-32-905.

In order to give notice of the dissolution to creditors and other parties, the statute provides for the filing of articles of dissolution, much like those that are expected when a corporation dissolves. § 4-32-906. These articles include the name of the LLC, the date the articles of organization and all amendments were filed, the reason for filing the articles of dissolution, the effective date of the articles if not effective upon filing, and any other information deemed important by the members or managers responsible for the filing. This filing is optional (with the statutory provision saying the LLC "may" file articles of dissolution), but it is required to limit the rights of claimants against the LLC.

The LLC Act also permits but does not require that known creditors be mailed notice of the dissolution. § 4-32-907(a). The benefit to sending out such a notice is that once this is done, those creditors will have a very short period of time in which to file claims against the LLC. The notice must: (1) describe the information that must be included in a claim; (2) provide the address to which claims must be sent; (3) give a deadline for when claims must be delivered of not less than 120 days after the later of the notice or the filing of the articles of dissolution; and (4) state that claims not received in accordance with those provisions will be barred. § 4-32-907(b). If this process is in fact followed and a claim notice is sent to a known creditor, that creditor's claim is barred if it is not delivered by the deadline, or if it is rejected by the LLC and the claimant fails to commence an enforcement proceeding within 90 days after being notified of the rejection. § 4-32-907(c). Claims that are contingent, unknown, or those that arise after the effective date of dissolution are not covered by this period of limitations. § 4-32-907(d). In addition, the statute specifies that any claim upon which the LLC does not act upon within 30 days is presumed to be rejected. § 4-32-907(e).

Publication notice takes care of unknown or contingent creditors, or those whose claims arise after the effective date of dissolution. § 4-32-908. In order to comply with the statute, the notice must appear at least once "in a newspaper of general circulation in the county where the limited liability company's principal office is located or in a newspaper of general circulation in Pulaski County if the company does not have a principal office in this state." § 4-32-908(b)(1). It must describe the information that is required to be included in a claim, it must provide the mailing address to which the claim should be sent, and it must state that claims are barred unless proceedings to enforce the claim are initiated within the earlier of five years after publication of the notice or the expiration of the applicable statute of limitations otherwise provided by law. § 4-32-908(b)(2)-(3). If articles of dissolution are filed, and the publication notice provided for in the LLC Act is given, contingent and unknown claims are barred after the earlier of five years from publication or the expiration of the statute of limitations that would otherwise apply. If a claim is made before the expiration of these time periods, it may be enforced either against the LLC, to the extent of any undistributed assets, or against a member to the extent of his or her pro rata share of the claim or assets distributed to him or her by the LLC, whichever is less, provided that a member's total liability for all such claims is not to exceed amounts distributed to such member in liquidation. § 4-32-908(d).

As for the winding up process itself, unless the written operating agreement provides otherwise, the members or managers who had authority to operate the business prior to dissolution will normally also have authority to wind up the business and affairs of the LLC. § 4-32-903(1)(A). On the other hand, if one or more of such members or managers have engaged in wrongful conduct, or if any other equitable basis exists, any member or member's legal representative may petition the circuit court to have the court supervise the winding up. § 4-32-903(1)(B). The person conducting the winding up has statutory authority to: (1) prosecute and defend suits in the name of and on the behalf of the LLC; (2) settle and close the business of the company; (3) dispose of and transfer the LLC's property; (4) discharge its liabilities; and (5) distribute any remaining assets to the members. § 4-32-903(2).

After the business and affairs have been wound up, and the assets of the LLC liquidated, the proceeds are to be distributed as follows. First, the LLC must either pay or make adequate provision for payment to creditors, including to the extent permitted by law,[21] members who are creditors. § 4-32-905(1).

---

[21] The phrase "to the extent permitted by law" recognizes that under certain circumstances claims of owners as creditors may be subordinated to those of outside creditors under the doctrine of equitable subordination. Equitable subordination may be ordered by a court in a number of different situations, but one of them is "when

This obligation is not subject to contrary agreement in the operating agreement. The second order of priority, which may be modified in a written operating agreement, is to pay members and former members what they are owed in respect of previously declared distributions. § 4-32-905(2). Although the LLC Act says that this may be changed in the operating agreement, the only possible modifications would be to either to reduce the priority of such payments in general or to reduce the priority of some of these prior distributions, because the rights of creditors to first priority may not be compromised in the operating agreement. Under the default rules, and again this is subject to contrary agreement, the final order of priority is to pay out any remaining assets to members and former members "first for the return of their contribution and second in proportion to the members' respective rights to share in distributions from the limited liability company prior to dissolution." § 4-32-905(3). The operating agreement cannot give members priority over creditors, but can certainly change the priority among the members or the extent to which a return of contributions must be made first.

---

a fiduciary of the debtor misuses his position to the disadvantage of the other creditors." Matter of Cajun Electric Power Co-Operative, Inc. v. Cajun Power Cooperative, 119 F.3d 349, 357 (5th Cir. 1997) (also noting that the other two commonly cited possibilities are when a third party controls the debtor to its advantage, or when a third party actually defrauds other creditors). See also In re Graycarr, Inc., 330 B.R. 741, 749 (Bkrtcy.W.D.Ark. 2005) (citing In re Bellanca Aircraft Corp., 850 F.2d 1275, 1282 (8th Cir. 1988)). Although an LLC member has limited fiduciary responsibilities, they do owe some duties to the company, and this may prevent them from standing on the same footing as other creditors. Section 510 of the Bankruptcy Code has been described as "an extension of the common law doctrine of equitable subordination." In re Raney, 132 B.R. 63, 67 (Bkrtcy.D.Wyo. 1991), referring to 11 U.S.C. § 510. The Arkansas Fraudulent Transfer Act works in a similar way, providing that the insider status is one of the characteristics that might make it easier to treat a debt as having been fraudulently incurred, so that it might be subordinated to the claims of other creditors. § 4-49-204(b)(1).

Obviously, a member who receives liquidating distributions may be forced to pay back such amounts to creditors of the LLC if an appropriate claim is made within five years of the dissolution (assuming articles of dissolution are filed and publication notice is given). However, the LLC is not required to hold any such assets for such contingent or unknown creditors, and the members may not normally be required to contribute more than they receive in liquidation (unless, of course, the veil of limited liability is pierced).

CHAPTER VII.   CONVERTING   FROM ONE BUSINESS FORM TO ANOTHER

VII.1. History and Overview

Traditionally, each Arkansas business organization statute contained language that addressed the rules for how that particular kind of business might be converted to, consolidated with, or merged into another business. Some of the statutes were very detailed, and some offered a variety of options for switching between business forms. Other statutes were less helpful, and the rules applicable to different forms of enterprise were not always consistent. In fact, for clients wanting to convert some forms of business into a different kind of business (rather than, for example, having a corporation simply merge into another corporation), it was necessary to form multiple businesses along the way in order to eventually wind up with the desired business structure. This was both unnecessarily time consuming and expensive, and was not the product of any particular policy-based rationale.

The option of simply converting one business form to another was apparently limited to partnerships. The Arkansas UPA (1996) permitted general partnerships to convert into limited partnerships (§ 4-46-902(a) now amended), and ULPA (2001) allowed limited partnerships to convert into general partnerships (§ 4-46-903(a) now amended). In addition, any general partnership could (and still may) "convert" into an LLP (§ 4-46-1001), and a limited partnership could (and still may) convert into an LLLP (§ 4-47-201(a)(4)). It was also possible, although typically less desirable, for LLPs to convert into general partnerships (§ 4-46-1001(h)), and LLLPs could (and can) presumably convert back to limited partnerships (§ 4-47-202 (allowing amendments to a certificate in which LLLP status must be claimed)).

If a partnership wanted to change to a form of business other than those listed above, or if another kind of business wanted to change its organizational structure, often the only options were to liquidate and reform in the desired business structure (which often had devastating tax consequences) or to reorganize in another state that had statutes authorizing conversion to the desired organizational form. For example, if an Arkansas corporation wished to become an LLC, and it did not want to liquidate and transfer each asset individually in the process, it typically had to reincorporate in a different state with more liberal conversion or merger options. The Arkansas corporation would cause a corporation to be formed in that other state, often Delaware, and then the Arkansas corporation would merge into the foreign corporation. The foreign corporation would then convert into whatever business choice was deemed most desirable, and then the new business would typically simply domesticate in Arkansas.

One might wonder why the Arkansas corporation could not simply merge with a Delaware LLC, and at least avoid the step of creating the short-lived Delaware corporation that existed only to be merged into the final Delaware LLC. The answer is that even this was not necessarily possible because Arkansas statutes offered only limited merger options as well. Prior to the recent legislation, the only statutes in place clearly authorizing mergers allowed corporations to merge with other corporations (§ 4-27-1101, now amended), partnerships to merge with other general or limited partnerships (§ 4-46-905(a), now amended), and LLCs into other LLCs (§ 4-32-1201, now amended). The LLC Act also purported to unilaterally allow LLCs to merge with other entities (§ 4-32-1201, now amended), but because the statutes generally applicable to other entities did not specifically authorize such mergers, it was unclear as to whether such combinations would be allowed.

The result of this collection of inconsistent and limited legislation was that converting from one form of business into another under Arkansas law was typically expensive, cumbersome, time consuming, and usually required substantial legal assistance. It also potentially reduced the amount of franchise taxes being paid in the state, as businesses that really needed a different form of organization often reorganized under the laws of other jurisdictions, and never converted back into an Arkansas business, although they did domesticate here in order to conduct business in this state.

The Arkansas general assembly recently remedied these concerns by enacting legislation that modified the Arkansas statutes governing corporations, general partnerships, LLPs, limited partnerships, LLLPs, and LLCs in order to make the statutes consistent, and to give every form of business a clear statutory option for converting one form of business into a different organizational structure, or merging an existing business into another (even if the second business is a different kind of enterprise).[22] Conversion and merger provisions still appear in each of the business organization statutes, but the language and structure of the provisions is basically parallel. Each business organization statutes now includes a set of common definitions, a provision authorizing a direct conversion, a description of the approval process and required filings to effectuate a conversion, a provision explaining the legal effect of a conversion, and similar provisions relating to mergers.

---

[22]   The new provisions relating to conversion and merger of corporations appear at §§ 4-27-1102 to -1111; the new provisions applicable to LLCs appear at §§ 4-32-1202 to -1210; the new sections governing general partnerships and LLPs are codified at §§ 4-46-902 to -913; and the provisions applicable to limited partnerships and LLLPs can be found at §§ 4-47-1101 to -1113.

This chapter will review the general structure and operation of each of the new provisions, and then will discuss conversion and merger in turn. The final section of the chapter will discuss some of the potential consequences of complying with these new provisions.

VII.2. Structure of the Statutes

The conversion and merger provisions in each distinct business organization statute start out by defining certain terms. "Constituent organization," for example means any entity that is a party to a merger. A converting or converted organization is an entity that has changed or is changing to another organizational form. "Organization" is defined to include general partnerships (including LLPs), limited partnerships (including LLLPs), LLCs, corporations, business trusts, and "any other person having a governing statute." This means that "organization" could include any other form of business, such as a cooperative. The term is also broad enough to cover domestic and foreign entities, and applies both to business organized for and not for profit. Organizational documents are defined differently for the differing forms of business. In general the organization documents of a domestic or foreign general partnership would be the partnership agreement, and if it has registered as an LLP, the filed statement registering the partnership as such. For a limited partnership, it would be the certificate of limited partnership and partnership agreement. An LLC's organizational documents would be the articles of organization and operating agreement or comparable records if governed by a foreign statute. For business trusts, it would be the agreement of trust and declaration of trust. For a domestic or foreign business corporation, the term "organizational documents" would include articles of incorporation, bylaws, and shareholder agreements or comparable records. For any other organization, the term would include records that create the organization, determine its internal governance, and govern relations among the organization's owners, members, and other interested parties. The definitions section for conversions and mergers of general partnerships and LLPs can be found at § 4-46-901; the equivalent provision for limited partnerships and LLLPs is codified at § 4-47-1101; the definitions section in the LLC Act appears at § 4-32-1201; and the parallel provision for business corporations can be found at § 4-27-1101.

In essence, the way a conversion works is that the converting entity adopts a plan of conversion, which must contain certain basic information. For a general partnership, LLP, limited partnership, or LLLP that wishes to convert, the statutory default rules require approval of all partners, although this may be modified by the partnership agreement. For a converting LLC, it normally takes approval of only a majority of the members, although this number can be changed in the operating agreement. Note that the requirement of approval by one-half of the members applies both to member- and manager-managed LLCs. A corporation's plan of conversion must normally be recommend to the shareholders by the directors, and approved by one-half of the shares entitled to vote, although there are exceptions to this process in the statute and these rules are also subject to modification in the corporation's articles of incorporation.

After the plan of conversion is approved, the appropriate persons must prepare articles of conversion and have those filed with the Secretary of State. The articles must include several standard statements that are set out in the statues. Filing of the articles completes the conversion process, and once this happens, the converted entity "is for all purposes the same entity that existed before the conversion." § 4-46-905(a) (general partnerships and LLPs); § 4-47-1105 (limited partnerships and LLLPs); § 4-32-1205(a) (LLCs); and § 4-27-1105(a) (corporations). Property that was owned by the business prior to the conversion is automatically owned by the converted entity, and its debts and obligations are automatically assumed as well. The conversion does not act as a dissolution of the original business, and the converted entity will generally continue to operate in the same way as the original business, with the exception of statutory benefits that might exist because of the conversion, such as tax status, management responsibilities or powers, or owner liability.

Similarly, a merger essentially starts out with two or more constituent entities, and at the end of the merger, only one survives. The surviving organization may either have been one of the original constituent entities, or may be created as part of the merger process. Each of the constituent entities must adopt a plan of merger containing at least a certain minimum of information. With general partnerships, LLPs, limited partnerships, and LLLPs, a plan of merger "must be consented to by all of the partners" unless the applicable partnership agreement provides differently. For LLCs, a plan of merger must have the consent of more than one-half of the number of members unless otherwise agreed in writing in the operating agreement. For corporations, the plan of merger must generally be approved by a majority of directors and shareholders, unless the articles require a greater vote, although there are exceptions to the voting rights set out in the corporate statute that are not mirrored in the statutes applicable to the other forms of business covered by these new provisions.

After each organization that is a party to a merger has properly approved the plan of merger, articles of merger must be prepared and filed. Regardless of whether a merging entity is a partnership, LLC, or corporation, these articles must be filed with the Secretary of State in order to complete the merger process. Once the merger becomes effective, "[e]ach constituent organization that merges into the surviving organization ceases to exist as a separate entity." § 4-46-909(a)(2) (general partnerships and LLPs); § 4-47-1109(a)(2) (limited partnerships and LLLPs); § 4-32-1209(a)(2) (LLCs); and § 4-27-1110(a)(2) (corporations). Property belonging to any entity that disappeared as part of the merger vests in the surviving entity, and all liability and obligations also become debts of the survivor.   Although the constituent entities that merge into the survivor cease to exist independently, they are not deemed to dissolve under state law as part of the merger process.

Because there are some differences in how these general rules apply to differing business forms, the following sections will examine the statutory rules governing conversions and mergers in greater detail.

VII.3. Conversions

VII.3.1.   General Partnerships and LLPs

An Arkansas general partnership or LLP may elect to convert into any other organizational format, and any other organization may convert into an Arkansas general partnership or LLP, provided that the other organization's governing statute authorizes the conversion, the requirements of that statute are complied with, and the conversion is not prohibited by the law of the jurisdiction that enacted the governing statute. § 4-46-902(a). Under the UPA (1996) a plan of conversion is required which must be in a record (kept by the organization at one of its offices or with the Secretary of State), and must include the following information: (1) the name and form of the organization before conversion;   (2) the name and form of the organization after conversion; (3) the terms and conditions of the conversion; and (4) appropriate organizational documents of the organization after conversion. § 4-46-902(b).

If the conversion is by a general partnership or LLP, the plan of conversion must be approved either in accordance with the partnership agreement or consented to by all partners. § 4-46-903(a). If the partnership agreement provides for less than unanimous consent, conversion that would result in a partner of the converting partnership having personal liability must either be approved by that partner, or that partner must have agreed in the partnership agreement to allow for conversion on less than unanimous approval. § 4-46-910. Agreeing to an amendment of the partnership agreement on less than a unanimous vote does not constitute agreement to convert into a new form of business involving personal liability, including a plan that would change the business from an LLP to a general partnership.

Following adoption of a plan of conversion, the converting general partnership or LLP must prepare and file articles of conversion. § 4-46-904. Until articles of conversion are prepared and filed, the plan may be amended or abandoned as provided in the plan, or with the same consent required to approve the plan (unless the plan prohibits such changes). § 4-46-903(b). If it is a general partnership or LLP that is converting, the articles that must be prepared and filed after adoption of the plan are required to include: (1) a statement that the partnership has been converted into another organization; (2) the name and form of the converted organization and the jurisdiction of its governing statute; (3) the date the conversion is effective; (4) a statement that the conversion was approved as required by the Arkansas UPA (1996); (5) a statement that the conversion was approved as required by the governing statute of the converted organization; (6) a statement confirming that the converted organization has filed a statement appointing an agent for service of process (unless the converted organization is foreign and not required to domesticate in Arkansas); and (7) a copy of the plan of conversion or a statement listing the address of the organization's office where the plan of conversion is on file and an agreement that a copy of the plan of conversion will be furnished by the converted organization on request and without cost to any partner of the converting partnership. § 4-46-904(a)(2). If the conversion involves another entity converting into an Arkansas general partnership or LLP, the converting organization must file a statement of qualification including: (1) a statement that the partnership or LLP was converted from another organization; (2) the name and form of the converting organization (and the jurisdiction of the original organization's governing statute); and (3) a statement that the conversion was approved as required by the converting organization's governing statute. § 4-46-904(b). For a general partnership or LLP that is converting, the conversion is effective when the articles of conversion indicate. For other organizations converting into a general partnership or LLP the effective date will be as provided in the governing statute of the converting organization. § 4-46-904(c).

For all purposes, an organization that converts under UPA (1996) is "the same entity that existed before the conversion," although obviously the laws applicable to the form of entity as converted will govern the converted organization. § 4-46-905(a). This means that the converted entity: (1) retains ownership of all property owned by the converting organization; (2) has all the debts, liability and other obligation of the converting organization; (3) is automatically substituted as a party in any action or proceeding that was pending against the converting organization; and (4) retains all of the rights, privileges, immunities, powers, and purposes of the converting organization. § 4-46-905(b)(1)-(4). In addition, upon the effective date, unless otherwise provided in the plan itself, the terms and conditions of the plan of conversion take effect. § 4-46-905(b)(5). Conversion does not dissolve a converting general partnership or LLP. § 4-46-905(b)(6).

For an Arkansas general partnership or LLP that converts into a foreign organization, the converted organization automatically "consents to the jurisdiction of the courts of this state to enforce any obligation owed by the converting partnership, if before the conversion the converting partnership was subject to suit in this state on the obligation." § 4-46-905(c)(1). If the converted organization is a foreign organization not authorized to transact business Arkansas, and if it fails to appoint an agent for service of process here, or no longer has one, or has one that cannot be served with reasonable diligence, the converted organization may be served by registered or certified mail, return receipt requested, addressed to one or more of the governors of the entity by name at its principal office or if that is not possible, by handing a copy to the manager, clerk, or other person in charge of any regular place of business or activity if the person served is not a plaintiff in the action. § 4-46-905(c)(2), cross referencing § 4-20-113.

The general partnership statute specifically authorizes conversion or merger under any other law as well. § 4-46-913.

In addition to the preceding provisions specifically governing the conversion process, there are a number of rules in the statute that apply equally to conversions and mergers. These provisions govern changes in operational structure that could result in the loss of LLP status, the liability of owners following change in structure, and the power of owners to bind the entity following a change in structure.

With regard to a conversion (or merger) that would result in a partner of a converting partnership (or a constituent partnership for a merger) possessing personal liability after the change in organizational form, the approval or amendment of a plan will be ineffective unless that partner consents, or the partnership agreement provides for approval of a conversion or merger without the consent of that partner and that partner consented to the provision in the partnership agreement. § 4-46-910(a). The same kind of approval requirement exists for any conversion (or merger) that would delete a statement of qualification for an LLP. § 4-46-910(b). A partner does not give consent as required in these provisions merely by agreeing that the partnership agreement may be amended upon a vote of less than all partners. § 4-46-910(c).

Neither a conversion nor merger discharges a partner or dissociated partner from liability for partnership obligations that existed prior to the change in structure, and the provisions of UPA (1996) continue to govern how any such obligation may be collected or discharged. § 4-46-911(a)(1). The converted or surviving organization is deemed to acquire the rights that were possessed by the converting or constituent partnership in order to enforce such obligations. § 4-46-911(a)(2). Anyone required to pay off any such partnership liabilities after a conversion or merger retains the right to seek contribution from everyone else who was liable as a partner when the obligation was originally incurred unless such other person has been released. § 4-46-911(a)(3)(A). Such contribution would be "in proportion to the right to receive distributions in the capacity of partner in effect for each other person when the obligation was incurred." § 4-46-911(a)(3)(B). In addition, the conversion and merger provisions specify that a partner in a converting or constituent partnership that was not an LLP will be personally liable for obligations of the converted or surviving organization, even after the change in organization, if at the time a third party enters into a transaction, the third party does not have notice of the conversion or merger and reasonably believes that the original partnership still exists, that it is not an LLP, and that the person is a partner in such partnership. § 4-46-911(b)(1). A dissociated partner of a converting or constituent partnership will also continue to retain liability that existed prior to the conversion or merger for a period of up to two years from the dissociation so long as the third party does not know of the dissociation, does not have notice of the conversion or merger, and reasonably believes that the original partnership still continues (not as an LLP) with the dissociated partner as a partner. § 4-46-911(b)(2).

Following the conversion or merger of a general partnership or LLP, a partner who had the power to bind the original partnership continues to be able to bind the converted or surviving organization if, at the time of a transaction, the third party to the transaction does not have notice of the conversion or merger, and reasonably believes both that the converted or surviving organization is still the original partnership and that the person is a partner in such partnership. § 4-46-912(a). A dissociated partner can also retain authority to bind the converted or surviving oganization for up to two years following dissociation, again so long as the dissociated partner would have had authority prior to the change in organization, and the third party does not have notice of the dissociation or the conversion or merger, and reasonably believes that the converted or surviving organization is still the partnership and that the dissociated partner is still a partner. § 4-46-912(b). If a partner or dissociated partner causes the converted or surviving organization to incur liability after knowing of the conversion or merger, he or she will be liable to the organization or any other person for damages that arise out of the obligation. § 4-46-912(c).

VII.3.2.   Limited Partnerships and LLLPs

The provisions relating to conversion of limited partnerships and LLPs are very similar to those governing limited and LLLPs. An Arkansas limited partnership or LLLP may elect to convert into any other organizational form, and any other organization may convert into an Arkansas limited partnership or LLLP, provided that the other organization's governing statute authorizes the conversion, the requirements of that statute are complied with, and the conversion is not prohibited by the law of the jurisdiction that enacted the governing statute. § 4-47-1102(a). Under ULPA (2001) a plan of conversion is required, and it must be in a record (kept by the organization at one of its offices or with the Secretary of State) that includes the following information: (1) the name and form of the organization before conversion; (2) the name and form of the organization after conversion; (3) the terms and conditions of the conversion; and (4) appropriate organizational documents of the organization after conversion. § 4-47-1102(b). This tracks exactly the rules applicable to general partnerships and LLPs.

If the conversion is by a limited partnership or LLLP, the plan of conversion must be approved either in accordance with the partnership agreement or consented to by all partners. § 4-47-1103(a). (This provision does not mention the possibility of approval by anything less than unanimous vote, but this is not one of the statutory default rules that cannot be modified by the parties.) If the partnership agreement provides for less than unanimous consent, conversion that would result in a partner of the converting partnership having personal liability with respect to the organization after conversion, must either be approved by that partner, or that partner must have agreed in the partnership agreement to allow for conversion on less than unanimous approval. § 4-47-1110. Agreeing generally to allow amendment of the partnership agreement on less than a unanimous vote does not constitute agreement to convert into a new form of business involving personal liability, including a plan that would change from an LLLP to a limited partnership.

Following adoption of a plan of conversion, the converting limited partnership or LLLP must prepare and file articles of conversion. § 4-47-1104. Until articles of conversion are prepared and filed, the plan may be amended or abandoned as provided in the plan, or with the same consent required to approve the plan (unless the plan prohibits such changes). § 4-47-1103(b). If it is a limited partnership or LLLP that is converting, the articles must include: (1) a statement that the limited partnership has been converted into another organization; (2) the name and form of the converted organization and the jurisdiction of its governing statute; (3) the date the conversion is effective; (4) a statement that the conversion was approved as required by the Arkansas ULPA (2001); (5) a statement that the conversion was approved as required by the governing statute of the converted organization; and (6) a statement confirming that the converted organization has filed a statement appointing an agent for service of process (unless the converted organization is foreign and not required to domesticate in Arkansas). § 4-47-1104(a)(1). If the conversion involves another entity converting into an Arkansas limited partnership or LLLP, the converting organization must file a certificate of limited partnership that includes: (1) a statement that the limited partnership or LLLP was converted from another organization; (2) the name and form of the converting organization (and the jurisdiction of the original organization's governing statute); and (3) a statement that the conversion was approved as required by the converting organization's governing statute. § 4-47-1104(a)(2). If the converted organization is a limited partnership or LLLP, the conversion is effective when the certificate of limited partnership goes into effect. § 4-47-1104(b)(1). If the converted organization is not a limited partnership or LLLP, the conversion is effective as provided in the governing statute of the converted organization. § 4-47-1104(b)(2).

As is the case for general partnerships and LLPs, the limited partnership statute specifically authorizes conversion or merger under any other law. § 4-47-1113.

Similar to UPA (1996), there are also a number of provisions that apply to both conversions and mergers, setting out the rules that govern issues such as the loss of LLLP status, the liability of owners following change in structure, and the power of owners to bind the entity following its change in structure.

With regard to a conversion (or merger) that would result in a partner of a converting limited partnership (or a constituent limited partnership for a merger) possessing personal liability after the change in organization, the approval or any amendment of a plan will be ineffective unless that partner consents, or the partnership agreement provides for approval of a conversion or merger without the consent of that partner and that partner consented to the provision in the partnership agreement. § 4-47-1110(a). The same kind of approval requirement exists for any conversion or plan that would delete a statement that the limited partnership is to be an LLLP. § 4-47-1110(b). A partner does not give consent as required in these provisions merely by agreeing generally that the partnership agreement may be amended upon a vote of less than all partners. § 4-47-1110(c).

Neither a conversion nor merger discharges a general partner or dissociated general partner from liability for partnership obligations that existed prior to the change in structure, and the provisions of ULPA (2001) continue to govern how any such obligations may be collected or discharged. § 4-47-1111(a)(1). The converted or surviving organization is deemed to have the rights of the converting or constituent limited partnership in order to enforce such obligations. § 4-47-1111(a)(2). Anyone required to pay such amounts after a conversion or merger retains the right to seek contribution from everyone else who was liable as a general partner when the obligation was originally incurred unless such other person has been released. § 4-47-1111(a)(3)(A). Such contribution would be "in proportion to the right to receive distributions in the capacity of general partner in effect for each of those persons when the obligation was incurred." § 4-47-1111(a)(3)(B). In addition, the merger and conversion provisions specify that a general partner in a converting or constituent partnership that was not an LLLP will be personally liable for obligations of the converted or surviving organization, even after the change in organization, if at the time a third party enters into a transaction, the third party does not have notice of the conversion or merger and reasonably believes that the original limited partnership still exists, that it is not an LLLP, and that the person is still a general partner in such partnership. § 4-47-911(b)(1). A dissociated partner of a converting or constituent partnership will also retain liability that existed prior to the conversion or merger for a period of up to two years from the dissociation so long as a third party does not know of the dissociation, does not have notice of the conversion or merger, and reasonably believes that the original partnership still continues (not as an LLLP) with the dissociated partner as a partner. § 4-47-1111(b)(2).

Following the conversion or merger of a limited partnership or LLLP, a general partner who had the power to bind the original limited partnership continues to possess the power to bind the converted or surviving organization if, at the time of a transaction, the third party did not have notice of the conversion or merger, and reasonably believes the converted or surviving organization is still the original limited partnership and that the person is still a general partner in such partnership. § 4-47-1112(a). A dissociated general partner can also retain authority to bind the converted or surviving organization for up to two years following dissociation, again so long as the dissociated partner would have had authority prior to the change in organization, and the third party does not have notice of the dissociation or the conversion or merger, and reasonably believes that the converted or surviving organization is still the limited partnership and that the dissociated partner is still a general partner. § 4-47-1112(b). If a general partner or dissociated general partner causes the converted or surviving organization to incur liability after knowing of the conversion or merger, he or she will be liable to the organization or any other person for any damages incurred that arise out of the obligation. § 4-47-1112(c).

VII.3.3. LLCs

Not surprisingly, the LLC Act contains most of the same conversion and merger provisions that apply to Arkansas general and limited partnerships, LLPs, and LLLPs; and the same general procedures apply to conversion of Arkansas LLCs or conversion of other entities into Arkansas LLCs.

An Arkansas LLC may elect to convert into any other organizational form, and any other organization may convert into an Arkansas LLC, provided that the other organization's governing statute authorizes the conversion, the requirements of that statute are complied with, and the conversion is not prohibited by the law of the jurisdiction that enacted the governing statute. § 4-32-1202(a). Under the LLC Act a plan of conversion is required, and it must be in a record (kept by the organization at one of its offices or with the Secretary of State) that includes the following information: (1) the name and form of the organization before conversion; (2) the name and form of the organization after conversion; (3) the terms and conditions of the conversion; and (4) appropriate organizational documents of the organization after conversion. § 4-32-1202(b).

If the conversion is by a LLC, the plan of conversion must be approved either in accordance with the terms of a written operating agreement or consented to by more than one-half of the members. § 4-32-1203(a). Following adoption of a plan of conversion, the converting LLC must prepare and file articles of conversion. § 4-32-1204. Until articles of conversion are prepared and filed, the plan may be amended or abandoned as provided in the plan, or with the same consent required to approve the plan (unless the plan prohibits such changes). § 4-32-1203(b). The articles must include: (1) a statement that the LLC has been converted into another organization; (2) the name and form of the converted organization and the jurisdiction of its governing statute; (3) the date the conversion is effective; (4) a statement that the conversion was approved as required by the LLC Act; (5) a statement that the conversion was approved as required by the governing statute of the converted organization; (6) a statement confirming that the converted organization has filed a statement appointing an agent for service of process (unless the converted organization is foreign and not required to domesticate in Arkansas); and (7) a copy of the plan of conversion or a statement listing the address of the organization's office where the plan of conversion is on file and agreement that a copy of the plan of conversion will be furnished by the converted organization on request and without cost to any "shareholder" of the converting LLC. § 4-32-1204(a)(2). (The word "shareholder" in this section probably should be "member.") If the conversion involves another entity converting into an Arkansas LLC, the converting organization must file articles of organization that include: (1) a statement that the LLC was converted from another organization; (2) the name and form of the converting organization (and the jurisdiction of the original organization's governing statute); and (3) a statement that the conversion was approved as required by the converting organization's governing statute. § 4-32-1204(b). For an LLC that is converting, the conversion is effective when the articles of organization are effective, and for other organizations converting into a LLC, the effective date will be as provided in the governing statute of the converting organization. § 4-32-1204(c).

For all purposes, an organization that converts under the LLC Act is "the same entity that existed before the conversion," although obviously the laws applicable to the form of entity as converted will govern the converted organization. § 4-32-1205(a). This means that the converted entity: (1) retains ownership of all property owned by the converting organization; (2) has all the debts, liability, and other obligation of the converting organization; (3) is automatically substituted as a party in any action or proceeding that was pending against the converting organization; and (4) retains all of the rights, privileges, immunities, powers, and purposes of the converting organization. § 4-32-1205(b)(1)-(4). In addition, upon the effective date, unless otherwise provided in the plan itself, the terms and conditions of the plan of conversion take effect. § 4-32-1205(b)(5). Conversion does not dissolve a converting LLC. § 4-32-1205(b)(6).

For an Arkansas LLC that converts into a foreign organization, the converted organization automatically "consents to the jurisdiction of the courts of this state to enforce any obligation owed by the converting limited liability company, if before the conversion the converting limited liability company was subject to suit in this state on the obligation." § 4-32-1205(c)(1). If the converted organization is a foreign organization not authorized to transact business in Arkansas, and if it fails to appoint an agent for service of process here, or no longer has one, or has one that cannot be served with reasonable diligence, the converted organization may be served by registered or certified mail, return receipt requested, addressed to one or more of the governors of the entity by name at its principal office, or if that is not possible, by handing a copy to the manager, clerk, or other person in charge of any regular place of business or activity if the person served is not a plaintiff in the action. § 4-32-1205(c)(2), cross referencing § 4-20-113.

The LLC statute specifically authorizes conversion or merger under any other law as well as under these procedures. § 4-32-1213.

VII.3.4.   Corporations

While the focus of this book is on unincorporated entities, it is also important to consider that one or more unincorporated entities might wish to change to the corporate form, or that a corporation might wish to become a partnership of one sort or another, or an LLC. This section will therefore look at the rules governing conversion of or conversion into corporations under the Arkansas Business Corporation Act (1987).

As is the case with the unincorporated entities previously discussed in these materials, a corporation may convert into any of the other forms of business described here, and any of those forms of organization may simply convert into a corporation. § 4-27-1102(a). If a foreign entity is involved, the other organization's governing statute must also authorize the conversion, and its terms must be complied with. § 4-27-1102(a)(1). In order to accomplish the conversion under the Business Corporation Act of 1987 a plan of conversion is required, and it must be in a record (kept by the organization at one of its offices or with the Secretary of State) that includes the following information: (1) the name and form of the organization before conversion; (2) the name and form of the organization after conversion; (3) the terms and conditions of the conversion; and (4) appropriate organizational documents of the organization after conversion. § 4-27-1102(b).

If the conversion is by a corporation, the plan of conversion is approved if it is recommended by the directors (or the directors determine that they cannot make a recommendation because of a conflict of interest or other special circumstances) and the shareholders who are entitled to vote approve the plan. § 4-27-1103(a). The directors may condition their recommendation on any terms that they decide, but they must call a shareholder meeting, and give every shareholder (whether or not entitled to vote) notice of the meeting. § 4-27-1103(b)-(c). Unless the articles of incorporation or the board of directors require a greater vote, or voting by groups, the conversion must be approved by a majority of the votes entitled to be cast, and separately by a majority of all the votes entitled to be cast by each group if voting by separate groups is required. § 4-27-1103(d).

Following adoption of a plan of conversion, the converting corporation must prepare and file articles of conversion. § 4-27-1104. Until this happens, the plan may be amended or abandoned as provided by the plan or, unless prohibited by the plan, by the same vote required to originally adopt the plan. § 4-27-1103(e). The right to amend or abandon the plan is subject to any contractual rights that may have been created upon the original adoption of the plan. The articles must include: (1) a statement that the corporation has been converted into another organization; (2) the name and form of the converted organization and the jurisdiction of its governing statute; (3) the date the conversion is effective; (4) a statement that the conversion was approved as required by the Business Corporation Act of 1987; (5) a statement that the conversion was approved as required by the governing statute of the converted organization; (6) a statement confirming that the converted organization has filed a statement appointing an agent for service of process (unless the converted organization is foreign and not required to domesticate in Arkansas); and (7) a copy of the plan of conversion or a statement listing the address of the organization's office where the plan of conversion is on file and an agreement that a copy of the plan of conversion will be furnished by the converted organization on request and without cost to any shareholder of the converting corporation. § 4-27-1104(a)(2). If the conversion involves another entity converting into an Arkansas corporation, the converting organization must file articles of conversion that include: (1) a statement that the corporation was converted from another organization; (2) the name and form of the converting organization (and the jurisdiction of the original organization's governing statute); and (3) a statement that the conversion was approved as required by the converting organization's governing statute. § 4-27-1104(b). For a corporation that is converting, the conversion is effective when the articles of conversion indicate, or for other organizations converting into a corporation the effective date will be as provided in the governing statute of the converting organization. § 4-27-1104(c).

For all purposes, an organization that converts under the Business Corporation Act of 1987 is "the same entity that existed before the conversion," although obviously the laws applicable to the form of entity as converted will govern the converted organization. § 4-27-1105(a). This means that the converted entity: (1) retains ownership of all property owned by the converting organization; (2) has all the debts, liability, and other obligation of the converting organization; (3) is automatically substituted as a party in any action or proceeding that was pending against the converting organization; (4) retains all of the rights, privileges, immunities, powers, and purposes of the converting organization. § 4-27-1105(b)(1)-(4). In addition, upon the effective date, unless otherwise provided in the plan itself, the terms and conditions of the plan of conversion take effect. § 4-27-1105(b)(5). Conversion does not dissolve a converting corporation. § 4-27-1105(b)(6).

For an Arkansas corporation that converts into a foreign organization, the converted organization automatically "consents to the jurisdiction of the courts of this state to enforce any obligation owed by the converting corporation, if before the conversion the converting corporation was subject to suit in this state on the obligation." § 4-27-1105(c)(1). If the converted organization is a foreign organization not authorized to transact business Arkansas, and if it fails to appoint an agent for service of process here, or no longer has one, or has one that cannot be served with reasonable diligence, the converted organization may be served by registered or certified mail, return receipt requested, addressed to one or more of the governors of the entity by name at its principal office, or if that is not possible, by handing a copy to the manager, clerk, or other person in charge of any regular place of business or activity if the person served is not a plaintiff in the action. § 4-27-1105(c)(2), cross referencing § 4-20-113.

The Business Corporation Act of 1987 specifically authorizes conversion or merger under any other law as well. § 4-27-913.

VII.4. Mergers

A conversion involves a single business entity changing its organizational structure into an alternative form of enterprise. A merger involves two or more constituent entities, where only one organization survives. It is possible that one of the original constituent entities will survive, or as part of the merger a new entity may be created and the new entity will become the sole surviving enterprise. Because at least two businesses are involved in a merger, the procedures required may be slightly more complicated than a simple conversion.

351

VII.4.1.   General Partnerships and LLPs

The UPA (1996) permits any Arkansas general partnership or LLP to merge with one or more other constituent organizations, which may but need not be partnerships. § 4-46-906(a). The governing statutes of all of the constituent organizations must permit the merger, the merger must not be prohibited by the jurisdiction that enacted the governing statutes, and every constituent entity must comply with its governing statute. § 4-46-906(a)(1)-(3). The plan of merger, like a plan of conversion, must be in a record (kept by the surviving organization at one of its offices or with the Secretary of State) that includes the following information: (1) the name and form of each constituent organization before the merger; (2) the name and form of the surviving organization; (3) the terms and conditions of the merger, including how the ownership interests in each constituent organization will be converted and into what; and (4) any amendments to the surviving organization's organizational documents. § 4-46-906(b).

All of the partners of any constituent general partnership or LLP must consent to the merger, although this rule is apparently subject to the contrary agreement of the partners. § 4-46-907(a). However, if the merger would result in a partner of a constituent partnership possessing personal liability after the change in organization, the approval or amendment of a plan will be ineffective unless that partner consents, or the partnership agreement provides for approval of a conversion or merger without the consent of that partner and that partner specifically consented to the provision in the partnership agreement. § 4-46-910(a). The same kind of approval requirement exists for any merger that would delete a statement of qualification for an LLP. § 4-46-910(b). A partner does not give consent as required in these provisions merely by agreeing that the partnership agreement may be amended upon a vote of less than all partners. § 4-46-910(c).

Following adoption of a plan of merger, articles of merger must be prepared, signed by an authorized representative from each constituent entity, and filed with the Secretary of State. § 4-46-908(a). Until these articles of merger are prepared and filed, and subject to any contractual rights that the plan may have created, the plan of merger may be amended or abandoned as provided in the plan, or with the same consent required to approve the plan (unless the plan prohibits such changes). § 4-46-907(b). The articles of merger are required to include: (1) the name and form of each constituent organization as well as the jurisdiction of each such entity's governing statute; (2) the name and form of the surviving organization and the jurisdiction of its governing statute; (3) the date the merger is effective under the governing statute of the surviving organization; (4) any amendments to the organizational document of the surviving organization if the organizational document is required to be filed; (5) a statement as to each constituent organization that the merger was approved as required by that organization's governing statute; (6) if the surviving entity is a foreign organization that is not domesticated here, a statement confirming that the surviving organization has filed a statement appointing an agent for service of process; (7) either a copy of the plan of merger or a statement containing the address of an office of the surviving organization where the plan of merger is on file and an agreement that a copy of the plan of merger will be furnished on request and without cost to any owner of any constituent organization; and (8) any additional information required by the governing statute of any constituent organization. § 4-46-908(b). If the surviving organization is a general partnership or LLP, the merger is effective upon filing of articles of merger in compliance with the above requirements or as specified in the articles of merger. § 4-46-908(c)(1). If the surviving organization is another form of organization, the effective date will be as provided in the governing statute of the surviving organization. § 4-46-908(c)(2).

When a merger becomes effective, the surviving organization either continues or comes into existence, and every other constituent organization ceases to exist as a separate entity. § 4-46-909(a)(1)-(2). All property that was previously owned by any of the constituent entities is now owned by the surviving organization. § 4-46-909(a)(3). In addition, the surviving entity automatically acquires all the debts, liability, and other obligations of the constituent organizations; is automatically substituted as a party in any action or proceeding that was pending against any converting organization; and except as prohibited by law, obtains all of the rights, privileges, immunities, powers, and purposes of each constituent organization. § 4-46-909(a)(4)-(6). In addition, upon the effective date, unless otherwise provided in the plan itself, the terms and conditions of the plan of merger take effect and any amendments provided for in the plan of merger for the organizational documents of the surviving organization will take effect. § 4-46-909(a)(7), (9). Except as otherwise agreed, a constituent general partnership or LLP is not dissolved even if it ceases to exist as part of a merger. § 4-46-909(a)(8).

If the surviving organization is a foreign organization, the surviving entity automatically "consents to the jurisdiction of the courts of this state to enforce any obligation owed by a constituent organization, if before the merger the constituent organization was subject to suit in this state on the obligation." § 4-46-909(b)(1). If the surviving organization is a foreign organization not authorized to transact business Arkansas, and if it fails to appoint an agent for service of process here, or no longer has one, or has one that cannot be served with reasonable diligence, the surviving organization may be served by registered or certified mail, return receipt requested, addressed to one or more of the governors of the entity by name at its principal office, or if that is not possible, by handing a copy to the manager, clerk or other person in charge of any regular place of business or activity if the person served is not a plaintiff in the action. § 4-46-909(b)(2), cross referencing § 4-20-113.

The general partnership statute specifically authorizes a merger under any other law as well as under these procedures. § 4-46-913.

As mentioned earlier, in the materials dealing with conversions of general partnerships and LLPs, a merger will not discharge a partner or dissociated partner from liability for partnership obligations that existed prior to the merger, and the provisions of UPA (1996) continue to govern how any such obligation may be collected or discharged. § 4-46-911(a)(1). The surviving organization is deemed to have the rights of any constituent general partnership or LLP in order to enforce such obligations. § 4-46-911(a)(2). Anyone required to pay such amounts after a merger retains the right to seek contribution from everyone else who was liable as a partner when the obligation was originally incurred unless such other person has been released. § 4-46-911(a)(3)(A). Such contribution would be "in proportion to the right to receive distributions in the capacity of partner in effect for each other person when the obligation was incurred." § 4-46-911(a)(3)(B). In addition, the merger provisions specify that a partner in a constituent partnership that was not an LLP will be personally liable for obligations of the surviving organization, even after the merger, if at the time the third party enters into a transaction, the third party does not have notice of the merger and reasonably believes that the original partnership still exists, that it is not an LLP, and that the person is a partner in such partnership. § 4-46-911(b)(1). A dissociated partner of a constituent partnership will also retain any liability that existed prior to the merger for a period of up to two years from the dissociation so long as the third party does not know of the dissociation, does not have notice of the merger, and reasonably believes that the original partnership still continues (not as an LLP) with the dissociated partner as a partner. § 4-46-911(b)(2).

Following the merger of a general partnership or LLP, a partner who had the power to bind the original partnership continues to be able to bind the surviving organization if, at the time of a transaction, the third party did not have not have notice of the merger, reasonably believes the surviving organization is still the original partnership and that the person is a partner in such partnership. § 4-46-912(a). A dissociated partner can also retain authority to bind the surviving organization for up to two years following dissociation, again so long as the dissociated partner would have had authority prior to the merger, and the third party does not have notice of the dissociation or the merger, and the third party reasonably believes that the surviving organization is still the partnership and that the dissociated partner is still a partner. § 4-46-912(b). If a partner or dissociated partner causes the surviving organization to incur liability after knowing of the merger, he or she will be liable to the surviving organization or any other person for any damages that arise out of the obligation. § 4-46-912(c).

VII.4.2.   Limited Partnerships and LLLPs

Arkansas' limited partnership statute works in very much the same way when a limited partnership or LLLP is one of the constituent organizations in a merger.

The ULPA (2001) permits any Arkansas limited partnership or LLLP to merger with one or more other constituent organizations, which may but need not be partnerships. §

4-47-1106(a). The governing statutes of all of the constituent organizations must permit the merger, the merger must not be prohibited by the jurisdiction that enacted the governing statutes, and every constituent entity must comply with its governing statute. § 4-47-1106(a)(1)-(3). The plan of merger, like a plan of conversion, must be in a record (kept by the surviving organization at one of its offices or with the Secretary of State) that includes the following information: (1) the name and form of each constituent organization before the merger; (2) the name and form of the surviving organization; (3) the terms and conditions of the merger, including how the ownership interests in each constituent organization will be converted and into what; and (4) any amendments to the surviving organization's organizational documents. § 4-47-1106(b).

All of the partners of any constituent limited partnership or LLLP must consent to the merger, including all limited partners, although this rule is apparently subject to the contrary agreement of the partners. § 4-47-1107(a). However, if the merger would result in a partner of a constituent partnership possessing personal liability after the change in organization, the approval or amendment of a plan will be ineffective unless that partner consents, or the partnership agreement provides for approval of a merger without the consent of that partner and that partner specifically consented to the provision in the partnership agreement. § 4-47-1110(a). The same kind of approval requirement exists for any merger that would delete or amend the certificate of limited partnership by deleting a statement that the limited partnership is an LLLP. § 4-47-910(b). A partner does not give consent as required in these provisions merely by agreeing that the partnership agreement may be generally amended upon a vote of less than all partners. § 4-47-910(c).

Following adoption of a plan of merger, articles of merger must be prepared, signed by every general partner of each preexisting limited partnership or LLLP and authorized representatives from every other constituent entity, and filed with the Secretary of State § 4-47-1108(a). Until these articles of merger are prepared and filed, and subject to any contractual rights that the plan may have created, the plan of merger may be amended or abandoned as provided in the plan, or with the same consent required to approve the plan (unless the plan prohibits such changes). § 4-47-1107(b). The articles of merger must include: (1) the name and form of each constituent organization as well as the jurisdiction of each such entity's governing statute; (2) the name and form of the surviving organization and the jurisdiction of its governing statute; (3) the date the merger is effective under the governing statute of the surviving organization; (4) if the surviving organization is to be created by the merger appropriate organizational documents; (5) if the surviving organization exists before the merger, any amendments provided for in the plan of merger for the organizational document creating that organization; (6) a statement as to each constituent organization that the merger was approved as required by that organization's governing statute; (7) if the surviving entity is a foreign organization that is not domesticated here, a statement confirming that the surviving organization has filed a statement appointing an agent for service of process; and (8) any additional information required by the governing statute of any constituent organization. § 4-47-1108(b). (Note that there are slight differences between the requirements for articles of merger for a limited partnership or LLLP as compared to those for a general partnership or LLP.) If the surviving organization is a limited partnership or LLLP, the merger is effective upon filing of articles of merger in compliance with the above requirements or as specified in the articles of merger. § 4-47-1108(c)(1). If the surviving organization is another form of organization, the effective date will be as provided in the governing statute of the surviving organization. § 4-47-1108(c)(2).

When a merger becomes effective, the surviving organization either continues or comes into existence, and every other constituent organization ceases to exist as a separate entity. § 4-47-1109(a)(1)-(2). All property that was previously owned by any of the constituent entities is transferred to the surviving organization. § 4-47-1109(a)(3). In addition, the surviving entity automatically acquires all the debts, liabilities, and other obligations of the constituent organizations; is automatically substituted as a party in any action or proceeding that was pending against any constituent organization; and except as prohibited by law, obtains all of the rights, privileges, immunities, powers, and purposes of each constituent organization. § 4-47-1109(a)(4)-(6). In addition, upon the effective date, unless otherwise provided in the plan itself, the terms and conditions of the plan of merger take effect, any organizational documents for a new entity take effect, and if the surviving organization existed before the merger, any amendments provided for in the plan of merger for the organizational documents of the surviving organization will take effect. § 4-47-1109(a)(7)-(9). Except as otherwise agreed, a constituent limited partnership or LLLP is not dissolved even if it ceases to exist as part of the merger. § 4-47-1109(a)(8).

If the surviving organization is a foreign organization, the surviving organization automatically "consents to the jurisdiction of the courts of this State to enforce any obligation owed by a constituent organization, if before the merger the constituent organization was subject to suit in this State on the obligation." § 4-47-1109(b). If the surviving organization is a foreign organization not authorized to transact business Arkansas, and if it fails to appoint an agent for service of process here, or no longer has one, or has one that cannot be served with reasonable diligence, the surviving organization may be served by registered or certified mail, return receipt requested, addressed to one or more of the governors of the entity by name at its principal office or if that is not possible, by handing a copy to the manager, clerk, or other person in charge of any regular place of business or activity if the person served is not a plaintiff in the action. § 4-47-1109(b)(2), cross referencing § 4-20-113.

The limited partnership statute specifically authorizes mergers under any other law as well as these procedures. § 4-47-1113.

As mentioned earlier, in the materials dealing with conversions of limited partnerships and LLLPs, a merger will not discharge a general partner or dissociated general partner from liability for limited partnership obligations that existed prior to the merger, and the provisions of ULPA (2001) continue to govern how any such obligation may be collected or discharged. § 4-47-1111(a)(1). The surviving organization is deemed to have the rights of any constituent limited partnership or LLLP in order to enforce such obligations. § 4-47-1111(a)(2). Anyone required to pay such amounts after a merger retains the right to seek contribution from everyone else who was liable as a partner when the obligation was originally incurred unless such other person has been released. § 4-47-1111(a)(3)(A). Such contribution would be "in proportion to the right to receive distributions in the capacity of general partner in effect for each of those persons when the obligation was incurred." § 4-47-1111(a)(3)(B). In addition, the merger provisions specify that a general partner in a constituent limited partnership that was not an LLLP will be personally liable for obligations of the surviving organization, even after the merger, if at the time the third party enters into a transaction, the third party does not have notice of the merger and reasonably believes that the original limited partnership still exists, that it is not an LLLP, and that the person is a general partner in such partnership. § 4-47-1111(b)(1). A dissociated general partner of a constituent limited partnership will also retain any liability that existed prior to the merger for a period of up to two years from the dissociation so long as the third party does not know of the dissociation, does not have notice of the merger, and reasonably believes that the original limited partnership still continues (not as an LLLP) with the dissociated partner as a general partner. § 4-47-1111(b)(2).

Following the merger of a limited partnership or LLLP, a general partner who had the power to bind the original limited partnership continues to be able to bind the surviving organization if, at the time of the transaction, the third party did not have not have notice of the merger, and reasonably believes the surviving organization is still the original limited partnership and that the person is a general partner in such partnership. § 4-47-1112(a). A dissociated general partner can also retain authority to bind the surviving organization for up to two years following dissociation, again so long as the dissociated general partner would have had authority prior to the merger, and the third party does not have notice of the dissociation or the merger, and reasonably believes that the surviving organization is still the limited partnership and that the dissociated partner is still a general partner. § 4-47-1112(b). If a general partner or dissociated general partner causes the surviving organization to incur liability after knowing of the merger, he or she will be liable to the surviving organization or any other person for any damages that arise out of the obligation. § 4-47-1112(c).

VII.4.3.   LLCs

Arkansas' LLC statute also works in very much the same way when an LLC is one of the constituent organizations in a merger.

The Arkansas LLC Act permits any Arkansas LLC to merger with one or more other constituent organizations, which may but need not be LLCs. § 4-32-1206(a). The governing statutes of all of the constituent organizations must permit the merger, the merger must not be prohibited by the jurisdiction that enacted the governing statutes, and every constituent entity must comply with its governing statute. § 4-32-1206(a)(1)-(3). The plan of merger, like a plan of conversion, must be in a record (kept by the surviving organization at one of its offices or with the Secretary of State) that includes the following information: (1) the name and form of each constituent organization before the merger; (2) the name and form of the surviving organization; (3) the terms and conditions of the merger, including how the ownership interests in each constituent organization will be converted and into what; and (4) any amendments to the surviving organization's organizational documents. § 4-32-1206(b).

Unless otherwise provided in a written operating agreement, more than one-half (by number) of the members of any constituent LLC must consent to the merger. § 4-32-1207(a). Following adoption of a plan of merger, articles of merger must be prepared, signed by authorized representatives from every constituent entity, and filed with the Secretary of State. § 4-32-1208(a). Until these articles of merger are prepared and filed, and subject to any contractual rights that the plan may have created, the plan of merger may be amended or abandoned as provided in the plan, or with the same consent required to approve the plan (unless the plan prohibits such changes). § 4-32-1207(b).

The articles of merger are required to include: (1) the name and form of each constituent organization as well as the jurisdiction of each such entity's governing statute; (2) the name and form of the surviving organization and the jurisdiction of its governing statute; (3) the date the merger is effective under the governing statute of the surviving organization; (4) any amendments to the organizational document of the surviving organization if the organizational document is required to be filed; (5) a statement as to each constituent organization that the merger was approved as required by that organization's governing statute; (6) if the surviving entity is a foreign organization that is not domesticated here, a statement confirming that the surviving organization has filed a statement appointing an agent for service of process; (7) either a copy of the plan of merger or a statement containing the address of an office of the surviving organization where the plan of merger is on file and an agreement that a copy of the plan of merger will be furnished on request and without cost to any owner of any constituent organization; and (8) any additional information required by the governing statute of any constituent organization. § 4-32-1208(b). (Note that there are slight differences between the requirements for a articles of merger for a LLC as compared to those for a limited partnership or LLLP.) If the surviving organization is a LLC, the merger is effective upon filing of articles of merger in compliance with the above requirements or as specified in the articles of merger. § 4-32-1208(c)(1). If the surviving organization is another form of organization, the effective date will be as provided in the governing statute of the surviving organization. § 4-32-1208(c)(2).

When a merger becomes effective, the surviving organization either continues or comes into existence, and every other constituent organization ceases to exist as a separate entity. § 4-32-1209(a)(1)-(2). All property that was previously owned by any of the constituent entities is transferred to the surviving organization. § 4-32-1209(a)(3). In addition, the surviving entity automatically assumes all the debts, liabilities, and other obligations of the constituent organizations; is automatically substituted as a party in any action or proceeding that was pending against any constituent organization; and except as prohibited by law, obtains all of the rights, privileges, immunities, powers, and purposes of each constituent organization. § 4-32-1209(a)(4)-(6). In addition, upon the effective date, unless otherwise provided in the plan itself, the terms and conditions of the plan of merger take effect, any organizational documents for a new entity take effect, and if the surviving organization existed before the merger, any amendments provided for in the plan of merger for the organizational documents of the surviving organization will take effect. § 4-32-1209(a)(7)-(9). Except as otherwise agreed, a constituent LLC is not dissolved even if it ceases to exist. § 4-32-1209(a)(8).

If the surviving organization is a foreign organization, the surviving organization automatically "consents to the jurisdiction of the courts of this state to enforce any obligation owed by a constituent organization if before the merger the constituent organization was subject to suit in this state on the obligation." § 4-32-1209(b)(1). If the surviving organization is a foreign organization not authorized to transact business Arkansas, and if it fails to appoint an agent for service of process here, or no longer has one, or has one that cannot be served with reasonable diligence, the surviving organization may be served by registered or certified mail, return receipt requested, addressed to one or more of the governors of the entity by name at its principal office or if that is not possible, by handing a copy to the manager, clerk, or other person in charge of any regular place of business or activity if the person served is not a plaintiff in the action. § 4-32-1209(b)(2), cross referencing § 4-20-113.

The LLC statute also specifically authorizes merger under any other law. § 4-32-1210.

VII.4.4.   Corporations

Arkansas' Business Corporation Act of 1987 works in very much the same way when an Arkansas corporation is one of the constituent organizations in a merger.

The statute governing corporations permits any Arkansas corporation to merger with one or more other constituent organizations, which may but need not be corporations. § 4-27-1106(a). The governing statutes of all of the constituent organizations must permit the merger, the merger must not be prohibited by the jurisdiction that enacted the governing statutes, and every constituent entity must comply with its governing statute. § 4-27-1106(a)(1)-(3). The plan of merger must be in a record (kept by the surviving organization at one of its offices or with the Secretary of State) that includes the following information: (1) the name and form of each constituent organization before the merger; (2) the name and form of the surviving organization; (3) the terms and conditions of the merger, including how the ownership interests in each constituent organization will be converted and into what; and (4) any amendments to the surviving organization's organizational documents. § 4-27-1106(b).

For any merger in which a corporation is one of the constituent organizations, the statutes set out relatively detailed approval requirements. With limited exceptions, unless the merger involves a subsidiary being merger into a parent corporation, the normal process is for the board of directors of the corporation to submit the plan of merger for approval by the corporation's shareholders. § 4-27-1107(a). As the initial step in the approval process, the directors must recommend the plan, unless they determine that because of a conflict or other special reason they can make no such recommendation. § 4-27-1107(b)(1)(A). The directors must also communicate the reason for their recommendation or determination at the time the plan of merger is submitted to the shareholders. § 4-27-1107(b)(1)(B). The second step is for the shareholders who are entitled to vote to approve the plan. § 4-27-1107(b)(2). All shareholders must be notified of the proposed shareholders meeting, and must be told that the purpose is to consider a plan of merger, a copy or summary of which must be included with the notice. § 4-27-1107(d). Although the directors may impose any extra conditions that they decide upon, the default rule is that (unless the articles of incorporation require otherwise) the plan must be approved by affirmative vote of stockholders holding a majority of outstanding shares entitled to vote, and/or by voting group if voting by separate groups is required. § 4-27-1107(c) & (e). Voting by separate groups is required if the plan increases or decreases the number of shares in that class, changes or reclassifies the shares in that class, adds shares to that class, changes terms applicable to that class of shares, creates a new class of shares with superior or equal rights to distributions or upon dissolution, increases the rights and privileges of any other class of shares so that they are superior or equal to that class, limits or denies an existing preemptive right of any shares of that class, or otherwise affects rights to distributions or dissolutions that have accumulated on any shares of that class. § 4-27-1107(f), cross referencing § 4-27-1004.

The shareholders of a constituent corporation that is the surviving entity are not required to approve the transaction if four requirements are met. The first requirement is that the articles of incorporation of the surviving corporation may only be amended to: extend the duration of the corporation if it was formed at a time when the articles were required to specify a date upon which the corporation was to be dissolved; delete the names or addresses of the initial directors; change the corporation's registered agent or address; change the corporate name in certain minor wars; or, if the corporation has only a single class of shares, increase the number of shares to a greater whole number of the same shares. § 4-27-1107(g)(1), cross referencing § 4-27-1002. The second requirement is that all pre-existing shareholders of the surviving corporation must continue to hold the same number of shares with identical rights immediately following the merger. § 4-27-1107(g)(2). The third requirement in order to dispense with the shareholder vote is that the merger must not increase the total number of voting shares of the surviving corporation by more than 20% (including shares to be issued upon the exercise of rights or warrants issued as part of the merger). § 4-27-1107(g)(3). The final requirement is that the number of participating shares may not increase by more than 20%. § 4-27-1107(g)(4). For this purpose, a "participating share" is one that entitles the holder to participate in distributions from the corporation, and a "voting share" is one that gives the holder the right to vote unconditionally in the elections of directors. § 4-27-1107(h).

Also, as is the case for mergers involving other entities, and subject to any contractual rights, the plan of merger may be abandoned at any time prior to filing articles of merger either as provided in the plan or as determined by the board of directors. § 4-27-1107(i).

Special procedures are set out where the merger involves a parent and subsidiary corporation as the constituent entities. If the parent corporation owns at least 90% of the outstanding shares of every class of the subsidiary, the parent corporation may merge the subsidiary into the parent without the necessity of obtaining approval of shareholders of either the parent or subsidiary. § 4-27-1108(a). For this type of merger, the board of directors of the parent corporation must adopt a plan of merger that includes the names of the parent and subsidiary corporations, and the manner in which shares of the subsidiary are to be converted and into what. § 4-27-1108(b). Although the statute first says that either a copy or a summary of the plan must be mailed to every shareholder of the subsidiary who has not waived the mailing requirement in writing (§ 4-27-1108(c)), the statute also says that the articles of merger may not be filed with the Secretary of State until at least 30 days after a copy of the plan has been mailed to each such shareholder (§ 4-27-1108(d)). To be safe, then, the parent corporation should deliver a full copy of the plan to each shareholder of the subsidiary who has not waived the right to receive the plan in writing. If this process is used, the articles of merger may contain only those amendments to the articles of the parent, which would not require shareholder approval (as described above). § 4-27-1108(e).

In order to effectuate the merger, after each constituent organization has approved the plan as required by the applicable statute for such organization, the articles of merger must be signed by an authorized representative of each such organization. § 4-27-1109(a). The articles of merger are required to include: (1) the name and form of each constituent organization as well as the jurisdiction of each such entity's governing statute; (2) the name and form of the surviving organization and the jurisdiction of its governing statute; (3) the date the merger is effective under the governing statute of the surviving organization; (4) any amendments to the organizational document of the surviving organization if the organizational document is required to be filed; (5) a statement as to each constituent organization that the merger was approved as required by that organization's governing statute; (6) if the surviving entity is a foreign organization that is not domesticated here, a statement confirming that the surviving organization has filed a statement appointing an agent for service of process; (7) either a copy of the plan of merger or a statement containing the address of an office of the surviving organization where the plan of merger is on file and an agreement that a copy of the plan of merger will be furnished on request and without cost to any owner of any constituent organization; and (8) any additional information required by the governing statute of any constituent organization. § 4-27-1109(b). (Note that there are slight differences between the requirements for a articles of merger for a corporation and those required for a limited partnership or LLLP. This language does, however, mirror the requirements found in UPA (1996).) Each constituent organization shall deliver a copy of the articles for filing by the Secretary of State. § 4-27-1109(c). If the surviving organization is a corporation, the merger is effective upon filing of articles of merger in compliance with the above requirements or as specified in the articles of merger. § 4-27-1109(d)(1). If the surviving organization is another form of organization, the effective date will be as provided in the governing statute of the surviving organization. § 4-27-1109(d)(2).

When a merger becomes effective, the surviving organization either continues or comes into existence, and every other constituent organization ceases to exist as a separate entity. § 4-27-1110(a)(1)-(2). All property that was previously owned by any of the constituent entities is automatically transferred to the surviving organization. § 4-27-1110(a)(3). In addition, the surviving entity automatically assumes all the debts, liabilities and, other obligations of the constituent organizations; is automatically substituted as a party in any action or proceeding that was pending against any constituent organization; and except as prohibited by law, obtains all of the rights, privileges, immunities, powers, and purposes of each constituent organization. § 4-27-1110(a)(4)-(6). In addition, upon the effective date, unless otherwise provided in the plan itself, the terms and conditions of the plan of merger take effect, any organizational documents for a new entity take effect, and if the surviving organization existed before the merger, any amendments provided for in the plan of merger for the organizational documents of the surviving organization will take effect. § 4-27-1110(a)(7)-(9). Except as otherwise agreed, a constituent corporation is not dissolved even if it ceases to exist. § 4-27-1110(a)(8).

If the surviving organization is a foreign organization, the surviving organization automatically "consents to the jurisdiction of the courts of this state to enforce any obligation owed by the constituent organization if before the merger the constituent organization was subject to suit in this state on the obligation." § 4-27-1110(b)(1). If the surviving organization is a foreign organization not authorized to transact business Arkansas, and if it fails to appoint an agent for service of process here, or no longer has one, or has one that cannot be served with reasonable diligence, the surviving organization may be served by registered or certified mail, return receipt requested, addressed to one or more of the governors of the entity by name at its principal office, or if that is not possible, by handing a copy to the manager, clerk, or other person in charge of any regular place of business or activity if the person served is not a plaintiff in the action. § 4-27-1110(b)(2), cross referencing § 4-20-113.

The Business Corporation Act of 1987 specifically authorizes merger under any other law. § 4-27-1111.

VII.5. Effects of Converting or Merging

As described above, a converted or surviving organization automatically steps into the shoes of the original entity or entities. It assumes the debts and liabilities, and acquires the assets and privileges of the original organizations by operation of law. It is automatically substituted as a party in any pending litigation or proceeding. No separate deeds or bills of sale are necessary to convey title to assets. No new filings are required to perfect security interests. And, for state law purposes at least, the surviving entity is a continuation of the original businesses, which are not deemed to dissolve as part of the conversion or merger.

While the focus of these materials is indeed compliance with the state business organization statutes rather than any other laws or regulations, it is probably worth emphasizing that the statement in the state business statutes that conversion and merger do not "dissolve" any of the original businesses is not necessarily binding on the IRS. This means that a conversion or merger might result in a deemed liquidation for tax purposes, with potentially significant negative tax consequences. This is particularly likely to create problems if any entity that is originally taxed as a corporation plans on converting to or merging into a business that will be taxed as a partnership. Conversion or merger of a tax partnership into an association taxable as a corporation is much less likely to involve any negative tax consequence, and a similar change from one tax partnership into a new tax partnership or a change from a tax corporation into a new entity also taxable as a corporation is unlikely to involve any taxable consequences at all.

A concrete example might frame the issue more clearly. Suppose the shareholders of an existing corporation seek your advice in connection with their desire to convert the business into an LLC that will have partnership tax status. Suppose also that the corporation has been in existence for a while and that it owns certain property that has appreciated in value since the corporation acquired it. This might be land, or securities, or any other property that has gone up in value since the date it was contributed or acquired. As is the case for individuals, no tax is owed by the corporation just because one or more of its owned assets goes up in value. Tax is owed only upon the sale or other disposition of the assets. If, however, the corporation elects to convert to an LLC that will be a tax partnership, and if the IRS determines for tax purposes that there has been a deemed liquidation and distribution to the shareholders, who are then deemed to contribute those assets to the LLC, there may be significant adverse tax consequences.

A corporation that converts into a form of business that will be taxed as a partnership may be treated for tax purposes as having made a liquidating distribution of all assets to the shareholders, who would then be deemed to have contributed those assets to the tax partnership. This would involve a taxable event for the shareholders when they receive that deemed liquidating distribution of assets. IRC § 331(a). There may also be tax consequences to the corporation, which may be deemed to have sold all of those assets at current fair market value. IRC § 336(a). These rules are not universally applied; there are, for example, exceptions to the rule requiring recognition if the payments are being made to a shareholder who owns stock representing at least 80% of voting rights and economic participation rights. IRC §§ 332 (providing that the shareholder need not recognize such gain), 337(a) (providing that the corporation need not recognize gain to the extent of deemed distributions to such a shareholder). However, the fact that such consequences are possible even though the state statutes specify that transfer of assets to the converted entity is automatic and that for all purposes the converted entity is deemed to have the status of the original organization, means that tax advisors need to be carefully consulted before business attorneys help clients arrange such conversions.

A merger can also involve very complicated tax consequences, which are well beyond the scope of these materials. Because there are various ways in which to structure mergers (i.e., by providing for different kinds of property to be offered to owners of constituent enterprises that are not to be the surviving organization), this is also something that requires the special expertise of a tax advisor.

Chapter VIII.   Piercing the Veil

VIII.1.   What Does it Mean to "Pierce the Veil"

Piercing the veil is an equitable doctrine developed at common law, which under certain circumstances allows a court to order that the separate legal existence of a business entity be disregarded. Originally, the doctrine was designed to allow creditors and other claimants to recover against the shareholders of a corporation, despite the usual rule that shareholders have no personal liability for debts of the corporation, and was available only if "the privilege of transacting business [had] been illegally abused to the injury of a third person."[23] This evolved over time so that, in very general terms, the modern rule seems to be predicated on the notion that if certain owners of a business fail to respect the separate existence of that business, third parties (and sometimes even insiders) need not recognize the business either. The language of these opinions often asks whether the corporation was "a mere instrumentality of the principals,"[24] or whether the corporation was no more than the "alter ego" of the person against whom recovery is sought.[25] In recent years, this doctrine has been applied to other limited liability enterprises, so it is no longer

---

[23]   If it is ever important to trace the history of piercing in Arkansas, Rounds & Porter Lumber Co. v. Burns, 216 Ark. 288, 290, 225 S.W.2d 1, 2-3 (1949), is an early case applying this rule . The opinion in Winchel v. Craig, 55 Ark. App. 373, 380-82, 934 S.W.2d 946, 950-51 (1996), traces the progression of piercing law in Arkansas through 1996.

[24]   In re Ozark Rest. Equip. Co., Inc., 816 F.2d 1222, 1224 (8th Cir. 1987).

[25]   For example, consider the discussion of the alter ego analysis in Winchel v Craig, 55 Ark. App. 373, 380; 934 S.W.2d 946, 950 (Ark. App. 19960), citing Humphries v. Bray, 271 Ark. 962, 611 S.W.2d 791 (1981).

accurate to speak solely in terms of piercing the "corporate" veil.[26]
The veil of limited liability can be pierced, when it is appropriate
to do so, for entities such as the LLC as well.

Before turning to the specifics of when it might be
appropriate to pierce the veil, some general observations may be
helpful. First, although the vast majority of piercing cases (in
Arkansas and elsewhere) still involve corporations, there are
enough opinions dealing with other forms of enterprise, and those
opinions are consistent enough, to be reasonably confident that the
general principles of piercing apply to more than just the
corporation. Second, there has never been a successful piercing
case involving a publicly held enterprise; all of the piercing cases
talk about closely held businesses, and usually a very small
number of active owners (often a single owner) are being pursued.
Third, the doctrine of piercing can also be used to collapse related
corporations and disregard to separate existence of parent and
subsidiaries or even sister corporations (this is sometimes called
triangular piercing). Fourth, reverse piercing is also theoretically
possible, where the separate existence of the corporation (or other
enterprise) is to be disregarded in order to enable an owner's
creditors to recover against the business' assets or even to allow
insiders to disregard the entity's existence in a legal proceeding.
Only in the case of reverse piercing do you see attempts by insiders
to disregard the entity's separate existence; traditional piercing was
generally limited to outsiders. Thus, a corporate shareholder or
director cannot normally pierce the veil of his or her corporation
in order to have the courts disregard its legal existence, unless the
doctrine of reverse piercing is invoked. Presumably, the same
limitations would apply to members or managers of an LLC, or
partners in an LLP, limited partnership, or LLLP.

---

[26]   For example, in Anderson v. Stewart, 366 Ark. 203, 234 S.W.3d 295
(2006), the court expressly held that piercing could apply to LLCs.

It is also worth emphasizing that piercing is not the only circumstance under which the owner of a limited liability business such as a corporation, LLC, LLP, limited partnership (as to limited partners), or LLLP might wind up being liable for a business debt. In addition to being liable if the veil of limited liability is disregarded, business owners are also liable for their promised contributions (provided that the promise to make the contribution is otherwise enforceable). Similarly, owners can be liable if they guarantee a debt of the business. Finally, owners are liable for their own conduct, and in this case their status as owner in a limited liability business will not shield their personal assets.[27] For example, if they act as agents of the business and in the course of acting, they commit a tort, they will be personally liable for any damage they inflict. The business may also be liable, for example under the doctrine of respondeat superior,[28] but the fact that the individual actors are corporate shareholders or LLC members will not insulate them from responsibility for their own misconduct. Alternatively, if they act as agents for the business and fail to fully disclose the existence and identity of the principle, they can be liable as agents for an unidentified principle under traditional agency law rules.[29]

---

[27]   See Scott v. Central Arkansas Nursing Centers, Inc., 101 Ark. App. 424, 434, 278 S.W.3d 587, 595-96 (2008), noting that while shareholders are "not ordinarily liable for the acts of their corporation or LLC," they "may be liable for their own acts or conduct."

[28]   The current Restatement of Agency specifies that "[a]n employer is subject to liability for torts committed by employees while acting within the scope of their employment." Rest (3rd) Agency § 2.04. "Employer" and "employee" are terms of art, designed to replace the old fashioned language of "master and servant" that was found in earlier restatements of the law.

[29]   See, e.g., Oliver v. Eureka Springs Sales Co., 222 Ark. 94, 95, 257 S.W.2d 367, 368 (1953), applying the doctrine but using the phrase "partially identified principal," which was the language of the earlier restatements rather than the current Restatement (3rd) of Agency. In Beech v. Crawford, Not Reported in S.W.3d, 1999 WL

The remainder of this chapter will examine in greater detail the rules applicable to traditional piercing in the corporate context (whether to hold shareholders or related corporations liable), piercing the veil as to other forms of enterprise, and finally, the doctrine of reverse piercing.

VIII.2.   Traditional Piercing of the Corporate Veil

As alluded to in the introductory section of this chapter, piercing the veil is a judicially-created and defined doctrine that allows courts to disregard statutorily authorized limited liability in business enterprises in order to allow persons who are ostensibly creditors of the business to access assets of owners or sometimes related entities. Originally developed and applied in the corporate context, the rule allowed courts to pierce the veil of limited liability traditionally available to corporate shareholders when the shareholders themselves failed to respect the enterprise as a distinct legal entity. The test for piercing in a corporate context has been formulated in a wide variety of ways, often asking whether the business is so controlled by its owners that it has become the mere alter ego or instrumentality of the owners. Of course those labels do not, in and of themselves, do much to help one understand when the "corporate facade" is likely to be disregarded by the courts.

1031310 (Ark. App. 1999), the Arkansas Court of Appeals applied these prinicples without referring to the restatement or its terminology. The court stated: "It is the agent's duty to disclose his capacity as agent of a corporation if he is to escape personal liability for contracts made by him, and the agent bears the burden of proving that he was acting in his corporate, rather than individual, capacity." Id, citing 19 C.J.S. Corporations § 540 (1990). Liability was imposed because there was no evidence showing that the agent told the third party "that he was contracting on behalf of the corporation."

Unfortunately, it has always been extremely difficult (some would say impossible) to articulate an accurate and predictive test for when the veil of limited liability will be pierced.[30] We are left with the task of searching through cases to see how similar situations have been handled in the past, and this task is hampered by the fact that many of the written opinions offer only conclusory observations rather than a helpful recital of the actual facts.

Commentators have been very active in this area, attempting to analyze and dissect the existing case law. One of the most influential and frequently cited articles was prepared by Professor Robert Thompson, after an exhaustive review of more than 1,600 reported piercing decisions. Professor Thompson listed the following factors as being most frequently cited by the courts when they were deciding whether to pierce the corporate veil: lack of meaningful separation between the shareholders and their corporation, commingling of corporate and individual assets, inadequate (or grossly inadequate) capitalization of the corporation, failure to observe corporate formalities, shareholder domination and control of the corporation, and overlap of corporate personnel and management (when multiple corporations are involved). Robert B. Thompson, Piercing the Corporate Veil: An Empirical Study, 76 Cornell L. Rev. 1036, 1063 (1991) (hereinafter Thompson II). Other commentators have prepared their own lists of factors, and if it becomes important to research this topic, two good (albeit older) articles are Cathy S. Krendl & James R. Krendl, Piercing the Corporate Veil: Focusing the

---

[30]   Frank Easterbrook and Daniel Fischel declared in the mid-1980s that veil piercing "seems to happen freakishly. Like lightning, it is rare, severe, and unprincipled." Frank H. Easterbrook & Daniel R. Fischel, Limited Liability and the Corporation, 52 U. Chi. L. Rev. 89, 89 (1985). Stephen Bainbridge once complained that its use is "rare, unprincipled, and arbitrary," and completely lacking in "bright-line rules for deciding when courts will pierce the corporate veil." Stephen M. Bainbridge, Abolishing Veil Piercing, 26 J. Corp. L. 479, 535, 513 (2001).

Inquiry, 55 Denv. U. L. Rev. 1, 16-17 (1978); and David H. Barber, Piercing the Corporate Veil, 17 Willamette L. Rev. 371, 374-75 (1980).

An even earlier treatise listed 11 factors that were considered by the author to be important in determining whether shareholders had improperly dominated their corporation, particularly in the context of parent-subsidiaries, where the corporate shareholder is itself another corporation: (1) the parent corporation owns all or substantially all of the subsidiary's stock; (2) the parent and subsidiary have common directors or officers; (3) the parent finances the operations of subsidiary; (4) the parent caused the subsidiary to have been incorporated; (5) grossly inadequate capitalization of the subsidiary; (6) the parent pays the salaries, expenses, and losses of the subsidiary; (7) the subsidiary's assets came solely from the parent, and the subsidiary conducts business only with the parent; (8) the parent's records refer to the subsidiary as a department or division of the parent, and the parent's records reflect the subsidiary's business as its own; (9) the parent uses the property of the subsidiary as its own; (10) the directors or executives of the subsidiary act on behalf of the parent rather than acting independently in the interest of the subsidiary, and (11) corporate formalities for the subsidiary are not observed. Frederick J. Powell, Parent and Subsidiary Corporations § 6 (1931). Powell also suggested that it was necessary to show some sort of impropriety in order to justify piercing, and listed these seven possibilities as bases for demonstrating such wrong-doing: (1) actual fraud; (2) violation of a statute; (3) stripping the subsidiary of its assets; (4) misrepresentation; (5) estoppel; (6) torts; and (7) other cases of wrong or injustice. For a more recent consideration of piercing particularly in the context of parent-subsidiaries, see John H. Matheson, *The Modern Law of Corporate Groups: an Empirical Study of Piercing the Corporate Veil in the Parent-Subsidiary Context*, 87 N.C. L. Rev. 1091

(2009).

There are a number of piercing cases in Arkansas. Most of them have involved situations where a third party sought to pierce the veil of a corporation to reach assets of either individuals or distinct corporate entities, generally on the theory that as a result of the shareholder's control over the corporations or the manner of operating the businesses in question, the shareholders or related corporations should also be held responsible. Arkansas courts typically state that they are "quite liberal" in protecting the limited liability of corporate shareholders, but commentators do not always agree with this assessment.[31]

Early Arkansas cases suggested that piercing should only occur if "the privilege of transacting business [was] illegally abused to the injury of a third person."[32] Gradually, Arkansas courts began to use other language to describe piercing factors.

---

[31] For example, one study found that in 1990 Arkansas courts pierced the veil in nearly 40% of the reported cases (or in 9 of the 23 reported cases where piercing was sought). Robert B. Thompson, Piercing the Corporate Veil: An Empirical Study, 76 Cornell L. Rev. 1036, 1039 (1991). A more recent study placed the percent at over 56%. Peter Oh, Veil Piercing, 89 Tex. L. Rev. 81, 115 (2010). Another commentator concluded that while Arkansas generally follows traditional rules governing piercing, the rules are applied so that the veil of limited liability has actually been pierced more easily here and that "it is particularly dangerous to fail to adhere to corporate formalities in Arkansas." Stephen B. Presser, Piercing the Corporate Veil, § 2:4. Arkansas.

[32] Rounds & Porter Lumber Co. v. Burns, 216 Ark. 288, 290, 225 S.W.2d 1, 2-3 (1949); Neal v. Oliver, 246 Ark. 377, 391, 438 S.W.2d 313, 320 (1969) (describing piercing as a method of avoiding "putting fiction above right and justice"); Banks v. Jones, 239 Ark. 396, 399, 390 S.W.2d 108, 110 (1965) (refusing to pierce because of lack of evidence to support a finding of illegal abuse of the corporate form to the injury of the appellant); Winchel v. Craig, 55 Ark. App. 373, 380-82, 934 S.W.2d 946, 950-51 (1996) (tracing the progression of piercing law in Arkansas through 1996).

Perhaps the most liberal example of piercing to date can be found in a 1981 opinion from the Arkansas Court of Appeals, Humphries v. Bray.[33] In that case, the Court of Appeals pierced the veil of limited liability to hold a sole shareholder liable under the Arkansas Workers' Compensation Act, apparently without any evidence of illegality or wrongdoing on the part of the sole shareholder. Technically, that Act applies only to businesses with five or more employees and the corporation in question had fewer employees. However, the sole shareholder also owned and operated two sole proprietorships, and if the businesses were considered together, there were more than five employees. The court found that none of the three businesses had more than two employees and that separate records were maintained for each of the three businesses; in its opinion it cited no evidence of any intent to circumvent application of the Workers' Compensation Act. The court did note that one bookkeeper kept accounts for all three businesses, that it was sometimes difficult to distinguish between the businesses, that the business were all in the same building with a single sign, that the businesses had a shared listing in the phone book, that some funds were moved between businesses to meet payroll, and that employee W-2 forms did not always use the correct business names. 271 Ark. at 965, 611 S.W.2d at 793. Although the court in Humphries cited language to the effect that piercing should be applied based on the circumstances of each case "when the facts warrant its application to prevent an injustice," it offered no explanation of how piercing the veil would in fact "prevent an injustice." Instead, the court merely offered its conclusion that "application [of the doctrine] in the instant case was warranted." Humphries, 271 Ark. at 966, 611 S.W.2d at 793.

---

[33]   271 Ark. 962, 611 S.W.2d 791 (Ark. App. 1981). Humphries has been an influential case on Arkansas law with regard to piercing. See, e.g., Epps v. Stewart Information Services Corp., 327 F.3d 642, 649 (8th Cir. 2003).

One commentator has suggested that the result in Humphries "may be to allow piercing the veil simply on the basis of a failure to adhere to corporate formalities, and without any evidence whatsoever on the part of the sole shareholder of an intent to perpetrate an injustice, wrongful act, or fraud."[34] This would be consistent with statements made in cases like Woodyard v. Ark. Diversified Ins. Co., 268 Ark. 94, 99, 594 S.W.2d 13, 17 (1980), where the court stated that the veil of corporate liability could be pierced and the corporate form ignored "where fairness demands it."

More recently, the Arkansas Supreme Court stated in Arkansas Bank & Trust Co. v. Douglass, 318 Ark. 457, 885 S.W.2d 863 (1994), that fraud or illegal acts need not be alleged; mere allegation of wrongdoing should be enough to pierce. 318 Ark. at 470, 885 S.W.2d at 870. The court in Douglass ignored the corporate form of a subsidiary on the grounds that it was a "mere tool" of the parent corporation, after concluding that there was sufficient evidence that the subsidiary had been established to do indirectly what the parent company could not do directly under statute.

On the other hand, there are recent piercing cases in Arkansas that suggest that fraud, illegality, or injustice are elements of piercing in Arkansas. Perhaps the leading Arkansas case suggesting that fraud or illegality is necessary in order to support an order of piercing is Anderson v. Stewart, 366 Ark. 203, 234 S.W.3d 295 (2006).[35] Citing EnviroClean, Inc. v. Arkansas

---

[34]   Stephen B. Presser, Piercing the Corporate Veil, § 2:4. Arkansas.

[35]   Technically, Anderson involved piercing the veil for a limited liability company. However, the court relied exclusively on corporate law, did not distinguish between corporations and LLCs, and in fact (inaccurately) referred to the LLC as a corporation and its members as "shareholders."

Pollution Control & Ecology Comm'n, 314 Ark. 98, 858 S.W.2d 116 (1993), and Don G. Parker, Inc. v. Point Ferry, Inc., 249 Ark. 764, 461 S.W.2d 587 (1971), the Arkansas Supreme Court noted that "[i]n special circumstances, the court will disregard the corporate facade when the corporate form has been illegally abused to the injury of a third party." 366 Ark. at 206, 234 S.W.3d at 298. The Anderson court then cited a legal treatise listing the following five common grounds for disregarding the corporate existence, all of which include some sort of fraud or other wrongdoing: 1) the corporate form is used to evade the payment of income taxes; 2) it is used to hinder, delay, and defraud creditors; 3) it is used to evade a contract or tort obligation; 4) it is used to evade the obligations of a federal or state statute; or 5) it is used to perpetrate fraud and injustice generally. Citing H. Murray Claycomb, Arkansas Corporations § 3–15 (1991). The Anderson court also bluntly claimed that "Arkansas cases in which the corporate veil has been pierced have generally involved some fraud or deception." 366 Ark. at 207, 234 S.W.3d at 298.

One of the cases cited in Anderson, EnviroClean, Inc. v. Arkansas Pollution Control and Ecology Com'n, 314 Ark. 98, 103, 858 S.W.2d 116, 119 (1993), ordered piercing on the grounds that there was abuse of the corporate facade in order to circumvent regulatory limitations on the transfer of certain facilities. While it did not specifically hold that fraud was required, it did cite the same language that was relied upon in Anderson, to the effect that "in special circumstances the court will disregard the corporate facade when the form has been illegally abused." *Id.*, citing Black and White, Inc. v. Love, 236 Ark. 529, 367 S.W.2d 427 (1963).

Some opinions from the Arkansas Court of Appeals have apparently embraced the notion that fraud or illegality should be required in order to pierce the veil. In a very recent opinion the court refused to award piercing where there "were no allegations, much less evidence, of fraud or other abuse of the corporate form." Bonds v. Hunt, 2010 Ark. App. 415, --- S.W.3d ----, 2010 WL 1904565 (2010). In Rhodes v. Veith, 80 Ark. App. 362, 363, 96 S.W.3d 734, 736 (2003), the Arkansas Court of Appeals reversed an award of piercing on the basis that the trial court had found no fraud, illegality, or overreaching. Similarly, the finding that there was no "illegal abuse" of the corporate form meant that the court declined to support piercing in Dalrymple v. Dalrymple, 74 Ark. App. 372, 47 S.W.3d 920 (2001).

On the other hand, other opinions tend to cite both the rules that piercing should be available when it is equitable as well as stating at least a preference for a finding of fraud or wrongdoing. In one fairly recent court of appeals decision not designated for publication, the court first acknowledged that the Arkansas Supreme Court "has stated that it is a nearly universal rule that a corporation and its stockholders are separate and distinct entities, and the court will only disregard the corporate facade when the corporate form has been illegally abused to the injury of a third party." Rush-Bradley v. Van Ore, Not Reported in S.W.3d, 2009 WL 262114 (Ark.App., 2009), citing Quinn-Matchet Partners, Inc. v. Parker Corp., 85 Ark.App. 143, 147 S.W.3d 703 (2004). The Rush-Bradley court then paid homage to the more liberal position, stating that "[t]he conditions under which the corporate entity may be disregarded or looked upon as the alter ego of the principal stockholder vary according to the circumstances of each case. The doctrine of piercing the corporate veil is applied when the facts warrant its application to prevent an injustice." *Id.*, citations to the same supreme court case omitted.

If, instead of focusing on the general discussion of whether fraud or illegality is necessary, attention is turned to the actual factors that are discussed in the cases, it does appear that the three most common grounds for piercing in Arkansas are significant failure to observe formalities, substantial undercapitalization of the corporation, and evidence that respecting the corporate form would allow the parties to evade the requirements of law. Not all of these factors need to be present, and in most cases only one or two of these are mentioned or appear to have been a factor in the decision.

Failure to observe formalities is mentioned in a number of cases as being essential in finding that the corporate veil should be disregarded. Unreported decisions are supposed to be those that break no new ground, and perhaps it is simply that the issue appears so well settled that the courts of appeal believe that they are saying nothing new. However, some of the clearest explanations of the importance of observing corporate formalities can be found in recent opinions not designated for publication. In Rush-Bradley v. Van Ore, Not Reported in S.W.3d, 2009 WL 262114 (Ark. App. 2009), the court (after reciting precedent to the effect that fraud or illegality should be present in order to pierce the veil), focused on the fact that the shareholder "failed to scrupulously follow corporate formalities." There were no minutes of annual shareholder meetings, and (despite the fact that the burden of proof in piercing cases is normally on the claimant, the court also relied on the fact that the shareholder "failed to introduce any financial records" proving the separate corporate existence. The court was also concerned with the omission of the word "Incorporated" from the corporation's signs and letterhead. The corporation in that case had converted property belonging to the claimant, but the court ordered that the veil be pierced so as to permit recovery against the shareholder as well.

The Eighth Circuit Court of Appeals, applying Arkansas law, found that failure to observe formalities and respect the corporate accounts as assets to be used for corporate purposes alone could result in piercing in Refco, Inc. v. Farm Prod. Ass'n., Inc., 844 F.2d 525, 529 (8th Cir. 1988).

In addition, when the corporate formalities are observed, Arkansas courts appear reluctant to pierce the veil. In Larco, Inc. v. Strebeck, 2010 Ark. App. 263, --- S.W.3d ----, 2010 WL 956194 (2010), the court relied on proper filing of tax returns, separate payroll records and reports, separate payments to employees, and separate workers' compensation plans in declining to combine related corporations even though the were both owned and operated by the same person, with the same employees. In Quinn-Matchet Partners, Inc. v. Parker Corp., Inc., 85 Ark. App. 143, 147 S.W.3d 703 (2004), the court focused on evidence that the failure to observe some formalities did not justify piercing when there was evidence that "the corporation adhered to corporate formalities by keeping its own financial records and bank accounts, by filing separate tax returns, and by recording the loans made." 85 Ark. App. 149-50, 147 S.W.3d at 707. Similarly in Indiana Lumbermen's Mut. Ins. Co. v. Phoenix Surety Group, Inc, Not Reported in S.W.3d, 2003 WL 22300304 (Ark. App. 2003), the court upheld a trial court's refusal to pierce the veil, relying on the facts that there was "no evidence that appellees failed to hold corporate meetings or otherwise disregarded the corporate form" or that the corporate account was ever used for non-business purposes.

A second factor that appears to play a critical role in multiple reported cases is significant undercapitalization of the corporation at issue. For example in Winchel v. Craig, 55 Ark. App. 373, 934 S.W.2d 946 (1996), a jury verdict ordering piercing of the veil was sustained on the basis that there was substantial evidence that the shareholders took no steps to provide for the contingent liability for personal injuries, and that the shareholders terminated the business and started a new one rather than making sufficient provision for such liability. 55 Ark. App. at 379, 934 S.W.2d at 949. The court also commented on the corporation's failure to provide insurance to cover such obligations. 55 Ark.

App. at 381, 934 S.W.2d at 950.   Failure to adequately fund corporate operations was also the primary concern that lead a bankruptcy court to pierce the veil in Mixon v. Anderson (In re Ozark Rest. Equip. Co., Inc.), 41 B.R. 476, 481 (Bankr. W.D. Ark. 1984). The factors that indicated undercapitalization in Mixon included the fact that the corporation never turned a profit, had a negative net worth, the other shareholder-owned companies turned a profit on this corporation's under-priced goods, and no interest was paid on accounts between the companies. *Id.* at 478-79.

The third factor that appears to be very commonly relied upon as a justification for piercing in Arkansas is a finding that failure to pierce would allow the corporation, often a parent and subsidiary, to avoid application of a statutory or regulatory requirement. Although the court emphasized that there was no fraud or illegality, use of a corporate subsidiary to allow the parent to accomplish "indirectly what they could not do directly" was found to be sufficient grounds for piercing in Arkansas Bank & Trust Co. v. Douglass, 318 Ark. 457, 470, 885 S.W.2d 863, 870 (1994). Similarly, the court in EnviroClean, Inc. v. Arkansas Pollution Control and Ecology Com'n, 314 Ark. 98, 103, 858 S.W.2d 116, 119 (1993), ordered piercing on the grounds that there was abuse of the corporate facade in order to circumvent regulatory limitations on the transfer of certain facilities. Woodyard v. Ark. Diversified Ins. Co., 268 Ark. 94, 594 S.W.2d 13 (1980), also permitted piercing in order to prevent a parent from avoiding application of statutes that would otherwise have applied to it. Interestingly, some of these opinions appear to suggest that this amounts to wrongdoing or illegality and some (like Douglass) simply say that this kind of "unfairness" is enough.

Obviously, the preceding cases emphasize and talk about piercing in the corporate context, and it might seem odd to start these materials with that information, because the focus of the book is on unincorporated business entities. The reasons for using this as the starting point are that: (1) as incomplete as it is, the Arkansas law on piercing in the corporate context is far more complete than for any other form of business; and (2) when piercing has been awarded to hold owners of other kinds of business liable, the same essential rules have been followed.

VIII.3.   Piercing the Veil of Limited Liability for Other Entities

There are only a handful of cases dealing with piercing of unincorporated entities in Arkansas, and they all appear to be focused on LLCs.

The first reported decision in Arkansas to grant piercing in the context of an LLC was Anderson v. Stewart, 366 Ark. 203, 234 S.W.3d 295 (2006), and it would be easy to overlook this case when researching because the court keeps referring to piercing of the "corporate" veil to hold the "shareholders" liable. [36] Technically, in the context of an attempt to pierce the veil of limited liability of an LLC, there is no corporation and there are no shareholders. Despite these errors in terminology, however, the analysis of the court is basically sound. As stated by the court, the issue was "whether the trial court erred in applying the doctrine of 'piercing the corporate veil' and holding shareholders in a limited liability company individually liable." 366 Ark. at 204, 234

---

[36]   Arkansas courts seem remarkably consistent in speaking about the doctrine of piercing the "corporate veil" to go after an LLC's "shareholders." For instance, In K.C. Properties of N.W. Arkansas, Inc. v. Lowell Inv. Partners, LLC, 373 Ark. 14, 280 S.W.3d 1 (2008), the court repeatedly used this terminology in declining to pierce the veil. The same language appears in the most recent LLC piercing case as of the date these materials were prepared, Marx Real Estate Investments, LLC v. Coloso, 2011 Ark. App. 426 __ S.W3d __, 2011 WL 2368343 (June 15, 2011) (saying only that "[t]he court pierced MREI's corporate veil to hold [its owners] . . . personally liable.")

S.W.3d at 296. The Court of Appeals determined that the trial court's decision to pierce "the corporate veil" to hold the individual defendants liable was not clearly erroneous because the owners did not properly maintain business records as required by the Check Casher's Act (see § 23–52–112(a)), withdrew assets in a manner designed to see that there were insufficient assets, and arranged for the same individuals to carry on the business even after closing of the LLC. 366 Ark. At 204, 234 S.W.3d at 296.

These are precisely the same kinds of issues that would lead to piercing in the corporate context–failure to observe required formalities and evading regulatory requirements.

A more recent opinion confirms that piercing of the veil for an LLC is possible in Arkansas, but offers no explanation of the circumstances under which is it appropriate. In Marx Real Estate Investments, LLC v. Coloso, 2011 Ark. App. 426 __ S.W3d __, 2011 WL 2368343 (2011), the court mentions almost in passing that the LLC's "corporate veil" was pierced so that its owners would be "personally liable."

There are other cases that suggest the Arkansas courts are willing to consider piercing of the veil for an LLC, such as Sherry Holdings, LLC v. Hefley, Not Reported in S.W.3d, 2008 WL 4820996 (Ark. App. 2008), in which the basis for declining to pierce the veil of the LLC was that evidence that a single member owned the business was insufficient grounds, just as there would be insufficient grounds to pierce a corporation's veil solely on the grounds that it had a single shareholder. In K.C. Properties of N.W. Arkansas, Inc. v. Lowell Inv. Partners, LLC, 373 Ark. 14, 280 S.W.3d 1 (2008), the court includes a long discussion of piercing in the corporate context before concluding that the facts then before it did not justify piercing the veil of the LLC. This was a rather stringent interpretation of the piercing doctrine since the owners of the LLC had apparently admitted in discovery that a number of formalities had been completely ignored, including failure to properly admit members, draft an operating agreement, keep books and records, maintain assets, pay for its own debts, or receive contributions. 373 Ark. at 33, 280 S.W.3d at 16.

This general approach of borrowing from corporate law in order to determine when it is appropriate to pierce the veil for unincorporated entities is consistent with opinions on the subject from other jurisdictions. One commentator has bluntly concluded that "[c]ase law suggests that corporate law piercing principles will be applied to LLCs and there is no reason to believe that LLPs will be treated differently." Harvey Gelb, Limited Liability Policy and Veil Piercing, 9 Wyo. L. Rev. 551, 554 (2009), citations omitted. For a general discussion of this issue under Arkansas law, see Emily A. Lackey, Piercing the Veil of Limited Liability in the Non-Corporate Setting, 55 Ark. L. Rev. 553 (2002).

VIII.4.   "Reverse Piercing"

Traditionally, piercing involved attempts to hold shareholders personally liable for corporate debts, even though the corporate form was supposed to offer owners protection against personal liability. As noted in the preceding materials, there are cases that have applied these rules to hold owners of other limited liability but unincorporated entities (most notably members of LLCs) personally liable. In some cases, however, the effort shifted from going after the owner of the limited liability entity, and instead focused on holding the corporate entity liable for the personal debts of its shareholders, generally based upon a showing that the corporate entity was really the alter ego of the individual owner(s). While there are, to date, no reported cases in Arkansas applying the doctrine of reverse piercing to any of the entities discussed in this book, because the courts have seemed so willing to borrow from corporate law in the context of traditional piercing, it is important to consider at least the general parameters of this doctrine.

Speaking in general terms, reverse piercing cases tend to arise in one of two different situations. "The most common reverse pierce cases involve 'insider' reverse piercing claims. Such claims involve a dominant shareholder or other controlling insider who 'attempts to have the corporate entity disregarded to avail the insider of corporate claims against third parties or to bring corporate assets under the shelter of protection from third party claims that are available only for assets owned by the insider.' Other reverse piercing cases, however, involve 'outsider' reverse piercing claims where third party claimants or judgment creditors with claims against a corporate insider attempt to disregard the corporate entity to reach the assets of the corporation to satisfy those claims." Leslie C. Heilman, *C.F. Trust, Inc. v. First Flight Limited Partnership: Will the Virginia Supreme Court Permit Outsider Reverse Veil-Piercing Against a Limited Partnership?* 28 Del. J. Corp. L. 619, 622-23 (2003) (citations omitted).

It appears that most courts dealing with a "reverse piercing" claim tend to apply the traditional veil-piercing analysis, which requires abuse or failure to respect the corporate form in a manner that results in fraud, injustice, or inequity in order to order piercing of the veil. Courts are often very concerned about the rights of innocent shareholders, and may be especially reluctant to order reverse piercing if their rights might be compromised.

Perhaps not surprisingly, there are very few reported decisions in Arkansas that seem to involve claims of reverse piercing at all. In 1974, the Arkansas Supreme Court (without actually confirming that the issue before it involved a claim for reverse piercing by insiders) refused to allow shareholders to disregard the corporate existence of an entity that they had formed and in which they each owned 50%. "A corporation is an entity separate from its stockholders. The fact these stockholders each held fifty percent of the stock in the Corporation does not make it tantamount to a partnership. The corporate existence cannot be so lightly regarded by its stockholders." Shipp v. Bell & Ross Enterprises, Inc., 256 Ark. 89, 97, 505 S.W.2d 509, 515 (1974) (citations omitted).

The only "express" reference to reverse piercing in a reported case from an Arkansas state court appears in a 1999 opinion from the Arkansas Court of Appeals in Thomsen Family Trust, 1990 v. Peterson Family Enterprises, Inc., 66 Ark. App. 294, 989 S.W.2d 934 (1999). That case involved an attempt by an outsider to recover against the assets of a corporation on the basis of alleged wrongdoing by the corporate shareholder. The court specifically acknowledged that this was an attempt to obtain "a 'reverse piercing of the corporate veil.'" 66 Ark. App. At 300, 989 S.W.2d at 937. In denying the request, the court recited the general principle that "[i]t is a nearly universal rule that a corporation and its stockholders are separate and distinct entities, even though a stockholder may own the majority of the stock." *Id.* Instead the court suggested that the corporate "facade" might be disregarded only in special circumstances where "corporate form has been illegally abused to the injury of a third party." *Id.,* citation omitted. Based on its conclusion that there was no evidence that the corporate form had been "illegally abused," the court declined to reverse pierce. *Id.*

In Nursing Home Consultants, Inc. v. Quantum Health Servs., Inc., 926 F. Supp. 835, 840 n.12 (E.D. Ark. 1996), a federal circuit court (applying Arkansas law) observed that "the 'reverse piercing' doctrine . . . . is itself controversial in that it allows corporations to be held liable for the acts of their shareholders. . ."

Logically, it would seem that reverse piercing might be an issue, in appropriate circumstances, for business that are organized as corporations or as any other unincorporated business offering its owners limited liability.   In advising clients, it is therefore important to warn them that they need to respect the separate existence of their business, and observe the formalities associated with having a business that is distinct from them. In addition, they should be advised that the privileges of conducting business through a limited liability entity should not be used to improperly avoid statutory or regulatory requirements, or to perpetrate a fraud or injustice on third parties. Because there is so little law on point, however, it is impossible to offer precise warnings about operational choices that are problematic.